Inside the White House in War Times: *Memoirs and Reports of Lincoln's Secretary*

By William O. Stoddard

Edited by Michael Burlingame

University of Nebraska Press

Lincoln and London

⊖

Library of Congress Cataloging-in-Publication Data
Stoddard, William Osborn, 1835–1925.
Inside the White House in war times: memoirs and reports of Lincoln's secretary / by William O. Stoddard;
edited by Michael Burlingame.
p.   cm.
"A Bison original"—P. [4] of cover.
Includes bibliographical references (p.   ) and index.
ISBN 0-8032-9257-0 (pbk.: alk. paper)
1. Stoddard, William Osborn, 1835–1925.   2. Lincoln,
Abraham, 1809–1865—Friends and associates.   3. Lincoln, Abraham, 1809–1865.   4. United States—Politics
and government—1861–1865.   5. United States—History—Civil War, 1861–1865 Personal narratives.
6. Washington (D.C.)—History—Civil War, 1861–1865
Personal narratives.   7. Secretaries—United States Bi-
ography.   I. Burlingame, Michael, 1941–
II. Title.
E664.S85A3   2000
973.7′092—dc21   99-30021
CIP

Contents

Editor's Introduction

Although William O. Stoddard (1835–1925) achieved renown as a journalist and the author of more than seventy books for boys, he is best remembered as "Lincoln's third secretary," assistant to the two main presidential aides, John G. Nicolay and John Hay, between 1861 and 1864. Like Nicolay and Hay, Stoddard wrote a biography of Lincoln; unlike them, he also published a memoir, *Inside the White House in War Times*, which appeared in 1890.[1] That volume is reproduced here, supplemented by thirteen "White House Sketches," reminiscences that Stoddard published in 1866 and that have escaped the attention of most historians.[2] Though much briefer than *Inside the White House in War Times*, the sketches, collected here for the first time, are more trustworthy, for they appeared shortly after the events described. In addition, their style is less self-consciously literary and fanciful than that of the memoir, therefore probably rendering them more accurate, if less aesthetically pleasing.

Stoddard has not impressed every reader as a reliable source of information about Lincoln. Nicolay criticized his "great tendency to exaggeration, which, useful to him as a writer of fiction of a certain kind, utterly unfits him for historical work."[3] Don E. Fehrenbacher and Virginia Fehrenbacher declared that "Stoddard probably overstated the extent of his intimacy with the President." They rightly observed that some passages in his memoirs stretch credulity beyond the breaking point.[4] But as Mark E. Neely Jr. noted, *Inside the White House in War Times* "contains some memorable vignettes of the Lincoln White House and is particularly good at describing the atmosphere of the tense and hard-working wartime administration."[5] Few people had a better coign of vantage for observing Lincoln during his presidency than did Stoddard, whose memoir, despite its exaggerations and self-serving nature, sheds a bright light on the sixteenth president's activities and character.

Born and raised near Syracuse in upstate New York, Stoddard as a youth "became much interested in the customs of the Indians who lived on a nearby reservation," according to his son. "In later years he used this knowledge in several of his most popular books."[6] His fondness for literature was stimulated by his father, Prentice S. Stoddard, a publisher and bookseller, and by his bookish mother, Sarah Osborn Stoddard. A precocious student, Stoddard composed poems and wrote for newspapers in his adolescence. In 1853 he entered the University of Rochester. As he approached his senior year, wanderlust induced him to head west in search of adventure. "Syracuse and Rochester seemed too small for my ambition," he recollected.[7] For a short time, he peddled books in Chicago, where he also wrote for the *Daily Ledger*. When the financial panic of 1857 killed that newspaper, he bought a farm near Tolono in eastern Illinois as a speculative investment. With the help of his sister, he tried cultivating the land, but a profound distaste for agricultural drudgery prompted him to move to the nearest town, West Urbana (now Champaign), where in May 1858 he began working for the *Central Illinois Gazette*, "an independent paper, devoted to agriculture, education, politics, temperance, literature, social reform, news and the interests of central Illinois." Stoddard described the paper's eccentric editor, Dr. John Walker Scroggs, as "a man of a million," one "of ability, for without school or academy training he had obtained a good deal of professional skill, medical, surgical, homeopathic, eclectic and universal." Ignorant of grammar and spelling, Scroggs nevertheless "could write after a fashion." A "fanatical temperance and antislavery man," he was, in Stoddard's estimation, "courageous and pugnacious." He had "strong prejudices against all ministers, and his feelings were pretty generally reciprocated. It must be said that the doctor was far from being a beloved citizen."[8] When he first met Scroggs, Stoddard, who admitted that he had not "a drop of humility," told him: "You can't run a newspaper, but I can." What Stoddard would later allude to somewhat apologetically as his "natural obstinacy" here worked to his advantage.[9] The skeptical doctor offered to let the brash young man try his hand at editing one issue, an experiment that turned out well. Soon thereafter Stoddard became a part owner and coeditor of the *Gazette*.[10]

In December 1858, Stoddard wrote to his friend and mentor Martin B. Anderson of the *Gazette's* increased participation in the political arena. He reported: "the Republican party of this region, dissatisfied with their present party organ[,] have requested publicly that the *Gazette* should take its place, and as an earnest have awarded us the entire public printing of Champaign County, an item of $1500." Stoddard feared that his "moderate

Whiggism" would not be "sufficiently radical" for a district represented by the militantly antislavery Congressman Owen Lovejoy, but Stoddard's ideology evidently suited his partner and the paper's readership.[11]

The following spring, Abraham Lincoln visited West Urbana and called on these journalists. In 1866 Scroggs recollected that "on the 27th of April 1859, Mr. Lincoln was in the *Central Illinois Gazette* office, where a conversation occurred upon the subject of the probable candidates for the Presidency in 1860. I suggested his name, but he—with characteristic modesty—declined. However his name was brought forward in the next issue, May 4th 1859."[12] In its "Personal" column, the *Gazette* noted:

We had the pleasure of introducing to the hospitalities of our sanctum a few days since the Hon. Abraham Lincoln. Few men can make an hour pass away more agreeably. We do not pretend to know whether Mr. Lincoln will ever condescend to occupy the White House or not, but if he should, it is a comfort to know that he has established for himself a character and reputation of sufficient strength and purity to withstand the disreputable and corrupting influences of even that locality. No man in the west at the present time occupies a more enviable position before the people or stands a better chance of obtaining a high position among those to whose guidance our ship of state is to be entrusted.[13]

Stoddard recalled vividly that April conversation with Lincoln:

He greeted me cordially as though we had known each other for a long time. There was no strangeness about him. He knew men on the instant. He wasted no time, but plunged at once into the causes of his coming. In a minute he had me not only interested but somewhat astonished. I had supposed that I knew the people and the politics of that county, and he had been told that I did, but so did he. He could ask about the different precincts and their leading men almost as if he had lived among them. As he was then studying Champaign County, so he was investigating the State of Illinois and other states and was getting into close relations with the current of feeling, North and South. The conversation was a long one.[14]

Lincoln, Stoddard said, "seemed to know my prairie neighbors almost man by man."[15]

Six months after praising Lincoln in its columns, the *Gazette* ran an editorial, "Who Shall Be President?" which endorsed him emphatically:

We in Illinois know him well; in the best sense of the word *a true Democrat*, a man of the people, whose strongest friends and supporters are the hard-handed and strong-limbed laboring men, who hail him as a brother, and who look upon him as one of their real representative men. A true friend of freedom, having already done important service for the cause, and proved his abundant ability for still greater services; yet a staunch conservative, whose enlarged and liberal mind descends to no narrow view, but sees both sides of every great question, and of whom we need not fear that either fanaticism on the one side, or servility on the other, will ever lead him into a betrayal of any trust.[16] Stoddard would later claim that he was the first editor to put forward Lincoln as a presidential candidate. In fact, several others had done so earlier, some in the fall of 1858.[17]

On 21 December 1859, the *Gazette* editors placed Lincoln's name at the head of the editorial columns, where it remained until after his election. "In the *Gazette* of January 18th 1860 an editorial appeared setting forth the claims and fitness of Mr. Lincoln and arguing at some length the absolute policy of nominating a western man, and especially Mr. Lincoln."[18] In February and May 1860, the *Gazette* again touted Lincoln's candidacy. After the Springfield rail-splitter won the nomination in May, Stoddard, as he later put it, "went into the political canvass, head over heels, heels over head." "I had nearly all the stumping of Champaign County on my own hands."[19]

Following the election, Stoddard expressed interest in joining the White House staff; Lincoln asked him to put his request in writing and said he would see to it.[20] But by late December 1860, the young journalist, in despair at the silence of the president-elect, wrote Lincoln's law partner, William H. Herndon:

As nearly two months have passed without my receiving any reply as to my application it is not unnatural that I should become a little nervous and desire to know what the indications are, if any. I am fully aware that the chances were from the first against my success, and am most painfully conscious that my request was bold, even presumptuous. Very likely, also, others with greater ability . . . may apply for the same position. The "President-elect," knowing so little of me, must necessarily, if he has thought of the matter at all, have doubts as to my fitness for a post of so much responsibility, and hesitate about according to me the degree of confidence which a man must place in his "private secretary."[21]

On the same day, Stoddard urged Illinois senator Lyman Trumbull to help him secure a job with Lincoln. Stoddard assured the senator that he had the support of Herndon, Lincoln's good friend Leonard Swett, and Sen. Ira Harris of New York.[22] He later alleged that he won his White House job in part because Senator Harris wrote him a strong letter of recommendation.[23]

The president-elect was unsure whether to offer the post of private secretary to Stoddard or to Benjamin F. James, a journalist who had helped Lincoln in his quest for a seat in Congress in the 1840s and who had applied for the job in September 1860.[24] Lincoln's friend Henry C. Whitney reported that both Stoddard and James told him that "Lincoln entertained with favor the idea of appointing one but not wishing to offend the other, [and] he concluded to keep Nicolay," who had started working as his secretary in May 1860.[25] Stoddard later admitted that Nicolay "was much better qualified" for the secretary's job than he was, for Nicolay was "older, more experienced, harder, had a worse temper, and was decidedly German in his manner of telling men what he thought of them," whereas Stoddard was, by his own admission, "more reticent."[26]

Eventually Lincoln summoned Stoddard to Washington as the secretary to the president to sign land patents.[27] On 23 February he arrived in the capital, where he found that "[o]ffice-seekers abound in untold and seedy looking multitudes. They roam the streets, seeking introductions, button-holing unfortunate great men."[28] At first Stoddard worked in the Interior Department, affixing Lincoln's name to some nine hundred documents each day; soon he was transferred to the White House.[29]

The day that war broke out, Stoddard volunteered for a three-month term in the National Rifles, a militia outfit that he described as "a company of select and eminent young gentlemen who regarded themselves as the pink of chivalry." While serving with them, he signed land patents in his spare time.[30] Eventually, as Nicolay recalled, land-office business "became very slack so that he [Stoddard] had scarcely any official work to do. He was therefore assigned to duty as one of my clerks at the White House, being able just as well to sign there the few Land Patents which were issued from time to time. Also on one or two occasions when Hay and I were both absent, he carried a message to Congress."[31] Stoddard's main job was to open and sort through the White House mail, which led people to call him "the paper-cutter."[32] He described his duties as "exceedingly hard work" that kept him busy until mid 1864, when "a siege of typhoid fever and a relapse unfitted me for so arduous a position."[33]

In his memoirs, Stoddard claimed that he and John Hay, Lincoln's assistant personal secretary, got along well together. He noted that not long after he had been transferred to the White House, Hay came down with a brief attack of Potomac fever: "I took care of him and when he got out at the end of it I heard him say that he could not have been more assiduously watched if his own mother had been with him."[34] It was during Hay's illness that Stoddard began to assume some secretarial duties. As he later recalled, the "business of Private Secretary, per se, was generally pretty well absorbed by Nicolay and Hay, but there were odd days, first during Hay's illness, when I had to go over and take Nicolay's place in the opposite room."[35]

Hay's letters, however, tell a somewhat different story of their relationship. In 1863 he complained to Nicolay, "Stod[dard] is more & more worthless. I can scarcely rely upon him for anything."[36] That same year Hay commented on his preference for another assistant secretary, Nathaniel S. Howe: "[Howe] is better than Stod[dard] as he is never stuffy and always on hand."[37] Hay thought Stoddard asinine as well as stuffy. "Stod[dard] has been extensively advertising himself in the Western Press," he told Nicolay in August 1864. "His asininity which is kept a little dark under your shadow at Washington blooms & burgeons in the free air of the West."[38] The following month Hay sarcastically observed that Stoddard had "been giving the Northern watering places for the last two months a model of high breeding and unquestionable deportment."[39]

Stoddard recorded milder criticisms that Hay made to his face. For example, Stoddard wrote the following in his memoirs: "[Hay was] angrily telling me that he considered me a kind of miracle of hard work and that I could do more without showing it than any other man he had ever seen. He abused me also for being what he called 'statuesque' and always inclined to strike attitudes and take positions—but I replied that the latter was just what we were wishing the army would succeed in doing."[40]

Stoddard's relations with Nicolay during the Civil War were, he remembered, "from the start, of an entirely satisfactory character."[41] In 1895 Nicolay called Stoddard "a very good fellow, and a man of considerable talent."[42] Ten years earlier, however, when Stoddard sent John Hay a copy of his Lincoln biography and asked for comments and criticisms, Stoddard reported, "Nicolay has not left me at liberty to write to him [Nicolay] or to send him a copy."[43] Nicolay was probably hostile toward Stoddard for the same reason he was hostile toward another Lincoln biographer, Ida M. Tarbell, to whom he complained: "You are invading my field. You write a popular Life of Lincoln and you do just so much to decrease the value of my property."[44]

A month after sending Hay a copy of his work, Stoddard wrote him: I did not suppose I was crossing your track or "taking away your market," and so said in my preface. I have left that unchanged in the edition now going out. Long ago I wrote you and Nicolay that I had a book in my mind and it was my idea, year after year, that yours would come out first. Is it too much to say that that idea died of old age? I hope you will make as full and valuable a work as I have thought of your making and that it will succeed *enormously*. Mine seems to find its place. So will yours. I have certainly done something in the way of advertising you. Never mind if your note nettled me a little but I certainly have not intentionally stolen a march on anybody.[45]

Stoddard's 1884 biography of Lincoln was not his only work to address Lincoln's presidential years. Stoddard's memoir, *Inside the White House in War Times*, is as much devoted to Lincoln's daily activities as it is to Stoddard's own. Likewise, in unpublished sections of his autobiography, Stoddard describes some episodes he observed that do not appear in *Inside the White House in War Times*.[46] For example, he recalled that in late November and early December 1863, when Lincoln was ill with the varioloid (a mild form of smallpox), Nicolay, Hay, and he "held mournful consultations over the idea that all the country would go to ruin if Abraham Lincoln should die of the dread disease, or any other." Stoddard's memoirs continue:

But it came to pass, as he was convalescing, that he was informed of my ironclad condition [Stoddard had been vaccinated] and sent for me. I went right in and attended to whatever the business was[,] telling him how glad I felt that he was doing so well and adding that now at least he was safe from officeseekers. He might do well, afterwards, to have his office in one of the smallpox hospitals. His laughing reply contained the information that one eager hunter had already replied to his doorkeeper: "O! That doesn't matter. I'll see him. I've been vaccinated."

As to the hospital experiment he declared almost sadly that "[t]he officeseekers would only wait until they had been vaccinated and would then come buzzing back around me like so many greenhead flies."[47]

Another episode not appearing in Stoddard's published autobiography or in *Inside the White House* involved Mary Todd Lincoln, whose dislike of presidential secretaries extended to Nicolay and Hay, but not to Stoddard. (When Stoddard left the White House in 1864, Nicolay exclaimed to Hay, "John! What'll we do with the Madam after Stod goes? You and I can't manage her.")[48] Stoddard recalled, "I was so entirely in charge of the social side of the White House that funny people used to describe me as Mrs. Lincoln's Secretary."[49] In his memoirs he recorded: "On the occasional absences of either Nicolay or Hay, I was expected to leave Mrs. Lincoln to her own resources and take the vacant place on one side or the other of the President. After the arrival of my sister Kate she became a great help to me in some of these matters, for Mrs. Lincoln took a fancy to her and liked to have her assistance at receptions."[50]

Stoddard's tact was evident when he helped solve a thorny problem related to the First Lady's notorious ball, held in February 1862. As he later recorded:

I had some fun with it. It was a rigidly formal or rather official affair. The invitations were limited to certain kinds or species of men and women. Senators, Congressmen, Judges of the Supreme Court, members of the Cabinet, generals and high naval men. . . . [F]rom all over the country there came to prominent Washington men urgent applications for invitations, as if these were but free tickets to "the Greatest Show on Earth." To have granted any of these requests, by favoritism, would have given just offence to the multitude who could not be gratified. The first applicants to be disappointed and to get mad about it were the local representatives of the great northern journals, nearly all of whom appeared to consider themselves sufficiently official or military or naval or judicial or diplomatic to be entitled to tickets. Nicolay and Hay were masters of the situation but for some reason, perhaps because it was disagreeable and I was young, it was shunted over upon my shoulders, in part, and I found all explanations in vain. A certain number, of course, could be admitted as "reporters" but when I mentioned that fact the fat was all in the fire. In the language of one excited scribe, "If we cannot come as gentlemen, we will not come at all!"— Which was hard upon any fellow who ceased to be a gentlemen when he became a reporter. I was in my room, one day, when Nicolay sent Hay to see me, in hot haste. Two of Mrs. Lincoln's favorite Congressmen, one of whom was my old friend Caleb Lyon, of Lyonsdale, New York, and the other my especial friend Gen. Daniel E. Sickles, had asked for tickets for two New York litterateurs, an editor of the *Herald*, a daily paper, and Mr. George Wilkes of the *Spirit of the Times*, both of which journals had been anything but complimentary to Mr. Lincoln.[51]

"Stoddard!" exclaimed poor Nicolay. "I can't do anything! It will make all sorts of trouble. 'She' is determined to have her own way. You will have to see to this. 'She' wouldn't listen to me."

"Give me the tickets," I said, "and I'll attend to it."

Down to the Red Room I went and there were present all the parties to the case and Mrs. Lincoln was smilingly expecting the cards which she had sent for under the pernicious beguilement of Dan Sickles and Caleb Lyon. They also smiled at me, as I came in.

"May I see you for a moment, Mrs. Lincoln?" I said, and she could see that I was boiling over, wild mad about something, furious but restraining myself, and she followed me into the Blue Room at once. "What is it, Mr. Stoddard?"

"Mrs. Lincoln! O! But won't I give it to Dan and Caleb!"

"Why? What for? What have they done?"

"Why, Mrs. Lincoln, I suppose you have a right to *know*. They have demanded of Mr. Nicolay invitations for those two fellows in there that have been abusing you, personally, and Mr. Lincoln, as though you were both pick-pockets. If we are to give out extra cards, we had better send them to our friends, not to our enemies. Besides, it would offend some of the best friends we have. I wish you would put your foot down on this and stop it. They can't have the invitations."

"Of course they can't!" she said. "I'll go right in and tell them so."

"And I'll give Sickles and Caleb a wigging!" I declared.

Into the Red Room she went again, to say very firmly: "Gentlemen, Mr. Stoddard, who has absolute charge of this business, tells me that I cannot give you the invitations. I am sorry, of course, but I must abide by his decision."

There was no help for it and they had to give it up, but I did have an interesting little mill with Caleb and the General in the vestibule. As for Mrs. Lincoln, I had felt sure of her. She never really went back on me and she was wide awake to any attack upon her husband. Nicolay and Hay were ready to pat me on the back when I went up stairs, and they expressed much wonder as to how I did that thing. At all events, in this case as in some others, all the ugly part of it fell on me and sometimes I was not making friends. [Stoddard alleged, "[T]here were those who did not like me. Many of them."][52]

Stoddard considered Mary Todd Lincoln a friend. Many years after the war, he told Nicolay, "I am glad to have had several chances for defending Mrs. Lincoln."[53] When solicited to contribute money to finance a college building in her honor, Stoddard replied:

I shall take a deep interest in the proposed memorial to a noble hearted woman who was one of the best friends I ever had. During nearly the whole of her husband's first term I was half jocularly described as "Mrs. Lincoln's secretary," her constant attendant at all receptions, public or social, and her adviser in many affairs. She was a woman much misrepresented and scandalously abused. For instance, the slanders assailing her patriotism, which was sincere and earnest, accusations of correspondence with "secessionists," etc. During all that time she would open no letter or parcel until I had opened and decided whether or not she should see it. The mass of vituperation sent her by

mail never reached her. . . . Mrs. Lincoln's course in the White
House was admirable, unexceptionable, patriotic!"[54]
Stoddard did acknowledge, however, that he found it difficult "to understand why a lady who could be one day so kindly, so considerate, so generous, so thoughtful and so hopeful, could, upon another day, appear so unreasonable, so irritable, so despondent, so even niggardly, and so prone to
see the dark, the wrong side of men and women and events."[55]

Nicolay and Hay did not share Stoddard's generally favorable view of the
First Lady, for they knew about her ungovernable temper and her misap-
propriation of public funds, padding of expense accounts and payrolls, ac-
ceptance of bribes, and similar violations of legal and ethical standards.[56]
Stoddard himself was accused of unethical conduct while in the White
House. What he would later call his "old besetting sins of careless extravagance and rash speculation" landed him in trouble.[57] In 1877 a New York fi-
nancier, Clinton Rice, told investigators looking into the McGarrahan claim
scandal:

> [In 1862] I became acquainted with William O. Stoddard, . . . [who]
> imparted to me that he enjoyed superior facilities for obtaining in ad-
> vance all information of a political, official and diplomatic character
> likely to affect gold, stocks, and other commodities. I entered into an
> arrangement with him to furnish me telegraphic cipher dispatches. I
> was, by way of reciprocation, to use the said information among the
> stock, gold and commercial brokers of New York, and divide with
> him, share and share alike, and during the years 1863 and 1864 we
> worked this together under said arrangement. The usual course pur-
> sued was for Stoddard to telegraph me in cipher, as agreed on, imme-
> diately upon any important action of the Cabinet, or on receipt by the
> President or heads of departments of any important military or naval
> or other official operation or of any diplomatic movements, in time to
> use the same at the boards, or at the produce exchange, or upon the
> street, before the announcement had been decided upon, and then, on
> the next day or by the next mail north, to post me a letter of explana-
> tion and advice, signed "Two Hundred."[58]

To corroborate his testimony, Rice provided copies of Stoddard's letters and
telegrams, dating back to October 1863. On the fifteenth of that month,
Stoddard informed Rice: "I am anxious to see you and talk over matters. I
have made a grand combination which will give me the entire control of the
New York press through their Washington correspondents. This alone is an
immense thing. In order to keep it up, however, we must make some money,
and that soon." The following day, Stoddard told Rice: "The victory busi-

ness at Bristow Station is hollow enough, for we did not win any, but they are making the people believe that we did. I think I could run a gold line here better than anywhere else. Will pay all the expenses for half the net proceeds. About ten thousand would do. Account rendered every thirty days."[59]

When this story appeared in the press, Stoddard emphatically denied that he "used his position to sell Cabinet and other government secrets for effect in Wall street and for other purposes." He acknowledged that the letters showed that he had speculated in stocks and gold, adding, "[B]ut all who knew me at the time were already well aware of that fact. Stock and gold gambling was the mania of the day, and for a time I had it very badly, but I made no concealment of it, for I thought [it] no evil." He protested, "I attended no Cabinet meetings, received no government despatches, had no access to hidden matters of state. . . . [T]he President and my official associates were well aware of my operations at the time. A man so young as I was then may well be pardoned if, in such a day of feverish excitement, he drifted for a while with the tide."[60]

Stoddard also defended himself in his memoirs:

Among other incidents of my official life at this time was the discovery that fifteen hundred dollars was a small salary for a man attempting to hold such a position as had somehow come my way and which involved larger expenses than might have been those of a clerk now or of even a Secretary in Andrew Jackson's time. It was therefore something worth while when a New York banker whose friendship I had acquired told me that two thirds of the up and down movements in stocks and gold were caused by false rumors or misunderstandings of current events. He proposed that I should keep him advised of the true state of affairs, as far as I could, and he would open a stock and gold account for me. I was just the man for him and there was nothing in my position or sources of information which rendered it improper. It happened that my early guesses at truth were singularly correct and my bank accounts grew rapidly, both in New York and Washington. There was no manner of secrecy about my varied speculations. President Lincoln laughed at my investments[;] but one day, a gentleman who loved me not was at Mrs. Lincoln's afternoon reception and struck me a deadly blow by remarking:

"Madame, I understand that your favorite Secretary has been quite successful on the gold market. He has cleared half a million!"

"Is it possible!" she exclaimed. "I'm so glad to hear it! I think a great deal of Mr. Stoddard. Glad to hear of his good luck."

He subsided and that very evening she warmly congratulated me on my good fortune, advising me, however, not to lose all my money.[61]

Just as Lincoln overlooked Stoddard's questionable financial dealings, so too he pardoned many a court-martialed soldier. Stoddard recalled one instance, however, when the president did not issue a pardon:

It [Lincoln's mail] included many of the applications for pardons and all of these were at one time in my keeping. I remember some of them and what became of them. There were those who grumbled at Mr. Lincoln's strong objection to any kind of capital punishment and his tendencies toward mercy for all sinners. I may have been one of these. There came, one day, a pile of influential petitions on behalf of a southwestern guerrilla of the most cruel sort. He was unquestionably a redhanded murderer but the movement in his favor was a strong one. It included even loyal politicians and [the] next day a gang of big men of several kinds came up to see the president about it. They spoke of the high character of the papers in the case and these were sent for but they were not in my possession. They may have been duly referred and transferred to the War Office, as was sometimes the custom. Inquiry was made there but the papers could not be found. The delegation went its way and that application for pardon was hung up. So was the woman-and-child killer who was the most interested party in the case and hardly had that fact been telegraphed before all the missing papers arrived at the White House. I think Mr. Lincoln did no more than look sidewise at me and I am sure he made no verbal commentary.[62]

Evidently Stoddard had withheld the papers in hopes that the guerilla would be executed, for he added: "There may have been other exceptional instances of the power of the 'paper-cutter' but I have forgotten them."[63] The episode illustrates John Hay's observation that, when considering pardons, Lincoln "was only merciless in cases where meanness or cruelty were shown."[64]

During the war, Stoddard became friendly with a prominent Washington journalist, Whitelaw Reid. As he later recalled, "I used to meet him almost daily at his office or at the White House, for he was soon a close friend of my next friend and office associate, John Hay. With Mr. Nicolay, also, his relations were peculiarly friendly. I can remember his always bright and cheery face as he would hail me or John to ask us for any news or to tell us what we did not know."[65]

Stoddard himself continued his journalistic career while in the White

House, sending regular dispatches to a Baptist weekly paper in New York using the pen name "Illinois." (Stoddard was a devout Baptist who taught Sunday school and led church meetings.) He recorded in his memoirs, "[A]t an early day I received an invitation from my uncle [Edward] Bright [Jr.], of the *New York Examiner & Chronicle*, to write news letters for that journal. I was glad to do so and the success which I attained led to my subsequent staff connection with the *Examiner* during many years."[66] From May 1861 to the summer of 1864, "Illinois" commented regularly on events in Washington and on military developments. Stoddard also submitted material for publication to the *New York Tribune*.[67]

In the spring of 1863, Stoddard suffered a near-fatal attack of typhoid fever, and the following year he endured a setback.[68] "All my business operations had been more or less interrupted by my long bout with typhoid," he recalled. "The one thing most apparent was my need of out-of-door air for as long as might be. I was no longer fit for close confinement and late hours." When he suggested that he undertake an inspection tour of Union armies in the West, Lincoln approved and, as Stoddard remembered, "provided me with abundant passes and letters of introduction, endorsing me as his secretary, entitled to go everywhere and be well received by everybody."[69]

In July 1864 Stoddard departed for Arkansas. On the eighth of that month, he told Manton Marble, editor of the *New York World*: "I have called to see you on my way to a new field of duty. I am going as heretofore to do my uttermost for Uncle Sam and Abraham Lincoln."[70] A few days later he announced to readers of the *New York Examiner* that he was, after more than three years, ending his career as a Washington correspondent.[71]

On 13 August Stoddard wrote to Hay from Little Rock: "Affairs here do not look well, and it is *not* the fault of the loyal citizens. I shall have much to say when I return. I do *not* want Orville Jennings appointed Dist. Attorney. He is not the sort of man at all. *Any* good, sound northern lawyer, but *not* a half converted rebel. I am down with 'summer complaint' today, but shall be up and on my way home shortly. I have got a big job before me here, but think it can be accomplished."[72]

In September, Stoddard returned to Washington and briefed Lincoln on the situation in the southwest. In his memoirs Stoddard recalled that because the war was drawing to a close, his imagination "burned with the desire to get into, to become a part of, the great new venture, the building of a truly united country," and he approached Lincoln with a request to be appointed marshal of Arkansas.[73] On 24 September Lincoln nominated Stoddard to be marshal for the eastern district of Arkansas.[74] Stoddard's son reported that "[i]n taking this position, he had in mind running for the Senate on the Republican ticket, when the war was over."[75] Stoddard ascribed his decision to his "love of adventure," which led him into "about the most dangerous post in the United States."

Stoddard wrote of his position: "As Marshal I represented the federal government, and my responsibilities were practically those of governor of the state."[76] From Little Rock he sent Lincoln lengthy reports on political and military conditions.[77] He also wrote to Illinois congressman Elihu B. Washburne, urging that Confederate lands be distributed to Union troops:

We want twenty thousand soldiers to settle here. I tell you, my dear Sir, you *cannot* build up a new and free state with the worn out and demoralized *debris* which is all that this war will leave of the old population of Arkansas. It always was ignorant and wanting in energy, but *now*—upon my soul Sir they are *trash*!

We want settlers, working *men*, not "*Proprietors*." Imagine, sir, the great impulse which would be given to our prosperity as a state by the actual settlement of twenty or thirty thousand brave and hardy Union men. What better mode of destroying guerilla-banditti, restoring order, and securing our state forever in the interest of freedom and law![78]

When word of Lincoln's assassination arrived in Arkansas, Stoddard told Hay:

The terrible news was some time in reaching us. Now that the first stunning effects are over, I feel for the first time how much I loved and venerated Abraham Lincoln. I cannot write about him, even to you. I only wish to say that something of personal sympathy for you and Nicolay mingles tonight with my sorrow for the man who has done more for me than all my other friends. Men who had never seen him wept when the news came. How shall *we* say our sorrow,—who knew him as he really was. To others, the *President* is dead. I can only remember my benefactor. God bless you, my dear fellow—God have mercy on us all, for we are sorely tried![79]

Ill health forced Stoddard to abandon his Arkansas post in May 1866.[80] Then, according to his son, "he came north to New York and about this time his hearing was seriously affected, so that certain occupations were closed to him." Between 1871 and 1873 he served as chief clerk of the bureau of engineering in the New York Dock Department, a post he secured with the help of John A. Dix and Andrew H. Green. Stoddard "made and lost various fortunes in those unstable years after the war and finally settled down to authorship" after the panic of 1873 ruined his business career.[81] He had published his first book, a satire of Tammany Hall entitled *The Royal Decrees of Scanderoon*, in 1869.[82]

In 1870 Stoddard married Susan E. Cooper of New York City. Their son, William O. Stoddard Jr., was born four years later. The younger Stoddard considered his father "a born fighter"[83] and portrayed him thus:

Father had straight black hair, and black eyes that flashed on occasion, but which were always kindly. He was the most dynamic creature I have ever known, and utterly fearless. He was a crack shot with both hands. I have seen him plug a visiting card right and left at twelve paces. He used a short-barreled Derringer, to me an impossible weapon. . . . Father was a notable raconteur. When he stepped into a room he immediately became its center. While he was quick on the trigger in repartee, he was never unkindly to an opponent. He was and still is my ideal American gentleman. He maintained poise and self-control under all circumstances.[84]

That characterization would have pleased the elder Stoddard, who in 1898 told Nicolay: "Mine has been a toilsome life, with many changes and vicissitudes, but I have fought it through without flinching—not a hair."[85] He claimed that reviewers of his books had dealt with him kindly, adding, "I ought to be comfortable. It is not exactly what they call fame, but it will do."[86] Twenty-seven years later, Stoddard died at the age of ninety.

1

Inside the White House in War Times

Opening the Door

Before me on the table lies a small brass latch-key. It has a worn-out look, as if it had served its time and had been honorably discharged, but if it had a tongue few other keys could tell so notable a history. During the administrations of seventeen successive Presidents of the United States, it opened the front door of the Executive Mansion at Washington. The lock it belonged to was put on when that house was built, and was replaced by a new one in the time of President Grant. In my own mind and memory, this key is associated with the years which I spent in and about the White House; the years of Lincoln's administration; the days of the Civil War; the terrible furnace time, during which, as it then and ever since has seemed to me, the old nation melted away and a new nation was moulded.

This is the year 1861, and although it is so early in the spring the weather is warm. Suppose we stroll toward the White House.

The short, thin, smiling, humorous-looking elderly Irishman in the doorway is Old Edward, the all but historic doorkeeper, who has been so great a favorite through so many administrations. He is as well liked by his seventh President as he was by even General Taylor. There is no end of quiet fun in him as well as intelligence, and his other name is Fidelity. He is said to have been the first man met in the White House by Mr. Lincoln who succeeded in making him laugh.

"Mr. Secretary"—and he is holding out something upon the palm of his open hand—"I've been getting some new latch-keys for the young gentlemen. I don't know what's become of the keys we had. Maybe they've gone South and mean to come back, some day, and open the door."

Two of the keys are bright and new, but one is old and tarnished.

"There's one for Mr. Nicolay, and one for Mr. Hay, and one for yourself. That's the old one, that belonged to the lock when it was put on."

"That's the key I want, Edward. Give Nicolay and Hay the new ones."

"It's like meself—it can open the door as well as ever it could," laughs Old Edward.

We have the key, therefore, and we can go into and out of the house as we please.

Americans are sufficiently familiar with the external appearance of this simple white oblong structure, built upon this low rise of ground sloping to the Potomac. Yonder, westward, are the dingy old War and Navy buildings. Eastward is the Treasury, half built, part old, part new, and beyond it lies most of the city, and just one mile distant, in that direction, is the Capitol. This pillared portico and covered carriage-way, on the north front of the house is where Lincoln will stand in a few days to review the first troops that are coming from the North. The secessionists hold Baltimore and claim Maryland, and Washington City is in a besieged condition. Its communications with the rest of the world are almost cut off, and there is no use in saying how easily it might be captured by a small body of daring men—Ethan Allens of the Confederacy.

A sort of uncanny glamour seems to have been settling upon the city, week after week. It has grown under the shadow of the tremendous events which are to come. It will remain long, and it will not entirely depart until the end of Andrew Johnson's term. It is a strange and shuddering kind of thing, and its central, darkest, most bewildering witchcraft works around this Executive Mansion.

The stones of the pavement of this portico are foot-worn into furrows, and every furrow is a kind of historical wrinkle. There! When you try it, the door opens to this key, now, in these early days of the Civil War, as it may have opened to it in the hands of Thomas Jefferson or Andrew Jackson.

Within the doorway there is a mere coop of a lobby, and beyond that is an ample vestibule. This is where they sometimes set up the racks for hats and coats on grand reception evenings. All along through March, after the inauguration, this was one of the most anxious places on the face of the earth, but it was not at all on account of the Rebellion. Men gathered in groups up and down the walks, outside, and filled the portico, and there was anxiety out there; but in here there was more of it, for the crowd was denser. They were all patriots and they loved their country and they were willing to serve it, here or at their homes, and they were all anxious to see the President.

This door, to the left, leads into a broad entryway. That flight of stairs goes up to the business part of the house. That is the door of the great East Room, the White House drawing-room. There, at the heel of the stairway, is the place for the Marine Band to sit and make music on reception evenings, but no band could have found any footing there during that first rush of office-seekers. The greater part of each day the East Room itself was thronged. The first men who volunteered for the defense of any part of Washington were a full battalion of these very patriots who crowded the White House. They bravely proposed to have guns furnished them and to bivouac in the East Room on the floor all night, so they would be here in the morning, first thing, ahead of anybody else, with their muskets stacked around them, and with better chances for interviews with Lincoln. Those were exciting days when, for hours and hours, the anterooms and halls upstairs were so full that they would hold no more, and when this broad staircase itself was also packed and jammed, stair by stair, from top to bottom, so that you could hardly squeeze your way up or down. It was all cut short by one of Lincoln's decrees. He decided not to interfere with his Cabinet officers in the selection of their clerks and other subordinates. As he expressed it, he "ceased to have any influence with this Administration" in the matter of appointments to minor offices.

The East Room has a faded, worn, untidy look, in spite of its frescoing and its glittering chandeliers. Its paint and furniture require renewal; but so does almost everything else about the house, within and without. Westward from the East Room, facing south, are the three reception rooms—the Blue Room, another, and the Red Room. The latter is the special private and public reception-room of the lady of the White House. Between these and the vestibule runs a broad hall, from the East Room to the entrance of the State Dining-room. The remainder of this floor, westward, belongs to family uses, and beyond all, without, is the conservatory, a respectable affair, and containing many rare and valuable plants.

The anxious throng of office-seekers long since dwindled from a river into a brook of manageable size. There is nobody at all here this morning, and we will go upstairs. At the head of them is a spacious entryway, and as we stand here, looking southward, to the right of us are apartments which are used as sleeping-rooms, but which, hereafter, will be turned into offices.

This fine broad hall that we next walk into runs the entire length of the building, east and west. Yonder, across the hall, is a large room which serves as a citadel and place of refuge for Presidents to retreat into when they are too severely pressed in their own business office adjoining, on the east. Beyond that, in the southeastern corner of the house, is the private secretary's office, occupied now by Mr. Nicolay and his immediate assistant, Mr. Hay. This large chamber on the north side of the hall is their sleeping-room. The northeastern room, next to it, a narrow room, corresponding to Mr. Nicolay's office on the other side of the hall, contains three desks. The two upright, antiquated, mahagony structures in the further corners belong to Mr. Hay. This heavy-looking table-desk of drawers, green-clothed and curiously littered, out here in front of the door, with its left elbow toward the fireplace, is to be yours through several years to come. It is, in some respects, a kind of breakwater, and the duties attached to it will be almost entirely separated from those performed by the other private secretaries.

We have a good reason for visiting the White House so very early, before the beginning of its official business hours.

It is the morning of the 12th of April, 1861, and at no previous date has the cloud hung so low above the White House, nor has the air here and throughout the country been so painfully dense with doubt and suspense, and with the dread of that which must surely come. The Civil War really began long ago, but it has not yet been wise for the President to say as much, nor to ask for troops to carry it on with. Leaving the northeast room, and walking westward along the hall, it seems a gloomy, shadowy, chilly corridor, and not a living soul is to be seen in it. The hall is severed here, near the head of the stairs, by folding doors, but they are wide open. Beyond, to the left, in the middle, is the very pleasant library, and adjoining it is the chamber in which Mr. Lincoln will one day lie, sick with the varioloid. Then come other folding doors, and behind them are the rooms of the family.

A remarkably tall and forward-bending form is coming through the further folding doors, leaving them carelessly open behind him. He is walking slowly, heavily, like a man in a dream. His strongly marked features have a drawn look, there are dark circles under his deep-set eyes, and these seem to be gazing at something far away, or into the future.

The President knows, as only a few others know, that the bombardment of Fort Sumter, in the harbor of the city of Charleston, S.C., has probably, has almost certainly, begun already, although positive official information of the fact cannot arrive until tomorrow.

We ourselves have no idea that all his soul is listening for the Sumter gun, while all his mind is busy with its consequences.

"Good morning, Mr. Lincoln."

For a moment he stands still, looking down into your face, but the faraway expression of his own does not change. He may be looking, prophetically, at future battlefields, and hearing the roar of other cannon than those in Charleston harbor, but you do not understand, and you exclaim, in astonishment:

"Why, Mr. Lincoln! you don't seem to know me!"

"Oh, yes, I do," he responds, wearily. "What is it?"

"I wish to ask a favor."

His lips contract as he asks, half petulantly,

"Well, well—what is it?"

Every man, almost, that he is meeting, every day and all day long, is saying about the same thing.

"It's just this, Mr. Lincoln: I believe there is going to be fighting, pretty soon, right here, and I don't feel like sitting at a desk in the Patent Office, or here, either, while any fight is going on. I've been serving with a company already, and if it's ordered on duty I want to go with it—"

"Well, well," he interrupts, but with a quickly brightening face, "why don't you go?"

"Why, Mr. Lincoln, only a few days ago I took a pretty big oath to obey your orders, and now I'm likely to be asked to take another to obey somebody else. I don't see how I can manage them both without your permission. I may be ordered to service outside of the District of Columbia—"

He is all but smiling as he cuts the explanation short with:

"Go ahead! Go ahead! Swear in! Go wherever you are ordered to go."

"That's all I want, Mr. Lincoln."

You have turned away, but he has called you back, and he says to you, earnestly,

"Young man, go just where you're ordered. Do your duty. You won't lose anything by this!"

A memorable morning interview with Lincoln is over, but it will seem, at a later day, listening back through the years, as if the roar of the "Sumter gun" broke through the brooding, ominous silence almost instantly. You will know, however, that the news did not reach Washington until the next day, the 13th; that the proclamation calling for troops went out on Sunday, the 14th; and that while the country was reading it in the papers of Monday morning, the 15th, the first company of volunteers that was mustered in, "Company A, Third Battalion," was drawn up in front of the War Office to be sworn, and that you became a three-months' volunteer private soldier by special permission of the President.

There is an accumulated heap of land patents, waiting the pen of a secretary to sign patents for land. They are old affairs, and not many new ones are making out now, and your entire work is soon to be transferred from your snug office in the Interior Department building to the former table-desk in the northeast room.

The duties of a private in Company A are severe, but furloughs of a few hours' each can be had, now and then, to sign important papers or to make flying visits to the White House. Going or coming, or in camp, or on guard duty, you are more and more convinced that all the young women of Washington, and some that are older, know more or less how to play the piano. The tone of the piano-playing part of Washington society, moreover, is in romantic sympathy with "the sunny South," and there is a perpetual tinkle of the favorite secession airs pouring through the windows, which they leave open for the benefit of any Northern vandals who may happen to pass within hearing.

The first favorite of all is "Dixie's Land," and its music has sounded almost day and night until it has taken on a weird, spell-like influence, and it seems a part and a voice of this horrible glamour that sweeps in upon the souls and hearts of men. It fairly makes one shudder to have that tune spring out upon him when he least expects it. A little behind "Dixie," in persistency of repetition, are the "Bonnie Blue Flag," and "Maryland, my Maryland."

The Pennsylvania Fifth has arrived, but it came without any muskets, and it brought no music. The New York Seventh is here, and the Massachusetts Eighth, and the blockade of Washington is broken through. Splendid bands, fine music, a magnificent river of steel points glittering down the avenue, but the bands play only commonplace national music, and the like. Company A is too busy to more than know that relief has come, although it met the Seventh at Annapolis Junction; but to-day the New York Twelfth has arrived, and is forming at the railway depot near the Capitol, and the orders you are obeying will take you with them.

Full company front, in excellent drill, perfect equipment, bayonets glittering, flags flying, and a brass band that makes a rank all the way across the avenue. The drums beat, and your heart beats for a moment as the gallant boys step off. What's that?

"I wish I was in Dixie! Look away!"

Hurrah! They are playing as if for a wager, and the cheering along the thronged sidewalks answers uproariously. Suddenly, as if a counter spell had been uttered, the weird and mocking power has passed away from the boding melody, and yet, somehow, it will never sound to you like any other tune.

We are half-way down the avenue, keeping step with the Twelfth. There is again only a roll of drums for a moment, and then that blessed band puts all its musical energies into the "Bonnie Blue Flag," past square after square. On sweeps the splendid regiment until it wheels around the Treasury corner to the front of the Executive Mansion, and pours through the wide gateway to pass in review before the waiting President. Again the music changes, and the serried ranks swing forward to the noble cadences of "Maryland, my Maryland," for Baltimore has been occupied by General

Butler and his men, and the National Government can safely call the old State "mine."

The young women of Washington City cease playing "Dixie." They shut their windows and mournfully declare that the Yankees have stolen even the national music of the South. Northern or Southern, we are none of us altogether sane in these feverish, bewildered, half-delirious days, but cannot a fever be cured without bleeding the patient?

There are sanguine people who express that kind of hope in spite of all that has been done, including the Sumter affair, but the State of Virginia is to take an important vote on the 23d of May, and at sunset of that day it will be known whether or not the Old Dominion is to join the Confederacy. Can anybody know beforehand the result of a State election? Perhaps not; but the President is so sure in his own mind that Virginia will adopt the Ordinance of Secession that he has ordered the Union forces to be ready to cross the Potomac at sunset of May 23, this very week upon which we are entering.

Nothing, however, could be more peaceful than is the White House as we enter it this Sunday morning. The President and Mrs. Lincoln are beginning with an effort to keep Sunday, and they have gone to church. They try to be private citizens once a week, but the circumstances are against them. Robert is away at college. The children are in the other part of the house. The two private secretaries may be at church for all we know—they are not in their office. The doors of the rooms are all wide open.

"Hullo, Ellsworth, are you here?"

"Yes, I'm all the President there is on hand this morning. I got away from camp to run over and see him and the boys."

He is a brilliant young fellow, and you like him, and you have an idea that if a war is to come he will play a prominent part in it. He is brimming, running over with health, high spirits, ambition, hope, and all the exuberant life of a rarely vigorous nature. You have been drilling hard as a soldier since a fortnight or so before you were sworn in, and he has picked up a carbine that was leaning against the wall. Put him through the manual of arms, for he has the name of being the most perfect master of it in the army. How like a piece of human mechanism are all his clock-work movements! There! He was standing too near the south window, and the order which brought the butt of that piece against his shoulder sent the muzzle of it through a pane of glass. So much for your defective tactics, and this war is to be a record of badly directed forces. You and he are boys, and when the private secretaries come in, for they too are boys, you can tell them that some assassin, lurking in the shrubbery down yonder, must have mistaken Colonel Ellsworth for the President. His bullet missed its mark, but it ruined the pane of glass. It is but a passing jest, but it illustrates the strong hold which the idea of probable assassination has already taken upon the minds of men.

Has a whole week passed since then? Yes; and here we are, in the same room, standing by the same window. Virginia has been invaded, and on the night in which Ellsworth was slain you were with Company A, and it was given by General Stone the honor of being the first to cross the bridge. The Twelfth New York came next, and now, indeed, they are in Dixie.

"Yes, General Leavenworth, last Sunday morning Ellsworth was here, about this time, and he stood exactly where you are standing. Do you see that?"

The marks of the glazier's fingers on the new glass illustrate the story, but the bright and gay young soldier has fallen on the very threshold of the war in which he hoped to be a leader. The river, down there, at which he and you were looking, has become the northern boundary line of the Confederacy. This White House itself has become the headquarters of a frontier post as well as the armies of the Republic. The heights, yonder, on the south bank of the Potomac, are within the enemy's country. A Confederate flag floated upon Arlington House last Sunday, but it is not there now, and one reason why the heights were so promptly occupied and fortified by the national troops was that a battery planted upon them could have pitched its shot and shell through the windows of the White House, or into the halls and chambers of the Capitol.

Persons and Papers

This large south-fronting room has been the business office of all the Presidents who have lived in this house. In one sense it is the nerve-centre of the Republic. It is a wonderful historic cavern to move about in. The hearts and brains of a great people are somehow in connection with it, and they send to this chamber their blind impulses, their thrills of hope, their faintnesses of disappointment, their shivers of fear, and even their sinking of despair.

Mr. Lincoln will be here in a few minutes. He was always an early riser, and it is a good habit for him to have in these overworked times. He is apt to come striding along the hall at farm hours, as if he were in haste to get here and finish something left over from last evening, or attend to some crisis which came in the night, before the daily procession of visitors can set in.

That long table in the middle of the room is the board around which the Cabinet sits in council, and they are gathered there frequently, nowadays. How they appear when they are gathered will be very well imagined by future generations after looking at Carpenter's picture of the first reading of the Emancipation Proclamation, which is to be painted a few years hence and hung upon a wall of the Capitol. In that picture, however, without purpose of the painter, Mr. Montgomery Blair, the Postmaster-General, will be made to stand upon the square yard of carpet he occupied when he and the President took leave of each other, coldly, formally, without any hand-shaking, the day he ceased to be a member of the Cabinet.

These meetings are wonderfully secret affairs. Only a private secretary may enter the room to so much as bring in a paper. No breath of any "Cabinet secret" will ever transpire, so faithfully is the seal of this room guarded.

There is hardly an ornamental or a superfluous article of furniture in the room. This second-hand mahogany upright desk, from some old furniture auction—or that is what it looks like—here by the middle window, is Mr.

Lincoln's working-desk. This is the place where he is expected to perform his political and military miracles. Matters of all kinds are put into shape here for after-consideration by the Cabinet, when they assemble around the long table to be informed why they were sent for. It is not often, however, that a paper or plan prepared by Mr. Lincoln is much changed in its appearance at the end of a meeting.

The opposite rule prevails at the Capitol, for Congress is all the while in a bubble and boil over business which goes to it from this desk. It is their privilege to cut and slash, very much as Tad and Willie are cutting and slashing something or other, on the floor, under and behind and all around this Republican throne. There is nothing on the desk but a few bundles of papers and an outspread map. It is a map of part of the regions which are beginning to be overrun with armies, and now that the President has come in and has dropped into his chair, his forehead wrinkles more deeply than usual as he leans forward. No doubt he knows what he means when he removes a red-headed pin on the map from the junction of the Ohio and Mississippi, at Cairo, and sticks it in again, further down the river. Next goes a black-headed pin away over into Missouri, and it may be that he is thinking of Frémont; but nobody can guess why the blue-headed pin is transferred from Cincinnati down into the heart of Kentucky. It is a way he has of studying the movements of the forces on both sides, and a lot of fresh telegraphic dispatches has just been brought in from the War Office and put down upon the Cabinet table.

There must be something in them, by the brightened look on the President's face as he reads them and puts them down.

What a yell! But it comes from the forces belonging to quite another seat of war. Tad has been trying to make a war-map of Willie, and there are rapid movements in consequence on both sides. Peace is obtained by sending them to their mother, at the other end of the building, but the President does not return to his desk. He is studying one of the maps he has pulled down from the spring-roller above the lounge on the eastern side of the room. It is an outline map of West Virginia and the mountain ranges, and it is likely that something important is going on there.

In the northwestern corner of the room there are standing racks, with many map-rollers, and there are folios of maps on the floor and leaning against the walls. The area of this war, by land and sea, is widening, but the operations at all points are watched and studied, and in their general outline are governed from, and are continually reported to, this central heart and brain room in this civil and military headquarters of the nation.

Hunting for generals? That is it exactly. The President is collecting and equipping armies, and he is compelled to direct them, more or less, during the processes of creation, but he is all the while searching for men who can take that responsibility off his hands. The men who are willing to take it are hunting him, too, and he could make up a regiment out of the applicants for stars.

The stack of papers on the Cabinet table, when we were in that room, related entirely to brigadier appointments. So do all these rubber-banded bundles in this deep drawer and in that. They gather day by day, and each batch must have a written digest made of its character. It is hard to digest some of them. Men ask authority to lead brigades, who cannot place a company in line, or put an awkward squad through the manual of arms.

There is a world of mournful fun in some of these brigadier papers, and Mr. Lincoln now and then succeeds in laughing over them, as well as in losing his temper.

What is in that other cram-full drawer? Post chaplains, and their papers also require much digestion. The President has an idea that most of the men who are anxious for the rank and pay of religious majors, without the toil and exposure and peril of keeping company with a regiment in the field, are what he calls "loose-footed ministers," and he does not take to them kindly.

Here is our special work coming in. The big sack that Louis, the President's messenger, is perspiring under, contains the morning's mail. What a pile it makes, as he pours it out upon the table! Why, no, it is no larger than usual. Heaps of newspapers? Yes, and no. We have to buy the newspapers we really need and read, like other people, but a host of journals, all over the country, supply the White House gratis. Open them if you wish to learn how the course of human events, and of the President in particular, is really influenced. How very many of these sagacious editors have blue-and-redded their favorite editorials, and have underscored their most stinging paragraphs!

That is because they fear lest Mr. Lincoln may otherwise fail to be duly impressed. He might even not see the points! His first complete failure was an attempt he made to watch the course of public opinion as expressed by the great dailies East and West. After he gave up reading them, he had a daily brief made for him to look at, but at the end of a fortnight he had not once found time to glance at it, and we gave it up.

Besides all other difficulties, the editors are dancing around the situation in such a manner that no man can follow them without getting too dizzy for regular work.

Put aside the journals now, and take up the kind of written papers which come through the post in bundles and bales, mostly sealed a great deal. Do you see what they are? That pile is of applications for appointments to offices of every name and grade, all over the land. They must be examined with care, and some of them must be briefed before they are referred to the departments and bureaus with which the offices asked for are connected. We will not show any of them to Mr. Lincoln at present.

That other pile contains matter that belongs here. They are "pardon papers," and this desk has the custody of them, but their proper place, one would think, is in the War Office. That is where they all must go, after a while; but the President wishes them where he can lay his hands upon them, and every batch of papers and petitions must be in order for him when he calls for it. He will surely do so when some more or less mournful delegation comes to see him about it. He is downright sure to pardon any case that he can find a fair excuse for pardoning, and some people think he carries his mercy too far. There was a vast amount of probable pardon, for instance, in a bale of papers which should have been here day before yesterday. It came from a guerrilla-stricken district in the West, for the pardon of the worst guerrilla in it, and the petitions were largely and eminently and influentially signed. There came up to the President's office in great haste a large and eminent and influential delegation, and the papers were sent for. Somehow or other they were not here. They may have been at the War Office, but the people there denied it. They may have been somewhere else, but the people there denied it, and the delegation had to go away, and the application still hangs fire.

"What did you say? A telegram from—? You don't tell me! Has that man been actually hung? It's a pity about his papers! Seems to me—well, yes, I remember now. I know where—"

"Well, if I did, I guess I wouldn't; not now; but if they're ever called for again, and they won't be, they ought to be where they can be found."

"Certainly, certainly. But it's just as well that one murderer has escaped being pardoned by Abraham Lincoln. Narrow escape, too! The merest piece of luck in all the world!"

There is no sameness in the sizes of the White House mails. Some days there will be less than 200 separate lots, large and small. Some days there will be over 300. Anyhow, every envelope must be opened and its contents duly examined.

Are they all read? Not exactly, with a big wicker waste-basket on either side of this chair. A good half of each mail belongs in them, as fast as you can find it out. The other half calls for more or less respectful treatment, but generally for judicious distribution among the departments, with or without favorable remarks indorsed upon it.

It is lightning work, necessarily, but have you noticed this fine-looking, well-dressed, elderly gentleman, who is sitting in the chair by the mantel? He has been watching, with increasing feverishness, the swift processes which dispose of the President's mail. He has narrowly noted the destructions and the references, and not while he has sat there has a solitary letter been discovered of the kind which seems to require the personal inspection and decision of Mr. Lincoln. It is not often that a mail, morning or evening, brings more than two or three envelopes of that kind. Upon all others the President's judgment is passed as nearly as his proxy can imagine it, and, at all events, the verdict is absolute and final.

The elderly gentleman looks as if he might be a judge, or a college president, or even a Governor, at home, but he is not at home now. The chances are two to one that he has at some time written letters to Mr. Lincoln, and now he is here, and he has sent in his card and he is waiting for an interview. His face is waxing very red and he squirms upon his chair, but we will not let him know we are watching him, and we will put aside that little heap of opened letters by themselves.

The explosion is coming! He actually stamps with anger as he exclaims:

"Is that the way you treat the President's mail? Mr. Lincoln does not know this! What would the people say if they knew that their communications to their Chief Magistrate are dealt with in this shameful manner? Thrown into the waste-basket! What does Lincoln mean? Putting such an awful responsibility into the hands of a mere boy! A boy!"

It is a storm of hot and fiery indignation, but it pauses for breath, and you can hand him the selected lot of opened letters at your elbow.

"Please read those, sir, and give me your own opinion of them. I may be right about them. Do you really think, now, that the President of the United States ought to turn from the affairs of the nation to put in his time on that sort of thing?"

He has them and he is reading, and his fiery face is getting redder yet as he goes along. Now he has struck something that makes him go the other way, and he is positively white with wrath. It was almost too mischievous to give him that horrible selection.

The letters in the hands of that dignified but angry critic tell stories of partisan bitterness and personal hatred; of the most venomous malice, seeking to shoot with poisoned arrows of abuse; of low, slanderous meannesses; of the coarsest, foulest vulgarity to which beastly men can sink; of the wildest, the fiercest and the most obscene ravings of utter insanity; and the elderly gentleman throws them upon the table and sinks back in his chair, for a moment almost speechless with shame and indignation. He has found his breath:

"You are right, young man! You are right! He ought not to see a line of that stuff! Burn it, sir! Burn it! What devils there are!"

He is pacing hotly up and down the room, but the messenger has come to summon him to an interview with the President, and he probably will not complain of what he saw doing here.

Nevertheless, this mail has not contained a larger percentage than usual of the evidence that when any man goes clean crazy in these war-days he at once sits down and pens an epistle to the President. That close-lined, four-page letter, written in red, which professes to be blood, comes every day, and is always signed "The Angel Gabriel," but the contents are the reverse of angelic. This long, elaborate, remarkably well-written, seemingly wise and sound volume of advice concerning the policy to be pursued by the Adminstration is a curiosity. It is calm, sane, dignified, but it professes to be signed, through a medium, by the spirits of nearly a score of old worthies of the Republic. There are the familiar signatures of George Washington, John Hancock, Benjamin Franklin, Thomas Jefferson, John Adams, and so on to the end of the list, all as perfectly made as they themselves could write them, or as the most expert living forger could imitate them, using the same pen for all. Keep that document and show it to the President some day.

There is all the while a host of letters that are altogether sane, but which give a curious presentation of the fact that the average American, male or female, knows almost nothing about the machinery of the National Government. Simple-minded people send their business to Father Abraham, no matter what it is, and it is the business of this desk to not neglect what they send. There may even be written upon their papers endorsements asking for prompt and favorable consideration, if there is a sufficient assurance that Lincoln would have done so, had he seen them before transmitting them to their proper bureau in one or other of the departments. At some later day, some gratified citizen may tell an admiring neighbor:

"Tell ye haow I did it. I jest cut the red tape and dodged the loryers and writ to Linken, and he searched the matter up and had it 'tended to. He's a good man, he is!"

There is about as large a throng of writers who are ready to offer advice and even instruction upon the management of the war. It is marvelous how they can, theoretically, swing troops back and forth about the country. It is plain that they all have played the game of checkers, and have learned how to "jump" the Confederate forces and forts with their men.

The assassination idea has taken possession of so many minds that not many days go by without the coming of some kind of epistolary threat or warning.

There is no end to the mere fault-finding, nor to the suggestions of plans of campaigns and of proposed improvements in management. Here is one now, just opened. It is from a man in Tolono, Ill., and he proposes to open the Confederate blockade of the Potomac from Washington down to Fortress Monroe. He says he has invented a cross-eyed gun, with two barrels, set at an angle so as to shoot in both directions; and he proposes to raise a regiment of cross-eyed men to use the new weapons.

"I know enough of cross-eyed men to fill up the regiment, and, by thunder! Mr. Lincoln, I'm cross-eyed enough to be colonel of it. We could march down the river and clean out both banks at once."

We will take that letter across the hall.

"How do you think it would work, Mr. Lincoln?"

"Well, I don't know but what there's about as much in it as there is in some of the other plans they want me to take."

He got a laugh out of it, anyhow, and that is something.

Written acknowledgments of the receipt and disposal of papers are frequently necessary, and it is well that you have the right to frank letters through the mails, for you never could get the President to spend time in franking.

The sack that Louis brings from the post-office is not so large as it would have to be but for the fact that no subordinate military or naval officer communicates directly with the commander-in-chief, the President. The latter may follow the armies as closely as he pleases upon his maps, but the men who make the movements do not report to him, and he does not meddle with the details of their work.

Mrs. Lincoln receives many letters. There lies her mail, ready to be taken to her.

"Somebody has been opening those letters."

Is it possible that such a blunder could have been made? Well, the only thing to be done is to go and see her at once. Take them along, and ask her to meet you in the Red Room.

Mrs. Lincoln is a pleasant-looking woman, and she is in fine health and spirits this morning.

"You sent word that you had a complaint to make to me. What is it?"

"This rascally paper-folder, Mrs. Lincoln. A lot of your letters—here they are—were lying on their faces on my table, and he got at them and opened every one of them. I caught him and choked him off before he had time to read them, but I'd like to know what I am to do about him?"

She does not seem to be at all angry with your long slip of polished ivory.

"Oh, dear me! Is that all? I wish you would open and read every letter that comes. You know my sister's handwriting?"

"Perfectly. That and that are from her."

"Read them, too, if you have any doubt. Don't let a thing come to me that you've not first read yourself, and that you are not sure I would wish to see. I do not wish to open a letter, nor even a parcel, of any kind, until after you have examined it. Never!"

She is suddenly called away, and you have no full explanation until you have carried that correspondence upstairs again.

The President's wife is venomously accused of being at heart a traitor, and of being in communication with the Confederate authorities, to whom, it is said, she sends information as to the plans of Union generals, as these are minutely confided to her by Mr. Lincoln. The newspapers, some of them, assert it openly, and their editors refuse to believe that she is intensely patriotic, and utterly devoted to her husband. She may be thinking of that—

Read! Read! You know now why she wishes you to inspect her letters. The insane, the depraved and the fiendish have by no means restricted themselves to the President in their infamous penmanship. His vilest foes are willing to vent their infernal malice upon his unoffending wife, but from this day forward they will but send their missives to the waste-basket and the fire. That is where some of the writers are going, too.

Weapons and War Ships

Inmates of the White House get accustomed, after a while, to this strange, unnatural, wartime atmosphere, but they cannot escape from some of its effects. Mr. Lincoln bears it better than could another man in his place, perhaps, but it is telling upon him perceptibly. The sense of not breathing so easily here as elsewhere is a false impression, no doubt, but all sorts of men are suffering from moral malarial fever. Some of them say and do different things from what they intended saying or doing before they came to Washington. All kinds of people come on all kinds of errands, and most of them, nowadays, besiege the Capitol and the Departments, but there is a long list of persistent visitors who hang around the White House and wait for chances to see the President, even after they are assured that he cannot and will not see them.

For a while the private secretary's room was overflowed, like the others, but the excess worked a reaction, and the door of that office is now under wholesome restrictions. The door of this northeast room cannot so well be closed, and it has become a favorite waiting-place for those who consider themselves privileged to make use of it. Hullo!

"I want to see Old Abe!"

He is six feet high, in shining black broadcloth, shining pin and watch-chain, shining black hat and hair, and his face is all one shine of serene, hearty, boisterous self-confidence. He knows exactly how to swing into the affections of a rail-splitter, and he has swung right past the usher, and the common people—Senators, Congressmen and the like—who are loitering so patiently near the President's office door. His entrance here suggests the word "bulge," if there is such a word.

"Is Old Abe in?" and the smile on his face ripens into a haw-haw of asserted old acquaintance and personal familiarity with—well, with the Government and with all creation.

"If you mean the President of the United States, this is Congress day. Are you a member of the Senate or of the House? The messenger will take in any member's card."

"I want to see Old Abe!"

"Oh, well! He isn't here!"

The smile which vanishes from the haw-haw's face brightens audibly upon the faces of several more or less venerable statesmen who are loitering near the desk, and a shining suit of black broadcloth fades limply away along the hall.

All sorts of people come upon all sorts of errands, and the broad-shouldered, plain-looking fellow sitting there seems to have his lap full of joiner-work, painted black. It reminds one of the Noah's arks he used to get at Christmas, only that it is very low and wide, and has no procession of wooden animals. There are toy cannon, too, looking out of the windows, instead of giraffes. That man was in to see the President yesterday, and they sat down together and discussed Western steamboats and flatboats and gunboats, and they turned that thing inside out. It has been here a good while, sitting on the mantel. It is the first model of a "tin-clad" gunboat, for use upon the shallow waters of the West, and the President has had more to do than most men are aware of with the beginnings of the Mississippi flotilla.

The other day there came another sort of man to sit here and wait his turn to see the President. He was a massive, vigorous, fine-looking man, and he said his name was Bushnell. He brought, to show to the President, a model of a strange, altogether new sea-going war-monster, devised by another man named Ericsson. Mr. Lincoln made a careful study of what was said to resemble a cheese-box on a raft, and he ordered a board of naval officers to get together and examine it. Then he turned himself into a naval officer and met with Bushnell and the board. There were adverse opinions from several other old salts, but Mr. Lincoln said he was like the fat girl when she put on her stocking—she thought there was something in it, and so did he, and the building of the *Monitor* was ordered, and is now quietly going on.

The new inventions that come and sit here are not by any means all of them of wood. Look at that thing on the table. It has been there week after week, and everybody stops and turns it over. No, it was not dug up from any old feudal-time battle-field. The surliest remark yet made upon that pretty blue shell of polished steel came from a grim old soldier with stars upon his shoulders:

"So that's a cuirass! Well, the inventor must be a queer ass to think a man could lug that thing on a march in a hot sun, or on the double-quick."

It claims to be bullet-proof, and Mr. Lincoln says that if that's the case, he approves of it; but that there must be a thorough test made. The inventor can put it on, and a detail of sharpshooters can practice at it, to see whether or not a bullet will go through. The test seems to be postponed, but it is a good enough table ornament.

So is the round cast-iron bulb that is serving as a paper-weight. There is hardly any other contrivance more thoroughly infernal than that proposed hand-grenade. Pick it up, so, and give it this twist, and it unscrews its shell and falls into a dozen pieces of irregular shapes and angles. In the middle of these, when they are screwed up again, there is a chamber for fulminate and powder. Charge it, throw it among a crowd, and it will drive those pieces in all directions. Put it on the ground where men or horses are to walk. It can be capped so delicately that a touch or a jar will explode it. A horrible thing for close combat, but of no practical use in these days of long-range rifles.

The brass cannon model, holding down those land patents, has a promise of slaughter in it. So has the semblance of a musket leaning against the wall, but the danger in that thing is to the man who fires it off. It is to be a speculation for somebody, if the agent who represents a shipload like it can induce the President to force an unwilling Ordnance Bureau to buy them. They were made by a fraudulent contractor for the Austrian army, and were rejected as worthless. No bribe could get them into the Austrian service, and here they are, under the supposition that Americans never have seen any guns. That specimen will be quite enough, for the President really knows something about gunnery. He takes an especial interest in the new idea of breech-loaders and repeaters, but the Bureau officials are against him. This Henry rifle is a sixteen-shooter. This other invention will go off nine times; but the single-shooting breech-loader is his idea of the army rifle of the future. He studies every new pattern that comes, and he has been looking closely at this. It's the very latest. An old Springfield musket barrel, fitted with a cartridge chamber that goes on and comes off with a screw twist.

"Ah! Mr. President."

"They say you're a pretty good marksman. I want you to be here early tomorrow morning; say half-past six. We'll go out on the Mall and try some of these guns. I can get a better idea—"

The talk on gunnery gets to be so interesting that they come to call him to his dinner, with a reminder from Mrs. Lincoln that it is a company day, and he has to go.

The Mall is that great slope of grass and weeds and rubbish between the White House grounds and the Potomac. Away out in the middle of it there is a pile of old lumber as large as a small house. It is just the thing to set up a target against. There will be no danger of our killing anybody.

One's nerves are all the better for rifle practice after a good night's sleep, and this is a clear, still, beautiful morning.

If Mr. Lincoln is not yet up—

"Well, you didn't keep me waiting. Now, you take that thing and I'll take this, and we'll go right along."

"That thing," as he calls it, is the old Springfield, with the screw-twisting additions, and it takes in cartridges of the full service size. His own choice is a kind of Spencer, and is neatly finished at about sporting caliber. No Union force ever yet marched out armed precisely as the Commander-in-Chief and his detachment are this morning.

"General Ripley says, Mr. Lincoln, that men enough can be killed with the old smooth-bore and the old cartridges, a ball and three buckshot."

"Just so. But our folks are not getting near enough to the enemy to do any good with them just now. We've got to get guns that'll carry further."

He is in a talking mood, and the entire breech-loading and muzzle-loading question is rapidly analyzed during the walk to the Mall.

A hundred yards is fair trial-distance, and a board against the pile of lumber is a good enough mark.

They make good gun-barrels at Springfield, and this thing carries straight, but oh, what a kick it has, with this loose twist at the heel of it!

He never was a first-rate shot.

"I declare, you are beating me! I'll take a good sight this time."

Down he crouches, to hold his piece across his knee, but he has entirely forgotten one thing. There are stringent orders out forbidding all firing within the camp limits of this frontier post called Washington City. Mr. Lincoln should have borne them in mind, for he got into difficulties with an order of that kind once. Away back, when he was a captain of militia in the Black Hawk War, he had to wear a wooden sword a whole day for emptying his horse-pistols too near the camp limits.

There they come! There is a short sergeant, or a short corporal, and four or five men of the regiment on guard duty, and they are on a clean run from the avenue, but the President's protracted squint along that blue barrel must not be interrupted.

The short sergeant, or he may be a short corporal, is beginning to make remarks, and he has forgotten all he learned in Sunday-school.

"Stop that firing! Stop that firing!"

That is his duty, no doubt, but where did he pick up so many "battle words?"

"Stop that firing—"

Bang goes the rifle, just as the sergeant, or corporal, arrives within a few paces and is putting out an eager, angry hand, as if he had an arrest to make. Here comes the fun!

Perhaps Mr. Lincoln heard him, and perhaps not, but his tall, gaunt form shoots up, up, up, uncoiling to its full height, and his smiling face looks down upon the explosive volunteers.

Their faces, especially that of the sergeant, or corporal, look up at his, and all their jaws seem to drop in unison. No word of command is uttered, but they "right about face" in a second of time. Now it is a double-quick, quicker, quicker, as they race back toward the avenue, leaving behind them only a confused, suppressed breath about having "cussed Old Abe himself."

His own laugh, in his semi-silent, peculiar way, is long and hearty, but his only remark is:

"Well, they might have stayed to see the shooting."

There is not a great deal more to be done, for he has answered the questions he had to ask of these rifles, and the back-action faculty developed by the old Springfield has kicked the secretary's shoulder black and blue. It will be a week before any very rapid writing is done in the northeast room.

We are back in it, lame enough, and in no humor to listen to the old one-wheel rifle orator, if he comes. Here he is, too, with his kill-at-three-miles rolling along beside him. It's nothing but an overgrown muzzle-loader, on a great spider-web wheel, but its inventor is persuaded that the people and the Army demand its adoption. He is loaded up, himself, with the popular dissatisfaction over the inefficient management of the war.

"The President must be made to understand, sir, that the eyes of the people are on him, sir! They are watching him, sir! This way of doing can't go on, sir! He must meet the requirements of the age, sir! Or he must take the consequences, sir!"

All of it, and of every reiterated form of it, is to be interpreted: "Woe to him, if he does not order the Ordnance Bureau to contract for at least 10,000 of enemy-slaughtering, far-shooting, spider-wheel-mounted, two-ounce-ball rifles, like this, sir!"

One way and another, this day's work has been much interrupted, and the mail was large. It must be cut into again by gaslight, and here we are.

Here is another of those queer communications from the ghost of Andrew Jackson. He was not particular about his grammar or his spelling, when he lived here, but he never wrote or talked such bald nonsense as this is, and the signature is decidedly not his own. That chair, yonder, was such a favorite with him that to this day it goes by the name of Andrew Jackson's chair. It is of Mexican material and workmanship, and was presented to him by citizens of that republic in token of their appreciation of his friendly policy, and is one of the heirlooms of the White House. Its strong but graceful and unique mahogany frame sustains a hollow morocco leather seat that is peculiarly comfortable. Old Hickory was accustomed to lean back in it, of winter evenings, before the fireplace in the President's room, and smoke his corncob pipe and put his stockinged feet upon the middle bricks of the fireplace arch. Mr. Lincoln expressed a wish to have those bricks preserved when the fireplace was reconstructed, but they were somehow mislaid and lost. Still, he has managed to step in Andrew Jackson's footmarks fairly well, so far as determination to preserve the Union is concerned.

"I want you to come along with me. I'm going over to Seward's."

It is the President himself, and he has a large portfolio under his arm.

"Here are some letters I had put aside to show to you."

"Not now. Not now. Come!"

He is intensely absorbed in something, and it is best to take the portfolio and follow him in silence. When he reaches the front door, and opens it and looks out, he discovers that a drizzle of rain is falling. The old doorkeeper is standing by, rubbing his hands as usual, and with his perpetual half smile of suppressed humor flickering across his face.

"Edward," says Mr. Lincoln, "go up to my room and bring me my umbrella. It stands in the corner, behind my table."

Edward is gone but a moment, while Mr. Lincoln stands peering gloomily out into the darkness, and now he is back again, but he brings no umbrella.

"Your Excellency," he remarks, washing his hands diligently, "it's not there. I think the owner must have come for it. I'll get another—just a minute, sir."

It was more the way it was said than the joke itself that makes the President laugh; but we are hardly out of the house, walking under the umbrella Edward found for him, before he tells a story about the doorkeeper.

"There's a great deal of fun in him. Just after Taylor's death, when Fillmore succeeded him, Fillmore needed to buy a carriage. Some gentleman here was breaking up housekeeping and had one for sale, and Fillmore took Edward with him when he went to look at it. It seemed to be a pretty good turnout, but Fillmore looked it carefully over and then asked Edward: 'How do you think it will do for the President of the United States to ride in a second-hand carriage?'

"'Sure, your Excellency,' replied Edward, 'you're only a second-hand President, you know.'

"Fillmore told the story himself," continues Mr. Lincoln; and then he adds something else about Fillmore which lasts to the door of Secretary Seward's house, a little beyond the avenue. In a moment more we are in the room on the right, a sort of business-like reception-room, and a bright wood fire is blazing upon the hearth, for the night is chilly. The portfolio is placed upon the center table and opened, and a number of maps and papers are spread out, for ready production when called for. In a minute more the door of the room again opens, and Mr. Seward enters, and with him is a slight, short, but firmly knit, self-possessed, intelligent-looking gentleman, in the uniform of a major-general, who is introduced to the President in spite of the fact that Mr. Lincoln's hand goes out to him at once.

"I'm glad to meet you, General Dix. My private secretary,—," and he adds a few words explanatory of his preference for holding a sort of council here rather than at the White House. There are grave matters before those three men. General Dix was in Buchanan's Cabinet, and he is aware of many things that are not so well known by other men. He has been taken into full confidence by the new Administration, and much authority and power have been given him. This evening he is here for consultation, and Mr. Seward and the President discuss with him the entire policy to be pursued with Maryland and the other border States. It is late when the conference ends, and when Mr. Lincoln goes out to return home it is still raining. If he is really watched and followed by would-be assassins, now is their time, for neither he nor his young attendant carries a weapon, and they are not dreaming of any danger from the few persons they are meeting.

"Mr. Lincoln, what do you think of General Dix? I never saw him before."

"Neither did I," replies the President. "This is our first interview. What do I think of him? Well, if I am going to judge by what he has said to-night—by the advice he has given—General Dix is, I should say, a wise man, a very wise man."

The White House is reached and entered, the umbrella is handed to Old Edward at the door, and the President returns to his room, directing that the portfolio be laid upon his table. It contains more papers than when it went out, and he has, he says, some work to do, but he is glad that no more dispatches came in during his absence.

Gifts and Visitors

There has never been and there is not now any excessive liberality in the appropriations made by Congress for paying Presidents and conducting the business of the National Executive. The President's salary, in 1861, is just what it was when such a dollar as is paid him, or even a silver dollar, would go twice as far in defraying household expenses. The salary of his private secretary is still only $2,500, with no provision for an assistant. When the work to be done imperatively demanded a second private secretary, it was necessary to appoint him, at first, a clerk in one of the departments, and then an army officer with special detail to duty in this office. His rank and position are fixed and recognized, however, by reason of the important functions he performs.

Since Mr. Lincoln's term began, something has been done toward refitting the "reception" part of the interior of the White House, but the remainder of that and of the outside are untouched, and the basement continues to carry somewhat the air of an old and unsuccessful hotel.

The northeast room has been as shabby as any, but it has assumed a suddenly disastrous look, this fine morning. The green cloth cover of the broad table was ink-stained and work-worn, last evening, but it was whole. It is by no means a unit, now. Tad and Willie Lincoln have been here, and they are the happy owners of brand-new pocket-knives. They are sharp knives, too, that will cut outline maps of the seat of war, or of anything else, upon green cloth table-covers. Such a looking mess!—Hullo! There goes the President's bell! He wants me in his room, but it isn't worth while to tell him what the boys have been up to.

That bell up there has a cord within the President's reach, and so have similar bells in other rooms, upstairs and downstairs. Any summons from him must be promptly responded to, especially when it is repeated in this furious manner. He is fire mad about something!

The door of the northeast room is opened and so is Nicolay's door, across the hall. See how he springs up! His bell, too, is ringing violently and repeatedly. There is Louis, the President's messenger, hurrying along the hall. Old Edward is coming upstairs as fast as his sense of propriety will let him. Here's Hay! There come Stackpole! Something is the matter with the President! This is something serious!

Not a bit of it. The trouble is that the bells of the whole house are bewitched, and the wizards who have done it are in wild glee over their success. One of them, named Tad, is sitting by a central pinion or "yoke" of the White House bell system, away up in the garret, tugging hard and bringing out at once all the jangle there is in the building. There is a very funny meeting of the miscellaneous crowd summoned to the President's room, but Tad and Willie have lost the *entrée* of the garret.

Speaking of the garret puts one in mind of what there is left of the antediluvian society of the Capital. The President is eminently social in his disposition and so is Mrs. Lincoln, but there have been many things in the way of even official sociability since their arrival in Washington. He has a superabundance of visitors, truly, and she has had no lack, but the old-time society of the city of Washington has been shattered to its foundations, and the new social structure takes form only slowly. It is semi-chaotic as yet.

The old society was based upon an aristocratic stratum of Virginian and Maryland families, reinforced from other parts of the South more largely than from the North. It possessed a subtle power for absorbing and assimilating whatever representatives of wealth or social rank drifted into it, from time to time, from what were then distinguished as the free States. There was a vast deal of conservative Union sentiment here until the Old Dominion joined the Confederacy and the army under McDowell crossed the Potomac. There has not been so much since then, but there is a manifest effort, which finds a singularly powerful echo in several of the great Northern cities, to associate Unionism with Plebeianism and to make secession proclivities a mark of social elevation, if not of some sort of distant relationship with the European aristocracies which are known to sympathize so strongly with the South.

There is no denying the attractiveness of Southern society—the charm of its manner, the attainments, the capacities of its leaders of both sexes. Its women were a power here, as much, almost, as were its statesmen; and those of them who remain are slow to yield their old supremacy, or to place themselves in relation with the changed order of things. Mrs. Lincoln came to Washington with a distinct understanding of her social duties and with an energetic purpose to perform them. Of a good Kentucky family and of very fair education, she had been early noted for the keenness of her wit, and the position held at the State Capital of Illinois during many years by her husband had prepared her for taking a leading part. That she should make a success here, under such circumstances, under the focalized bitterness of all possible adverse criticisms, was simply out of the question; but she has done vastly better than her ill-natured critics are at all willing to admit. They are a jury empaneled to convict on every count of every indictment which any slanderous tongue may bring against her, and they have already succeeded in so poisoning the popular mind that it will never be able to judge her fairly. Her first public reception was held in the parlors of Willard's Hotel, on the 25th of February, 1861, before the Inauguration, and it was largely but very promiscuously attended. The first of the regular series of Friday evening public receptions at the White House was held on the 8th of March following, and all that need be said of it was that during four hours there was a jam from the eastern gate of the grounds, of people coming in, to the western gate, of people going out; and that during two and a half hours the President shook hands with everybody that passed him. Mrs. Lincoln tried to follow his example, but had to give it up; and he asserted, at the end of it, that his hand, for once, was too lame to sign anything. There was at least this difference between the pack of 1861 and the memorable rush in Andrew Jackson's day, that all these hand-shakers were apparently well behaved and entirely sober—it was hardly so in 1829, if historians have correctly pictured the effect of the "superabundant refreshments" provided, according to the ideas of hospitality prevailing at that day.

A great deal of that old idea survives, lingering upon the sideboards of old Washington families; in the cupboards of professional offices; under the desks of officeholders, civil, military and naval; all over all of the hotels; meeting everybody in the street, whenever he meets anybody else; and it is powerfully intrenched under each of the two Houses of Congress, at the Capitol, and its very citadel is the famous "Hole in the Wall," convenient to the Supreme Court Rooms and operating as a half-way social house between the two legislative Houses. Sometimes one can understand the old time better after a late-in-the-day inspection of the sociability going on in the Hole in the Wall. There is nothing of the sort in the White House at present, for Mr. Lincoln is strictly abstinent as to all intoxicating drinks. His first printed paper, written while a mere boy, was a vigorous denunciation of the evils produced by whiskey among the settlers in the backwoods of his then own State of Indiana. We are to dine with him, to-day, by special invitation, and you will see for yourself that there is no wine upon his table; but a large number of Northern newspaper editors will tell you, afterward, that your eyes deceived you, and that the President was much the worse after dinner, according to his half-concealed custom. It is when he has been drinking, they say, that he does such things and tells such stories. The things, political and warlike, which the reporters may see fit to disapprove, may be the very acts for which some other men praise him; but we who have been in and out of the White House, day after day, have failed to hear any of those objectionable stories. We have heard pointed illustrations of many a keen-edged piece of common sense, but then they could have been uttered harmlessly anywhere. As for a vast number of so-called jokes, attributed to him, he has never so much as heard them; but one very, very witty and dirty and insolent pun, perpetrated by him upon a member of his own Cabinet, through the inventive brains of a well-known newspaper reporter, representative of a great Northern daily, has been carried to him, and the literary gentleman has been sent for. He has heretofore enjoyed special privileges of access to the President for news purposes, although his journal is a severely adverse critic. Here he is, now, waiting his turn to go into the President's room, with no idea whatever why he has been sent for.

He is a jolly fellow, full of wit, of some kinds, and that joke is too good and he must tell it. He cannot keep it in, and out it comes, while the paper-knife slices open the envelopes. He does not dream that his story is like so many of the documents the secretary is pulling out of their envelopes, and that it has been "respectfully referred," but to the Commander-in-Chief and not to any Bureau. He did not see the President's face flush and darken when the brand-new pattern of foul humor was given him, as being circulated in his name. He will see something now, however, and he will hear something, for Louis has come to summon him across the hall. He goes, all smiles and chuckles, for no doubt a lot of army and other news is ready for him, or even more than that, something from Europe. He has been in the President's room only a few moments. There he is, now, coming out again, and he is not smiling. Whatever new thing he has learned carries him out of the White House with unusual haste, and he may be taking with him the materials for another story.

Does the good-natured, soft-hearted, easy-going, easily led, easily deceived, simple-minded tenant of the White House ever really lose his temper?

The country generally does not believe that he ever does or can, but the right answer to the question is that under exceedingly trying circumstances he generally succeeds in keeping down the storm which is continually stirred up within him by the treacheries, cowardices, villainies and stupidities, which, almost daily and hourly, he is compelled to see and understand and wrestle with and overcome. He is an old criminal lawyer, practiced in observing the ways of rascals, accustomed to reading them and circumventing them, but he does not commonly tell any man precisely what he thinks of him.

Some of the best of men come to call upon the President, and there is a fine example, at this moment, standing near his office door, waiting for the audience he will surely obtain. Beyond a doubt that man is a clergyman of high caste—a doctor of divinity. He is probably a great gun of one of the great sects, sent by his convocation to administer spiritual advice and consolation to the wearied, over-burdened ruler of a sympathizing nation. His outfit is the perfection of clerical uniform. Shining silk hat, with a weed half way up its glossy cylinder. Costly and shining broadcloth, double-breasted, with an open-fronted waistcoat that discloses spotless linen and brightens the effect of his profusely voluminous white neckcloth and his high standing collar. Heavy gold guard-chain across his chest. Boots that are as black mirrors, and he is tapping one of them gently with a gold-headed cane which, perhaps, his loving congregation presented him. His eyes turn upward, now and then, and the corners of his mouth turn down, and not since Mr. Lincoln entered this house has there been so much apparent professional sanctity upon this floor. Thus he has gone in, and he will surely obtain his object, for the President invariably treats with marked respect all clergymen of all denominations, with an exceptional increase on behalf of Quakers, including the fat, unclerical Quaker whom he has placed at the head of a Bureau of the Interior Department.

Nobody knows or needs to know the nature of the interview which the saint in fine apparel has had with Abraham Lincoln. He is coming out now, smiling benevolently, with an upward cast of his eye-corners and a downward jerk upon each side of his mouth. He is satisfied, no doubt, with the way in which he has done his duty; but it is time for us to go to luncheon.

There is pleasant relief in getting away from work and out into the open air, and it is almost always worth while to look in at Willard's Hotel on the way. It is a great place to go to. Drop in there whenever you can, especially in the evening. More news; more great men from all over the country; more generals, of all sorts; and, if you can go up into the parlors without being ushered out as a trespasser, you will find more pleasant ladies there, and more of a strangely mingled society than you can anywhere else in Washington. There is always a stream of people coming and going between Willard's and the White House. The hotel rooms are not so full at this hour of the day, for Congress is in session; but there are a dozen generals, off duty. Some look like soldiers, and some do not. Pass through the military men, who are discussing other military men, as a rule. That wide door opens into the spacious and splendid bar-room. There is a knot of half a dozen startlingly well-dressed men standing by the bar, and the range of tumblers on the mahogany is in progress of being lifted by them. They wait, for a moment, while one of their number completes a seemingly interesting account of something he has been doing—that is, rather, of some person whom he has been doing. It is very interesting, and his account is sneeringly but uproariously applauded. Do you know him, with his white necktie and shining broadcloth? It is the same man we saw coming out of Lincoln's room a few minutes ago, and he is about the worst man in the United States; and these are thieves, counterfeiters, blacklegs—the scum and curse of the earth. Down go the corners of his mouth, up go the corners of his eyes, and he closes them with a pious roll, as he says, "Now, brethren, let us drink!"

He will go the White House once more, and only once, and he will go into the President's room, and he will come out; and when he then comes through the door there will be a strange vision of a large foot just behind him, suggesting to any naval constructor the idea of a propeller. Perhaps the most interesting part of the whole affair is the fact that he did not, for the twinkling of an eye, succeed in deceiving Mr. Lincoln as to his real character. He was received from the first as a rogue, a wolf in sheep's clothing, but his criminal audacity went beyond the limits of patient endurance—and so he was also sent beyond the limits.

It is about dinner-time, and we will walk over to the other side of the house. It is not necessary to go home first, and put on a swallow-tailed coat, for the President will come to his own family table in the same dress in which he just signed a European treaty and the commissions of a dozen generals. With the single exception of the absence of regulation dining uniforms, however, there will be dignity enough, even in an entirely homelike and informal dinner party; for the somewhat solemn fact that this house is not like any other is finding recognition and expression in many ways.

There are no preliminaries, but we watched the going of the President and are here with him, in ample time, although he himself is a little late. There are several of the more intimate friends of the family at table, now we are seated, and there is no reason why the plainest of them should not feel altogether at home. Mrs. Lincoln seems to be even more than usually full of life and hospitality, and everything goes along admirably well.

Are the foes of the family right, after all?

There is wine here, and a bottle of champagne has been opened! A glass of it has been put by the President's plate, and he seems to be taking more than a little interest in it. He takes it up and smells of it, and laughs merrily, but he does not drink. There is a story connected with that glass of wine, and after it is told he has more than one of his own to tell in return. Not all of those at table are as rigid abstainers as he is, however, and the story told by Mrs. Lincoln brings us into the Red Room with her, after dinner, for an important private consultation. Not by any means all of the wine-drinking people of the North are Mr. Lincoln's enemies, and not all of his fervent friends disapprove of his supposed use of vinous beverages. Some of them, liberal and kindly souls, have clubbed together and have decided that he is to be supplied with the very best, and of their own selection. It is possible that they have an idea of stimulating him to greater energy in the prosecution of the war. At all events, they have forwarded to him a notable assortment. It has arrived in safety, and it is waiting in one of the basement storerooms, while Mrs. Lincoln tells what there is of it, as far as she understands the cases, and laughs over it so heartily and wonders what she is to do with so very peculiar a testimonial elephant.

There are loads of champagne, green seal and other seal; red wines of several kinds; white wine from the Rhine; wines of Spain and Portugal and the islands; whiskey distilled from rye, and from wheat, and from potatoes; choice brandy; Jamaica rum, and Santa Cruz rum; and she suspects one case of containing gin.

"They do not seem to have forgotten anything, Mrs. Lincoln, unless he wanted some arrack or vodke."

"But what is to be done? I never use any, and Mr. Lincoln never touches any. Here it all is, and these gentlemen—what can be said to them?"

"There is only one thing to be done, Mrs. Lincoln. Acknowledge the gift and its arrival, with all kinds of thanks, and add that you have distributed it among your favorite hospitals. The doctors will know what to do with it, if they can keep it away from the hospital nurses."

Mrs. Lincoln accepts the proposition gladly, and she herself will carry it out to the letter. That is the destination of the whole consignment, and the purposes of the senders are to be somewhat more than fulfilled. Mrs. Lincoln has been a regular visitor among the hospitals all along, and it pleases her exceedingly to have the distribution of so carefully selected a medical supply. As for the President, he has gone back to his room to work, and he will do as much of it and quite as well as he would if he had been stimulated.

The Critics and the Gamblers

Mrs. Lincoln is absolute mistress of all that part of the White House inside of the vestibule, on the first floor, and of all the upper floor east of the folding doors across the hall at the head of the stairs. She has had varied assistance in the management of her domain since she came into possession of it. She was never less than a somewhat authoritative ruler of her own affairs, but it is entirely easy, for all that, to meet her with the most positive and strenuous negatives. She is always ready to listen to argument and to yield to plainly put reasons for doing or for not doing, provided the arguments come from a recognized friend, for her personal antipathies are quick and strong, and at times they find hasty and resentful forms of expression.

It was not easy, at first, to understand why a lady who could be one day so kindly, so considerate, so generous, so thoughtful and so hopeful, could, upon another day, appear so unreasonable, so irritable, so despondent, so even niggardly, and so prone to see the dark, the wrong side of men and women and events. It is easier to understand it all and to deal with it after a few words from an eminent medical practitioner. Probably all physicians and most middle-aged people will understand better than could a youthful secretary the causes of a sudden horror of poverty to come, for example, which, during a few hours of extreme depression, proposed to sell the very manure in the Executive stables, and to cut off the necessary expenses of the household. No demand for undue economy and no unhappiness of disposition could be discovered a week or so later. People in great need of something spicy to talk or write about are picking up all sorts of stray gossip relating to asserted occurrences under this roof, and they are making strange work out of some of it. It is a work which they will not cease from. They will do it, to the very end, so effectively that a host of excellent people will one day close their eyes to the wife's robe dabbled with her husband's blood. There will be, in that day, a strange blindness and brutality concerning the awful shock produced by an infernal murder which is to make Mrs. Lincoln a widow in the hour which will seem to her the zenith of her life and of her husband's career and her own. Then charity and chivalry alike will be forgotten in the sneering comments which will follow the remaining days of a disturbed mind and a shattered nervous system. Even the shadow of the tomb itself, at last, will not be regarded as a sufficient curtain to prevent an unjust judgment from peering through and looking back to this time and reading in it nothing but the prurient scandals of this feverish war-time.

It is indeed feverish to the last degree, for nobody knows what will be the end of this matter. The most hopeful of us walk by faith and not by sight. The nation is bleeding terribly, and it is spending oceans of money. We know that we must pour out more blood and more gold, while a host of solemn prophets, in this country and in Europe, are assuring us that it is all in vain, and that the Great Republic of the West is on its death-bed. The fever is in everybody's veins, and the men who hope for the death, and who rejoice over every apparent sign of its nearness, are numerous in the city of Washington, and they sometimes even pay visits to the White House.

It is still early, after the quiet dinner of the President and his family, and it may do us good to take an evening walk. We will go down to the White House grounds, instead of around by way of the gate. They are well laid out, these grounds, until you come to the Mall, and they present an attractive appearance on Saturday afternoons in summer, when the Marine Band is playing, and groups of ladies and gentlemen and children are strolling around over them. Just now they have a bare, deserted, withered look of winter and hard times, and we are depressed enough by some of the news from the seat of war, so that we will not linger. The unfinished Treasury building, that we pass in going out, reminds one of the paper promises to pay which are flowing from it in a river. There are vehement assertions made that the promises will not be kept, that repudiation will surely come, and that these greenbacks will one day be as worthless as so much Continental currency. If we walk on across to the avenue, it is of little consequence which way we go when we leave it; but there is a group of men upon the corner, yonder, who are in bitter antagonism to anything or anybody coming from the White House. Mark the tall man in a loose, drab overcoat, and wearing spectacles. He calls himself a Union man, from Kentucky, and he holds a commission in the Confederate army, and he is here as a spy. Even Colonel Baker, however, cannot yet get hold of proof enough either to lock him up or to send him beyond the lines.

You do not know Baker? The head of the detective service? There are many who do not, but if any other man has been here long enough, with anything dubious about him, Baker knows him. He sometimes comes to the White House, and he is a very useful officer. He is one of the long fingers of the Executive branch of the Government.

The dark-haired, eagle-nosed, brilliant-eyed, strikingly handsome man is a Copperhead Congressman. He is fastidiously well-dressed now, but there are some ways in life which lead inevitably downward. Next beyond him, with no beauty at all but such as the tailor has given him, is another Northern enemy of the Union. You cannot feel toward those men as you do toward Southerners with arms in their hands. The pair of dandies with them are mere sporting men, and it is asserted that the entire sporting fraternity here leans toward secession. Its best patrons and victims, heretofore, have been the reckless spendthrifts whose money was earned for them by the unpaid toil of other men, and the sportsmen have not yet made profitable connections with the present financial system. What are they all on that corner for? Well, that closed-up-looking brick building is the famous gambling establishment known as Joe Hall's, and it contains a great deal of one of the lessons of the day. There was always a gambling fever in Washington, which broke out in this spot, but now there are six or seven well-known dens right on the avenue, between this and the Capitol, and nobody knows how many more are scattered around on other thoroughfares. All the vice and profligacy of all the North and West and of part of the South seem to be sewering into this great frontier post and pay-station of the army. There are more dance-houses, and all that sort of thing, than you could consent to dream of, as if the gates of hell opened always in the rear of great wars. This gambling feature of the general fever is pestilential; but that entire group of men is entering the building, and if we go with them we may learn something. We belong to the class of men who are admitted, and, although we never play, we can put down five dollars somewhere, and lose it, to pay for what we are to learn. That's right—on the roulette table—it is gone, and we are free to look around. Look closely, for we shall not find one man here of doubtful social position. This is not a place for any but "gentlemen," and even now one of the managers, a handsome old man, with deep wrinkles and gray hair at thirty, is coming this way with a question to ask.

"You know everybody," he says. "Some of these men are strangers to me. Are there any Treasury men here? Any paymasters, or quartermasters, or commissaries, or Government clerks, or army or navy officers in charge of money, and so forth?"

"Not a man of the kind, so far as I am able to tell you. Why?"

"Strict orders from the War Department and Baker's men."

"Of course. They're here."

"We wish to obey orders. It's not for our interest to have any scandals traced here. It would hurt us."

He turns away; but he need not have any anxiety, for it is a rarely select assembly. That bent old gentleman, betting heavily at the faro table, is a wealthy Maryland planter, and he should not throw away money, for it is just as he says to the Congressman next him: all his slaves are leaving him, and there is no power on earth to bring them back. That is a judge, and those are jurists, and those are men of finance. Nearly a dozen Congressmen, mixed up with contractors, lobbyists of the successful stripe, business men from the North, travelers seeing the sights, and a very few army men on leave. That really noble-looking gentleman, playing high at the faro table, had a long interview with the President to-day. He is a political leader, and he was formerly a bosom friend of Daniel Webster. Near him is a keen-vis-aged politician, who was as near to Henry Clay. There are curious Washington traditions concerning the luck at cards, good and bad, of the old-time party idols. It is possible that this building contains, this evening, more of the "old time" than does any other in the Capital. Men are passing away fast, however, and with them is passing the era of American political history to which they belonged. It is very nearly a true saying that all that remains of that era is a clog and hindrance to the Administration.

It is too late to return to the White House to-night, but the lesson of Joe Hall's need not be forgotten. The difficulties which harass the President can be better appreciated by bearing in mind that he is dealing with an untell-able mass of defective human nature.

As for gambling, almost everybody played cards in the old society of Washington, and the custom of "making the game interesting" has by no means passed away. The limit at the club is five dollars a corner at whist, and half as much for euchre, but no rule really limits gambling. The mania for it has broken out in other forms, as one exhibit of the prevalent mental fever. Almost every man who can discover means for doing so is gambling in stocks and gold. The latter provides the more exciting game of chance be-cause of the card-like fascination of the sudden and unaccountable jumps and falls of what are called its prices, meaning the price of greenbacks. They are rather the pulsations of the public hope and fear concerning the national credit.

There are patriotic men not a few, who cannot bring themselves to the rashness of buying gold for a rise, lest they should go against the public good, but who grasp at every encouragement to play "bear" and sell gold short, in the wild idea that so they are helping to push it down, and are strengthening the Treasury and the Government while they are winning a little money for themselves.

Does the President take any interest in Wall Street gambling operations? Of course he does, for the currency is the life of his policy. He was talking about it at the dinner-table yesterday, when we were there. We must go right over now, and hand him that paper.

There is a peculiarly humorous expression on his face, as he looks up.

"What is the price of gold this morning? Is it going up or down?"

"Up, Mr. Lincoln. The Street is wild."

"Well, now, they don't know everything. If I were a bear on Wall Street, and if I were short of gold, I'd keep short. It's a good time to sell."

He never gives any explanations, but he adds something bitter about bulls that may be tossed themselves, and we will go back to work.

Is not that one of the most remarkable looking men you ever saw? The tall hawk-eyed man, who cannot stand still, but keeps on walking, walking, up and down the room. He is saying something to himself, aloud:

"I'll stop, right where I am! If it goes on up, it'll break me!"

"What's the matter, Dr. Durant?"

"Short of gold! Sold my head off! And now it's just booming. Time for me to take it in, I guess, and stand my losses just as they are."

"Now, Dr. Durant, they don't know everything. If I were a bear on Wall Street, and if I were short of gold, I'd keep short. It's a good time to sell."

"Is that so? Can you send a telegram from here, for me? Give me a blank!"

Telegram after telegram is dashed off rapidly by the relieved bear, and a messenger carries them out after him. It is to be hoped that the price of gold will drop heavily, for he needs all his money and credit. He is undertaking to build the Pacific Railroad, and to save the Pacific slope to the Union. As to the President's unintentional suggestion, no other such instance has occurred or probably ever will. Nothing done in or about the White House has anything to do with the course of things on Wall Street. The results of battles are known in New York even before they are in Washington, only that the reports received there never tally with those received by the War Office. The President and the Secretary of War would be ruined if they should attempt to play bulls and bears upon the strength of any dispatches sent them by the generals.

Speaking of society matters, the history of Capital cities shows that any political society must necessarily be somewhat loosely constructed. Queer candidates will surely gain admission and recognition, now and then. There was never a time when anything like censorship was more difficult than it is here at present.

The Secession Jacobites believe that they have a comparatively easy time of it, but there are anecdotes in circulation. They can, indeed, close their aristocratic doors against Vandals of every grade, and they have felt entirely safe in their seclusion. Now, however, it is heartlessly related that their zealous readiness to accept as pure gold every arrival from the sunny but persecuted land of the Stars and Bars has led to the reception of sundry ambassadors extraordinary from the wide and wonderful realm of Fraud. Even secretly exhibited commissions in the Confederate army have not always been drawn from the inner pockets of the irreproachable. Only too often, it is said, have the gates of gushing sympathy been opened to guests whose absence from their posts in the ranks of Lee, for instance, was largely due to the fact that such gentlemen as Lee had no use for them. The end of such things is generally borrowed money and a missing hero, whose duties here as a "spy" ended as soon as he discerned that his errand as a dead-beat was accomplished.

The Washington *côteries*, therefore, are as yet disposed to be somewhat narrow, but the business instincts of Northern theatrical and musical managers, especially of the lower grades, have done a great deal toward making up the deficiency. There is enough and to spare to fill up the evenings of those whose gas-light hours are unoccupied by duties.

There is to be a concert of music to-night, instead of a theatrical performance, at Ford's. A *prima donna* will sing there, with much help. She is one of the long procession of queens of song who are great for a season and then cease to be immortal, but she is advertised as the equal of any queen who has preceded her. Mrs. Lincoln has been urged to go, and to take the President with her, and she has succeeded in obtaining his assent. Down in the Red Room, just now, she was relating to two or three of us what a task it was, in spite of the fact that he is fond of music. He is also strongly averse to a swallow-tailed coat and kids, and the battle was nearly lost over the latter. She has invited quite a party to fill the President's box, and we are not wanted there. In fact, we have so much work on hand that we shall get in a little late, at the best.

So, in the result, does the President's entire party, for he was detained by national business, and hardly was able to keep his promise to Mrs. Lincoln. He put one of his gloves on after he left the White House, but the other will never all go on, for there is a Manassas Gap created between its thumb and forefinger, which tells of weak leather and a strong right hand.

What a dense pack there is in the theatre, and how many volunteers must recently have been paid off!

There is an immense amount of loyalty, no doubt, in this assembly, for it rises as the President enters, and gives him a round of cheers, after vigorously stamping at the first indication of his presence. He has but just seated himself when a harsh, croaking voice in the middle aisle, loud enough to be heard all over the house, exclaims:

"He hasn't any business here! That's all he cares for his poor soldiers!"

There was a second of angry silence. "Put him out! Put him out!" But even louder than that is the indignant declaration uttered in a wrathful accent, telling of the Rhine, as well as of common sense:

"De President has a right to hees music! He ees goot to come! He shall haf hees music! Dot ees vot I shay! He shall haf hees music!"

The somebody in the middle aisle is discovered not to be a soldier, but the discovery is made by soldiers, and they are not making any noise over it whatever. They do not hurt him. They only hoist him up bodily and carry him to the door, and, as John Bunyan says, "I saw him no more."

The President has seemingly paid no attention to the unpleasant little incident. The orchestra took a hint from somebody and struck up a storm of patriotic music, and now, as that dies away, out walks the *prima donna*, and Mr. Lincoln and all the volunteers present will have their music. Whether or not he will listen to it successfully is quite another matter.

Bronzes and Earthworks

There is hardly any other public question of greater interest, at the present, than is that of our national paper money. Every man has or wishes to have some of it in his pocket, and is greatly exercised in mind as to its value. The prevailing impression is that it is not a safe thing to keep, for there was never before so much reckless extravagance. So it was, the records tell us, in the days of the old Continental currency. Army officers lived fast then, as too many of them are living now, and it was that sort of folly which began the ruin of General Benedict Arnold.

There is a very deep interest in these national engravings, representing dollars, and one of the Washington papers last evening printed a stiffly formal notice that "the original greenback" would be on free exhibition at 8 o'clock this morning in front of the President's house. No doubt there will be a crowd gathered for a look at such a show as that, and we will be on hand half an hour or so ahead of time.

Almost all of these residences, larger or smaller, around this open square opposite the White House, are connected with historical reminiscences. We have no time now for anecdotes. Out there, in the middle of the square, is the equestrian marvel in bronze which did so much for Clark Mills. It also did something for Andrew Jackson, recording the fact that he was a good horseman, and could keep the saddle while the brute under him was on his hind feet. Also, that he always rode a horse with a high rolling tail, of a size and sweep sufficient to balance the animal himself after both were turned into bronze. Just before Lincoln got here, and when the city seemed to be all one hothouse of sympathy with Secession, that statue did someting better than to merely keep its balance. It was very much the fashion among the young women sympathizers and some others, to wear what were called secession rosettes. Early one morning, Andrew Jackson's brass horse got hold of altogether the largest and most brilliant rosette of that kind that had yet been seen, and he put it on at the beginning of his grand, sweeping tail, where it might swing joyously at its gay blue ribbon in the winds from north or south. The sharp iron spikes of the high railing protected the rosette until it had been seen by many passers-by. One of them remarked: "That's what makes him rear so! I would, if they put one of those things on me."

There were remarks in abundance, but the greater number of those who came and saw went away in hot indignation, and went so far as to say that their flag had been insulted.

It is getting near the hour for the exhibition of the "original greenback," and here we are in the White House portico. If you are curious about reminiscences, do you see that foot-worn stone, a couple of yards from the threshold of this republican palace? That is where Lincoln and Buchanan parted, it is said, after the inauguration ceremony, when the old republic passed away, and the new era began. Lincoln went into the house and upstairs to his workroom, and Buchanan went to Wheatlands, but they parted like two personally friendly and patriotic gentlemen, each hoping for the best and fearing the worst.

Those were troubled days, here and hereabout. Nothing has yet been done to remove the all but threadbare appearance of this place. Perhaps these foot-worn flagstones do much to give it its peculiar tone, but so does that mournful green-bronze statue of Lafayette, facing the other way, out there in the inclosure in front of the house. It is a sad-looking bit of statuary, and there is some talk of removing it, but nobody seems to know what to do with it, or with the bath-room statue of Mr. Jupiter Washington in the vacant lot beyond the Capitol.

It is nearly 8 o'clock, and there they come. Who would have thought that the "original greenback" would draw in this fashion? It is a regular procession all the way up the avenue, and its head is coming in at the gate. There is another procession coming from the opposite direction. No doubt those people are studying the currency question, some in one way, and some in another; but many of them look as if they had not seen a greenback in some time. They will see one now. The foremost files have reached the portico, and that fishy-eyed man is pointing out something. It is very green! It is the back of the bronze Lafayette!

Not a man in that procession confesses that he came to see any show, but file after file arrives and looks, and goes thoughtfully away about some business or other. We may as well go upstairs to work, for we also have business on hand.

The time was, long ago, when the generally accepted doctrine, even among civilized men, was that the natural state of men and nations is a state of war.

Interludes of peace were regarded as allowable, as provision for needful rest and preparation, but it was held that they ought not to be permitted to continue unhealthfully. The times and the doctrine have changed, and war is now looked upon as something exceptional and evil, but its presence brings with it a powerful suggestion that it has its moral uses, and that it may operate as a priceless social surgery.

Beyond a doubt this country had all but lost any knowledge of war, whether regarded as a good or as an evil, or only as an abnormal science or a questionable trade. The land was and is swarming full of "the cankers of a calm world and a long peace," as Captain Jack Falstaff called them, and a vast number of them have been swarming toward these frontier headquarters, from the roll of the first drum, which seems to wake them up and summon them as distinctly as it summoned the volunteers.

Perhaps actual insanity is not on the increase, but the war-fever may be bringing out much that was latent. Surely lunacy must be using the pen more freely than ever before, to judge by what one finds in the newspapers, and to think of the mass of stuff which even these excited editors must be inducing themselves not to print. The keepers of the front door of the White House are capable fellows, and it is not often that an out-and-out lunatic can pass by their keen inspection; but they are not infallible, and there are many kinds of insanity.

"I must see the President!"

"Have you sent in your card, madame? The messenger out in the hall will take it."

She is of medium height, and not ill-looking, now that you glance up from your work and see something in her face which compels you to look again. She is dressed in rusty mourning, with a preposterously large miniature pin fastening her wide lace collar, and she is scrupulously neat. She seems only a little nervous at first, but does not stand still while she is talking.

"I don't want any cards! I want to see the President. I will see him! He must give me my rights. I want my rights. He can give me the right."

"But madame—"

"I want my right. They have robbed me of my right. He can give it back to me. A divorced widow's right! I will have it! He is President!"

Not at all boisterous, but rather low-toned is her voice, and it is becoming more and more emphatic and she speaks more rapidly.

"I do not think the President can see you to-day, ma'am. He is very busy about the war."

"So he is. Busy about the war. I forgot that. But I want my right. A divorced widow's right. Yes, sir; if I can't see him now, I'll come some other time. He is President. I will have my right."

It is the saddest face you have seen for many a day. She is gentle, however, even in her madness, and she walks hurriedly away and does not come again.

There are crazy visitors whose peculiarities do not at once arouse sympathy, including the apparently perfectly sane little gentleman who dresses so well, and who comes again and again to urge upon anybody he may meet in the White House the obvious propriety of appointing him to the command of a brigade. He has served in the militia of his own State, and his grandfather was an officer in the War of the Revolution, and, as his circumstances are at present, he is really in need of the pay, he freely declares, as a suitable addition to his income. He may not be so wildly insane, when he modestly compares his own claims and qualifications with those of a number who have already been appointed. In fact, there are no other traces of actual lunacy about him, and he has loads of perseverance, which is a good thing for a general to have.

One reason for getting here early this morning had nothing to do with the "original greenback," and the table is decently cleared to be left for a few hours.

"Mr. President, I'd like to go over the river and inspect the army. I'm going as far as Wadsworth's camp."

"Going to dine with him? I'll give you a pass—"

He picks up a card, and says something in praise of Wadsworth while he is writing. He signs it, and it is as if your latch-key had been transferred to that card. It is an autograph to be treasured long, for it is your first general pass from the Commander-in-Chief, addressed, as it were, "to whom it may concern."

"There! Now you'd better get one at the War Department."

"Thank you, Mr. Lincoln. I'll report when I come back if I find the army."

"Oh, you will. It's there. That's just what's the difficulty."

The War Office officials readily provide an ample supplement to such a pass as the President has written, and now for the army!

Strangely enough, there is less army to be seen around Washington than there was earlier in the season, although the arrivals are continuous, and the entrenchments and forts are continually constructing on every side.

There is better discipline, no doubt, and fewer furloughs are granted, for General McClellan is an admirable organizer. At no other time has there been quite so much army in Washington, all at once, as there was just after Bull Run. Then, however, it did not come precisely as an army, although it was in uniform. It was rather a hungry mob in search of something to eat and of listeners to whom it could tell its story of the marvels of that remarkable field.

Among the listeners found were a number of intelligent penmen and pen-women, who immediately sat down and wrote accounts of the battle, as they heard them from men who had fought and bled and died and run away, and the accounts they wrote were printed, and some got into what is called "history." All through those days, however, the real "army," in good heart, and in sufficient force, was on the other side of the Potomac, and furnished the clear-headed Confederate commander with an answer to the hysterical question so fiercely propounded to him by his civilian friends, "why he did not at once go forward and capture Washington." There were too many rifle-men in the way, not at all panicky, and new earthworks, with more cannon, were going up every hour, while the Confederate forces were severely aware that they had recently won a victory. The result at Bull Run bore a singularly strong analogy to that of Sumter in its uses, as they were understood at the desk by the window of the President's room. The first "victory," gained in Charleston Harbor by the Confederacy, enabled Mr. Lincoln to sit down at that table and write a proclamation calling for 75,000 militia, under the pro-vision of law, and to issue orders for at once enlisting as many more, volun-teers, regulars and seamen, without any law whatever. The Bull Run affair put him into his chair again, pen in hand, to ask Congress for $400,000,000 and 400,000 men, and the legislators gave him more than he asked, mainly because they had all been talked to by the runaway soldiers, and had ob-tained new ideas about war.

This is the famous Long Bridge, and passes are of more importance and are more rigidly inspected here than at any point north or south of these watchful sentries. Right here, at the draw, lean over the railing and look down into the muddy water. That eddy is over the mid-channel, and a line drawn through it marks the southern boundary of the United States, as it is understood by the citizens of the Confederacy. You cannot make it real? They have pledged their lives, their fortunes, and their sacred honor, that they will make it real, and there are no other men on this earth who would more surely keep their pledge.

Did you ever see such tremendous earthworks as are these we reach and pass? Well, nobody else ever did, and it takes much riding and walking to really see all of one of them; but, after seeing, one can have a better idea of the true relations between one or all of these vast defenses and the White

House that is protected by them. It was so terribly hard to believe that the Government of the United States lived in a fort!

Did you ever before see a great camp, or a great army? No? We have ridden fast and far, and we have not seen one to-day. Nobody else ever saw one, unless looking down from some eminence upon forces in lowlands.

There are roads running in all directions. There are tents, wagons, lines of cavalry and infantry on the march or on parade, and there are trains of artillery, stationary or in motion. We have found dust, mud, earthworks, huts, guns in position, but where is this great army?

The fact that so little of it can be seen at once explains one mystery of the first reports from many a battle.

A great army covers a great deal of ground, and a great battle may be fought over three or four townships, or half a county, and so it is not always easy, at first, to know what has become of the victory, or who has the hold of it.

It is hungry work, this inspection of the Army of the Potomac, and it grows more and more pleasant to have a grand dinner to look forward to. There will be "style" at the headquarters of General Wadsworth. He is known as "Wadsworth of Geneseo," and he is about the richest brigadier in this army. When he is at home, he can ride up and down the Genesee, mile after mile, upon the lands of his own fair inheritance, and he is a gentleman of cultivated tastes, polished manners, and excellent mental capacity. Our newly appointed brigadiers, as a rule, are going in for style with energy. They are fine fellows, and their richly garnished tents are full of hospitality. Some of them had money before they received their commissions and some had not, but they all have good pay now and also credit.

These autumnal days, while the army is waiting for McClellan to move, are brilliant with fresh uniforms, stars, sashes, swords, spurs, plate, furniture, dinners, wines, cigars, dash, the pomp and circus dance of glorious war!

Is this Wadsworth's headquarters? Not in a tent-marquee? Only a little, old, paintless, frame farmhouse? Very well, he can fix it up inside to suit himself. Mrs. Wadsworth is with him, and she is said to be a graceful, dignified, accomplished woman. She, too, was born rich, of a high-caste family, and she was a beauty and a belle in her day.

We are just in time to avoid keeping the General's dinner waiting—that is, unless it is true, as it is said of him, that he would not really postpone it on account of anybody of less rank and importance than an attack in force by the Confederates.

Mrs. Wadsworth is at the head of the table, and she is admirable. The

General is here. So are his staff, and several distinguished officers as guests, and the table is indeed brilliant! But it is of pine boards, without any cloth to cover it, and the dinner placed upon it consists rigidly of the regular army rations, well cooked, served in such ware as the private soldiers of Wadsworth's brigade are eating from, around their camp-fires at this very hour.

This is style!

Can it be possible that, after all, the General is a humorist, and that this is a sarcasm upon the brigadiers, whose income is or should be measured by their pay and allowances? Or is it no rather a wise and simple-hearted fellowship with the men under his command?

Here comes a reminder that the White House is present, for the General rises and proposes the President's health, and you are to respond. You suppose they will bring a champagne glass.

What! A tin cup? A black bottle?

Exactly, and the President's health is drunk in weak whiskey and water instead of champagne. It is just as well, but you are thinking more of what you will tell Mr. Lincoln about this dinner than you are of responding to the toast.

That is the reason why you have made so poor and lame a response and feel so grateful to Mrs. Wadsworth for helping you out. There is no social reinforcement for a defeated and demoralized young man equal to one of these highly cultured women. It is true that they were never boys themselves, but then the General was one once, and you get such an idea of him now, that one day, hereafter, when you hear that he has fallen in battle, you will feel much more deeply about it than if the Confederate bullet had found some other mark of equal army rank.

The Reception

There is to be a grand public reception this evening. Hard work and no extra pay, at a time when every member of this household feels as if there were too much on his hands already, but there is no avoiding a kind of show which the popular will so imperatively demands. A President who would not put on his best clothes now and then, and stand up to shake hands with his fellow-citizens, would lose all influence over them, even if he escaped impeachment as a haughty tyrant and a gloomy, secluded despot.

"What is it, Edward?"

"Madame would like to see you in the Red Room before she goes out. Something about the reception, I think."

"I'll come right down."

Mrs. Lincoln is waiting in the Red Room, and she is bright, cheerful, almost merry. Her instructions are given in a very kindly and vivacious manner. As you look at her and talk with her, the fact that she has so many enemies strikes you as one of the moral curiosities of this venomous time, for she has never in any way harmed one of the men and women who are so recklessly assailing her.

She is going out for a drive, and the carriage is waiting for her, and so is a lady friend. You will not be wanted again until the evening, but you are requested to be on duty at an early hour.

Is Mrs. Lincoln fond of driving out?

Not very, but she must have exercise and fresh air, and there is hardly any other way than this. She has several times driven out to visit and inspect the forts and lines, and to wonder, as did her husband, why the men were kept at work upon additional defenses after so much hard spading had already been done. The military explanation, however, is perfect. It is true that the Confederate forces are numerically inferior, but they never tell us beforehand where they are going to strike us, and so we have no means of knowing. These lines are more or less concentric. Each outer line remedies some discovered defect or weakness in the line next behind it. Each inner line is a good thing for a defeated army to retreat into, after it has been whipped out of the line next outside of it. The inner lines, too, are shorter, and can be better defended by whatever is left of our army after it is defeated.

How about the defenses on the Maryland side?

They are pretty good. They are somewhat like those in Virginia, but there is not so much of them.

The very best Maryland lines thus far discovered, unless it be the Potomac River itself, are the Blue Ridge and its family of ridges.

Mrs. Lincoln is not going out to the fortifications to-day; only to the hospitals. She rarely takes outside company with her upon these errands, and she thereby loses opportunities. If she were worldly wise she would carry newspaper correspondents, from two to five, of both sexes, every time she went, and she would have them take shorthand notes of what she says to the sick soldiers and of what the sick soldiers say to her. Then she would bring the writers back to the White House, and give them some cake and—and coffee, as a rule, and show them the conservatory. By keeping up such a process until every correspondent that Colonel Baker can find for her has been dealt with, say twice, she could somewhat sweeten the contents of many journals and of the secretary's waste-basket. The directly opposite course, as she pursues it, has not by any means worked well.

It has proved a hard, vexatious day in the business part of the house, but evening has come at last, and the racks are set up in the vestibule. They are tall ranges of square holes, of about the right size for Shanghai hens' nests, and each box has its number and ticket. They are for the proper care of hats and wraps, but many men and women will go right along, not leaving anything in the racks. They will see all there is to be seen, and they will walk around and come out with all their wraps upon them. They are visitors who do not come to spend the evening, whether or not they become fascinated and stick to the end after they get here. You may be able to discern that the exceptionally noticeable air of American freedom which they also wear is a thin garment, through which very quickly penetrates a chilly blast of awe, if not of bashfulness, at finding themselves actually in the White House at Washington. They flinch a little, and have to stand still and rally at the moment when they realize that they, in their mortal bodies, are about to walk right up to the President, the greatest man upon this earth, or upon any other earth that they can think of.

There is not anything in the vestibule that they do not see, to begin with, before going further. Not many of them fail to ask each other, or one of the servants, or some benevolent-looking bystander, the name and rank of any men who are here in uniform, or wearing uncommon personal dignity.

There are not so many uniforms as one might perhaps expect. There is an idea afloat, even among officers righteously away from camp on furlough, that their presence elsewhere than at posts of active duty seems to be accompanied by a traveling interrogation point. Moreover, there are numbers of shoulder-strap wearers now in the city to whom the question "Why are you here?" might be an unpleasant conundrum to answer. No commander in the field is asking to have them assigned to duty with him, and they do not come in a swarm to look into the face of the President.

The human tide flows on from the vestibule through the open door of the Red Room, but this continues to be almost untenanted, for the attractions of the evening are not here. Just beyond its eastern door, and in the next room, there are groups worth studying.

How very tall the President looks, standing there in the foreground, between his two secretaries. That is their customary post of duty upon reception evenings, and we know by experience that it means an evening of hard work.

In no other land, or place, or time could there be gathered such a miscellaneous assortment of life and character as is now passing before Father Abraham.

A volunteer in the uniform of a private soldier is at this moment towering in front of him, and the hand of welcome which at once goes out is met by a weaker grasp than is expected. The man's face was pale, but it flushes.

"You're just a peg taller'n I am, Mr. Lincoln, but I reckon I'd ha' outweighed you 'fore I went into hospital."

"Where were you wounded?" asks the President, with evident interest.

"Reckon it was all over me. 'Twas one of these 'ere Potomac fevers."

"Worse than a bullet," responds Mr. Lincoln; "but it must have taken a heap of fever to go all over you."

"Well, it did!" The soldier swings cheerily on, with something to tell in camp, and he has hardly hindered the procession.

"I voted for you, Mr. Lincoln," chirps a short, fat, honest-faced man, who pauses in front of him. "I—I'm glad I did. I—I'd do it again. I—I'm putting in an application for paymaster. I—"

"Want to be a paymaster, eh?" laughs the President. "Well, some people would rather take money in than pay it out. It would about kill some men I know to make paymasters of 'em."

If that man meant to say any more he has lost his chance, for the President bends suddenly, and his long arm reaches through the press

"Come here, sister. I can't let you pass me in that way."

Sunny curls, blue eyes, cheeks delicately rosy, a child of seven or eight, warmly but plainly dressed, and now she is trembling with shyness and pleasure as he draws her to him for a kiss and to pat her golden hair. All children are favorites of his, and as she is released his arm goes out again and he has made another capture, but not without a vigorous kicking, and a short, half-frightened squall. Up, up, goes a chubby boy of four, and the squall changes to a boyish laugh, for he is a brave little fellow, and he knows a game of toss, even if it lifts him uncommonly high in the air.

We cannot hear just what the President says, but the children can, and both of them have hurried away, followed by parents and what seems a file of aunts and other relatives, all one chuckle of delight over this rare incident.

That is a noble-looking woman, whose hand the President is taking. Her features are fine, and there is a splendid glow of enthusiasm shining all over her face.

"I have three sons in the army, Mr. Lincoln."

"You may well be proud of that, ma'am."

Her eyes seem growing darker and yet brighter, and her bosom swells more proudly—if it is with pride. She hesitates, a breathing-space, but her lips do not quiver as she adds, quietly, firmly:

"There were four, Mr. Lincoln, but my eldest boy—" and somehow she can say no more and turns to pass onward.

"God bless you, madame," but she does not give him a chance to say any more.

One gone already? And so very few men seem to have been killed as yet! So many more must be. What will be the story of that mother's three younger boys? Nobody can guess, but day by day the President is vainly urging the commander of the forces along the Potomac to go ahead and fight battles. More men are dying in camp than would probably be killed in the field. It would be a saving of life to shorten the war, no matter how many men should die in shortening it.

Our own especial post of duty is over here by Mrs. Lincoln, and it is somewhat less arduous than is that of the other secretaries.

She stands a few paces to the right of her husband, and somewhat further back in the room. A large percentage of the procession which passes him sweeps inward for a word with her, but the greater part of it stares and smiles and bows, or does not bow, and surges forward. Her hand is not so hard as his, and could not endure so much grasping and shaking. Even his iron fingers get weary sometimes.

No guests are permitted to linger in this room—for it is of moderate capacity—without a special invitation, unless they are privileged characters. Such are members of the Cabinet and their families, the diplomatic corps, Supreme Court judges and those who accompany them, Senators and Congressmen. The line drawn is both certain and uncertain, and some whose privilege can hardly be discerned exercise it liberally, until, in some cases, it is needful to exercise tact and skill with them. Among the specially invited, this evening, are a number of distinguished officers of the army and navy, of the kind whose presence suggests the inquiry, "Where is he going to send them next?"

He has chatted with some of them inaudibly to others, but in a way which has stirred a buzz of curiosity. Have they orders which no one else knows anything about? They seem happy!

A splendid group of women has gathered around and near Mrs. Lincoln. Scattered around the room, and in the corners and by the windows, are other groups as notable. There is no excessive brilliancy of dress. There is even a relieving alternative of marked plainness. There is, however, an assembly of dignity, intelligence, beauty, noble womanhood, which does honor to the country which can fill its republican Court with such representatives. They are the wives and sisters and daughters of patriots, statesmen, jurists, legislators, financiers, heroes, and no Court in Europe can assemble their superiors.

It is a brilliant scene, this reception-room of the President and his wife. It is difficult to collect one's memories and thoughts, and to consider the fact that it is but a short drive from the door of these headquarters of the Commander-in-Chief to the trenches and camps, and to the fields of the bloodiest battles of this Civil War: battles fought and to be fought to prevent the Confederate flag from floating over the building in which we are spending the evening.

The presence of the war cannot be forgotten or put aside, however. The crowds who come and go, and even these smiling groups of distinguished ladies and gentlemen are busy from time to time with the reported movements of the forces which are said to threaten the National Capital. Nobody really believes it to be in danger, and conversation turns rather to the current rumors concerning the army movements preparing for the capture of the corresponding fortress and headquarters on the James River. President Davis may be holding a reception in Richmond this evening, and one of these posts, so near each other and yet so far, must change its flag and garrison before this war can be ended.

The members of the diplomatic corps never make their appearance early. They never arrive together, but singly, and the gentlemen only will present themselves at so very public and popular a reception as this. There is, more-over, a subtle understanding that the relations between the Lincoln Admin-istration and European diplomacy are out of joint; and the idea expresses it-self socially, for foreign Ministers of all the grades are not merely human beings, they are the finger-tips rather than the embodiments of Old World politics and policies.

Here comes England, and if Lord Lyons is out of humor with anything, nobody will guess it from his manner. No American has shaken hands more heartily than he with the President, in spite of the fact that our position with reference to Great Britain is to the last degree strained and dangerous.

"The British Neutral Service" is already putting to sea under the Confed-erate flag. The blockade-runners are as busy as bees and as daring as Vi-kings. The question of British recognition of the Confederacy still mutters in the air like distant thunder. General Chester A. Arthur is studying the fortifications of New York and the military capacities of its railroads, and the features of the Canadian frontier, preparatory to his reports upon those subjects. He and Governor Morgan have calculated with care, and have in-formed the President how many regiments of New York and other State mi-litia they can throw across the border in twenty-four hours, if need should be; but England, present here this evening, is as pleasant and conciliatory as if the two nations were really at peace with each other, instead of in a thinly veiled state of semi-hostility, with the White House as neutral ground.

France is not here, and it is understood that he will not come to-night; but if his absence has any ominous diplomatic meaning the hint is utterly lost upon Mr. Lincoln. Mr. Seward, who is chatting so cheerfully at your el-bow, may make something out of it. He can read such telegrams as if they were printed, but he never permits himself to be ruffled by them. This is not a good workroom for intrigue, and the razor-edges of school-diplomacy are of little value in dealing with a dictator whose first declaration of his foreign policy so strongly resembled axe-work.

Italy has now entered the room, and he is tall and dark, but not in the least romantic. Here is Germany, fat, hearty, sociable, and understood to be in personal sympathy with the popular feeling of his bond-buying, emigrat-ing countrymen, and with, if we are rightly informed, our friend, Count Bismarck. The short, dark, melancholy but suave and smiling man, with such fine teeth, is Mexico, and his greeting by the President may have some relation to the absence of France. At all events, the unscrupulous adven-turer who now poses as the French Emperor has no admirers among the gar-rison of the White House. Russia, yonder, with Mr. Seward at this moment, is a tremendous counter-poise to both France and England. He seems to put one in mind of the Crimea and Sebastopol and their unsettled account, which does but wait for a day of settlement. Spain, Brazil, Holland—all the list arrive, in turn and out of turn, coming in with the long American procession as if they were parts of it.

It is hard work for the President, but he receives and dismisses these varied hundreds of people with wonderful dexterity, the trained result of his natural tact and wit and of his long practice. It is one of the unavoidable duties of his position, from which he can no more escape than could his predecessors. It is a pity that the house has no picture gallery, with portraits of the Presidents and the ladies who have stood where Mr. Lincoln and his wife are standing, and whose hands have been shaken to lameness in this very room.

The hour has come, at last, for the President to make a promenade into and through the East Room. It is the breaking up of the reception, and it is performed without any prescribed order or formality. There are no rules of precedence, and this is dangerous coasting ground for what is called etiquette. The crowd in the East Room is dense. It is enjoying itself, and it will hardly get out of the way to let the President's official procession perform its walk around, although the Marine Band is manifestly changing its musical storm-mixture into the first notes of "Hail Columbia." There it comes, in full force and blast, and it is the signal for everybody to go home.

A Variety of Uniforms

The morning after a public reception is no more a time to be late in rising, or in getting at work, than is any other morning. No matter if, after the reception, there was a private party-crush somewhere else, and the process of being entertained and of enjoying one's self continued till the small hours. The President will be at his desk by the window as early as usual.

It is true that there do not seem to be any set hours for either beginning or ending work in the national business office. Mr. Lincoln himself keeps no hours, and he never once has asked what his assistants here are doing with their time. They are supposed to know their duties, and are expected to do them without throwing any burden of supervision upon him. Nevertheless, he is an unconscious driver, and he is unintentionally though unrelentingly exacting. No person employed in connection with Mr. Lincoln's work would willingly be out of call if he were wanted; but if the President should send for a man and couldn't find him, he would send at once for another. He manages his generals and sea-captains somewhat upon the same principle, excepting that he now and then drops one of them, and does not afterward make any effort to find him—not so much as to ring a bell for him.

What is that thing lying on the table?

It should speak for itself. It is an entirely new pattern of cavalry-saddle, and the inventor wishes the President to recommend it to General Stoneman and General Pleasanton and the rest as the best saddle for cavalry that was ever devised. It has new features all over it and in it and under it, and when Mr. Lincoln examined it he remembered a story that we forget, but it was something about saddles and cavalry, and the ancient practice of riding barebacked. This specimen has been gotten up tremendously, but it has ornamented the President's room long enough, and so they have brought it over here.

No, Mr. Senator, if you wish to try it, you'll have to take it downstairs. No horses are permitted up here.

It is not really the new saddle which has attracted such a crowd into the northeast room. It is a rush day, and it looks almost as if there was to be another reception. We are getting the overflow from the halls. There is almost every kind of man here already, except Indian chiefs and Governors of States. They never come. There were some great red men on a visit to their Great Father at Washington a few days ago, but the President went down to the East Room, and the council was held there. They did not smoke any pipes of peace nor bury any tomahawk, and it is believed that the treaty they have signed will last until they are again set loose upon the plains, but no longer. They came in their paint and feathers, and they were an imposing-looking group of men. One very good and friendly Indian wore, as fringes for his leggings of honor and glory, the scalp-tufts of ninety-three human beings who had fallen by his hand. Less than half of those tufts were black and coarse, and many of the others were long, soft, and of all shades, and curls from silver-silken to dark chestnut and even jet.

As for the absence of State Governors, there is a dim and floating tradition that no such officer should leave his State limits during his term of office, and that if he were to visit Washington he would make his trip a subject of jealous inquiry by any and all other Governors of States.

The uncommonly dignified gentleman standing by the mantel in such a picturesque attitude is an ex-Governor, and he has been watching you at your work, but he has not been half so interested, nor is he nearly so interesting, as is this grizzled, brawny, tobacco-chewing, farmer-like old man from somewhere away up North, who has captured Andrew Jackson's chair, and has pulled it up to the table-corner. He has watched the process of opening letters, and he has grinned as if he understood it. So has the ex-Governor, for he is accustomed to the reception and disposal of much correspondence; but this other man is paying more and more attention to the crowd out in the hall.

His curiosity has burst into questions at last.

"I say, mister, jest a minute. Couldn't you tell a feller something about these chaps? Who they be, and what they're here fur? No, not the Guvnor. I know him. Real sound, likely kind of man he is, too. Not the Senator, nuther. Everybody knows him, and he's a pretty level-headed old stick. But who in thunder is that there fat, red feller? Looks as though he'd been melted and poured into his clothes so they'd fit him 'thout any wrinkle. Red as a lobster! Is he a Britisher?"

"Oh, no, he is a Danish officer. He has come to serve in our army, if he can get a commission."

"They'll put him to work somewhar, I reckon. Hope he won't git shot.

Bleedin' wouldn't show on them clothes, though. Who's that there little gew-gaw-and-glitter feller?"

"That's a German officer. He has already served in Europe with distinction. He wants a commission, too. He's a baron!"

"He's a bar'n? Well, now! I never seed a bar'n before. Looks kind o' gritty, too. Do you git many on 'em?"

"Yes, one of our first volunteer regiments was said to be about half made up of barons and counts and that sort of men, that had got tired of living in Europe—or else, may be, Europe had got tired of them."

"You don't say! Is there any yurl out there? I never seed a nurl nor a dook. Do you have any yurls?"

"Well, no, we haven't enlisted an earl yet, that I know of. They're all English, you know, and they're not on our side. McClellan has a duke, and a prince, and a count on his staff."

"Not any kings? No? I'd like to see the kind they have in England. Who is that little rooster?"

There is a deal of good breeding in this world, for not a soul present smiled in such a way as to hurt the sensibilities of the distinguished German officer who is indicated.

"Awful clipped coat-tails."

And they are stiff as well as short, and he has nervously buttoned his coat tightly to the waist, with his coat-tails up, and now they cannot get down, and he goes in to see the President in the likeness of a gamecock trimmed for combat.

"No spurs on, but I guess he's game. Now, mister, who's that critter? Black mournin' veil down over her face. I'd say! If she isn't a-sobbin'! Wants Old Abe to give her somethin'."

"That's it. Don't you see? His messenger has just come out. Hear him."

"The President is too busy to see you, madame, but there it is. He has signed it, and you can take it to the War Office yourself. They know that it is signed."

So says Louis to the lady, as she gripes a paper hard in a withered thin white hand.

"Thank God! Thank Lincoln! Pardoned! Oh, my boy! my boy!" and a veiled storm of sobs totters out to the stairway on an errand to the War Department, the substance of which has preceded her.

The President very much dislikes to meet people, women especially, for whom he has done any favor, like saving a life for them, or that sort of thing. He prefers to hear no more about it after it is done.

"Mister, it's all right, isn't it? She's got the pardon? I'd ha' forgive him, if I'd ha' been Linken. I don't keer so much what he cut up, but then I reckon she doesn't feel quite so bad as she did. Who's that there tall feller that doesn't have to wait? And the short feller with him, that's mostly beard and spectacles? Three of 'em, and more beard, who are they, pushin' straight in?"

"One of them is War, and one of them is Honesty, and one of them is the Ocean."

"Was that there Stanton? Well, now, if he wasn't mad about somethin' he looked it. I'd ought to ha' known old Welles from his picture, but you didn't call the other feller."

"Yes, I did. His best name is Honesty, but his other name is Meigs. He buys things for the army. He is quartermaster-general, and when he gets clean through there won't be a stain on him, nor the smell of fire on his garments. Could you spend four or five thousands of millions of dollars and not steal some of it?"

"I guess I could. I wouldn't steal a cent, but some of it might stick, somewhere, or sift out into the backyard, somehow, while there was such an awful heap bein' carted."

"There won't any stick to old Honesty, nor sift into his backyard. He and a few men like him are the main reasons why we're going to win this fight."

"Win it? Of course we're going to win it."

He is intensely patriotic, and he is having a very interested audience, including the Governor, but that is the bell from Mr. Nicolay's room, and we must go over. Come.

It is not so crowded as the northeast room, and there is ordinarily an air of intense suppression here, for this is really an important part of the President's office adjoining. There is Mr. Nicolay, by the table, getting ready some paper or other for the President to sign. People who do not like him—because they cannot use him, perhaps—say he is sour and crusty, and it is a grand good thing, then, that he is. If you will sit in that chair a month or so, you will see what has become of any easy good-nature you sat down with. Hot-tempered fellows like you and me have no business in that chair. It takes a steady fellow like Nicolay, or somebody as quick-witted as John Hay. You have sat there often, when they were gone, but only for a day or half a day at a time, and did not like it. The President showed his good judgment of men when he put Mr. Nicolay just where he is, with a kind and amount of authority which it is not easy to describe. The ill-natured people call us all boys, and John Hay is nominally only twenty-four, and Mr. Nicolay is only a few summers farther on, if you count by the almanac; but is not this a time when a day is as a year often, and men grow gray internally? Mr. Lincoln must have lived at least a century since they telegraphed to him that he had been nominated for President by the Chicago Convention.

It seemed quiet here, as we passed through the door, but we did but inter-rupt a very striking lecture that is at once resumed as the lecturer walks up and down the room. There is a wide mirror over the mantel, and he pauses before it to survey himself all over while the lecture goes on, for the subject of it is dress—the dress now worn by the lecturer—black broadcloth, new, swallow-tailed, beautiful! He is tall and brawny and bearded, and his voice is hoarsely deep. He is a Union political brigadier-general from the far Southwest. He will never command a brigade in the field, for he is a mistake in a military point of view; but he has all his life been an orator, and he has drawn his first pay, and he has purchased the first good clothes he ever wore, and no Sioux chief at a big talk was ever prouder of his paint and feathers.

"Yes, sir; this is the only dress of a gentleman; he should never wear any-thing else. I never do."

Alas! that he should be interrupted by the pitiless Nicolay; but the Presi-dent will see him for a moment, and he goes in. Mr. Hay can let out now the laugh he has been keeping in, and the swallow-tailed brigadier can explain to Mr. Lincoln the condition of the people and the Union cause in his own part of the country. Again! Alas for him, that he should first repeat to the President his lecture of admiration of his new, beautiful swallow-tails, for Abraham Lincoln takes less interest in the tailoring business than do some other men. After the lecture is over there is less peril that the lives and for-tunes of a brigade of helpless volunteers will be entrusted to the skill and pa-triotism of the lecturer.

The endless reception held in this part of the house being ended at last, and the toilers of the President's office having adjourned for dinner, we can walk out to the westward, and we might as well get out through the conservatory. That is, you can do so if you have special permission from Mrs. Lincoln, or from the gardener, and that may or may not be easy to obtain. Just now we want some bouquets prepared for ladies who are to come here for a while, this morning, before they go to another affair which will keep them later. The flowers are doing well, are they not? Rare exotics, some of them, and the bouquets will be fine. The gardener has orders to give us anything we want in reason, and we will take liberally; but even while we are doing so the warm, fragrant, summer-like air of the conservatory suggests an idea that is just beginning to germinate in and about this White House. This very "greenhouse," the kitchens and laundry in yonder, the vegetable garden, not now in active operation, the bedrooms upstairs, this entire side of the house—is it not all absurdly out of place in the same building with the most important business office in the nation? Of course it is, but the moment you broach the idea of separating the President's dwelling from his workshop you will find how intense a jealousy your proposition must encounter. There is apparently a dread that if a private residence for the President were to be built, it would be made to cost too much, and would most likely become a palace, whatever that may mean to American imaginations. There is a greater fear that if he had a home of his own to take refuge in he would be less accessible, and could escape more completely from Congressional buttonholers. He might entirely get away!

Still, the mere business necessities which suggest and enforce the absurdity of having this incongruous greenhouse in the headquarters of the Commander-in-Chief will grow with the growth of the National Executive transactions. Much business which belongs here must now be attended to at the several Departments. We are not prophets, and you cannot now dream of the day when you will come to call upon President Andrew Johnson, but he will call you into the room next westward of the office Mr. Lincoln now occupies. That will then be an office for private secretaries. A few years later, President Grant will take you with him for a quiet chat in the library, one door further westward. You will spend an evening with President Hayes in the Red Room. Presidents Garfield and Arthur will make no important changes, but when at last you come to visit President Cleveland, you will find the whole floor east of the western folding doors turned into business offices, and that Mr. Lincoln's old bedroom, next to the library, is where President Cleveland expects you to talk with him.

One or two more administrations, following the star of empire at the same rate of progression, will find a President looking out of the windows of the western wing, up there, with a long range of business rooms left behind him eastward. Then, however, it is to be hoped that his kitchen and his bedroom will be elsewhere, whatever may have become of this conservatory.

What about the Soldiers' Home? No, that is only a kind of hot-weather retiring place, and will not answer for the palace of the Presidents.

Splendid flowers! Come, the gardener will have our bouquets ready at the right time. Come out this way, where even the gates and fences have not been changed since the War of 1812.

There are not any other old red brick buildings in the country as large as are the War Department and Navy Department buildings that present fewer external indications of the uses they are put to. Excepting for these uniforms which are coming and going so busily, and for the other uniforms and the soldierly looking men behind the desks of the offices, even their interiors would not tell much more.

We can go in, although it is after the hours for public admission. It is not because our latch-key fits any of these doors otherwise than theoretically, but because the doorkeeper is bound to suppose that it is upon business for the President. He has been here a long time, in charge of the door at which he is stationed, but even if he were a new hand and comparatively unacquainted with the latch-keys of the White House, he would at this moment be, as he is, in the attitude of holding his door open wide. We will ourselves step aside and let this party of gentlemen go by. We saw three of them, a little while ago, entering the door of the other office of the President, over yonder. These dingy old brick quadrangles are really parts of the Executive business arrangements, and belong to the White House more perfectly now than they have heretofore since Jackson's time. Two and two, Lincoln and Stanton walking ahead, Meigs and Welles following them, and there, on the steps of the Navy Department, for which they are aiming, is a strongly built, bright-eyed, good-looking man in a naval uniform. That is Captain Fox, a power in naval matters, the same officer who so eagerly undertook to relieve Fort Sumter, and was foiled by bad weather and slow subordinates. There is something up which requires a more select and secret council than can well be had to-day at the other office—most likely something about Burnside and the North Carolina coast. They all go into the Navy building together, and what they say and do after they get there we shall not know, for your errand and mine is ended, and we have had another given that carries us back to the White House.

Does the President do this sort of thing frequently?

Of course he does, going from one part of the Executive buildings to another, as he pleases; and by leaving the White House part of them at this hour he has escaped an ominous visit from a full corporal's guard of the Committee on the Conduct of the War. They arrive, but they do not go beyond the front door, where they are very politely and correctly informed by Old Edward that: "He's gone out, gentlemen. He didn't say where he was going, sir. Have you been to Mr. Seward's to see if he's there, sir? If he's not at Mr. Seward's, it's most likely he went to some of the other places. He'll not be gone long, or he may—I can't say. I'll tell him; yes, sir, I'll tell him."

And the estimable and influential and undeniably patriotic delegation departs, deeply engaged in a discussion of something relating to the Atlantic coast and the fleets, but they have not seen the smile on the face of Captain Fox when he saw the President coming, nor the other smile on the face of Old Edward, when he saw them going. There is nothing foxy about Mr. Lincoln. He did not know that a committee was coming, and that it had so nearly reached the White House, and he was not at all the man to run away from the Committee on the Conduct of the War.

The Two Chieftains

"Yes, sir, the hour may be at hand when the President's friends must stand by him in more ways than one. When that hour comes, you and I must be ready."

He was intensely in earnest, and his bright, handsome, young face is flushed with indignation, as well as stern with courageous purpose, and you never at any other time liked him so well.

"Nonsense, my dear fellow. What you mean is that we may have to get some rifles, and be ready to prevent the forcible occupation of the White House by somebody. We shall not need any guns. You are hinting at some like a *coup d'état*, a sudden stroke; something in the nature of a forward movement. There isn't a shadow of a danger of anything of the sort."

"If you had been present! If you had seen and heard what I have, you would feel differently."

"We can get as mad about it as we please, but the general is not at all that kind of man. He does not dream of any such thing, nor do the men around him. It couldn't be done, if they should all go crazy, unless they could control the army, and they couldn't control a corporal's guard!"

The talk is a trifle wild, considering the place and the time, but it has its meaning, and it illustrates the intensities of the situation. There is rapidly increasing, and spreading from Washington over the country, a clear, but as yet cautiously undefined, unformulated understanding that there is a struggle going on between the Constitutional supremacy of the civil authority, represented by the President, and the war-created strength of the military commander. There have been many startling surprises, and who knows but what another, yet more surprising, is in course of preparation for the country? Who knows how large a part of the population is preparing, unconsciously, for precisely such a surprise as has been indicated, and would welcome it as offering a solution of the problem before them?

Mr. Lincoln and General McClellan have been differently educated. They hold and have held adverse political opinions. They are at variance, now, as to questions with which, strictly construing his position, a military chief has nothing to do in this country. Frémont got into hot water by going too fast and too far in one direction, and now McClellan, taking a path opposite to that of Frémont, is capturing the leadership of a gathering political party.

This party is making up of the shreds and tatters of old parties, but it will inevitably be a tremendous power.

It will not do to call it a Cave of Adullam unless there is to be an indefinite expansion of the supposed capacity of that cavern. It might even be useful to so enlarge it that it will take in the border States, if not the entire South.

All the threads and wires of information which centre in this central den of the national spider-web are tremulous with suggestions of intrigue, and with warnings of oppositions, and with the increasingly bitter criticisms of friends and foes alike. It almost seems as if the President has no friends, so sharply do his own find fault with him; and, while they also denounce McClellan and his asserted pro-slavery leanings and his ambitions, they offer no apparent counterpoise to the unstinted praises heaped upon the young general by his supporters of all sorts. It will be no wonder at all if he shall fail to rightly interpret the signs of this time, or if he makes the mistake of supposing himself stronger than the sad-faced, silent man, who is at this hour at work in the room across the hall.

Your mail is at last all read, and is either transmitted or destroyed. Dinner was returned from two hours ago, and the gas is lighted, but it does not seem to burn well. It flickers and flares, and there is something blue in it. It must be a shade or two worse over in the President's room.

One cannot help thinking of him and feeling for him, for the Northern press, loyal and otherwise, has been abusively sarcastic to-day. It is a good thing that he does not read any of these stinging leaders in these sheets which litter the floor. There lies one that was torn lengthwise by the reader, as a faint expression of his feelings, and it is easier to understand why the old-time people used, now and then, to rend their garments.

This bitterly caustic essay which we have been reading, upon the art of war, as it is understood by the writer, who evidently thinks the road from Washington to Richmond to be something like Broadway, only better paved and wider, is annoyingly interesting, but we are not to finish it. The door into the hall is open, but no footstep is heard approaching, nor any other sound, until a low-toned, weary voice says:

"Leave that and come with me. I am going over to McClellan's house."

Reply of any sort seems to be shut off, as if anything more than rising with a bow of silent acquiescence would be disrespectful, for there is a world of natural majesty in this man's manner and presence at times. He is a born leader of men, and he is one of the great kings of the earth, ruling with wisdom and with power. He strides on to the stairs, and down them, and out at the door in utter silence. The secretary has no portfolio to carry this time. He is nothing in the world but an attendant. The subordinate commander we are going to visit will doubtless have members of his rarely brilliant staff about him, and it is fitting that the Commander-in-Chief should also bring along a member of his own staff, if only by way of contrast. The walk through the streets is brief enough; a bell is rung, and we are ushered by a servant into an elegant reception-room.

Why did not the President send instead of coming?

Well, it is his way. He is not always careless of the dignities of his position, but his heart and head are full just now.

It is bad diplomacy, as between two such contestants!

That kind of fencing-school diplomacy is worth about as much in a contest with Abraham Lincoln as foils and masks would be in the battles he is ordering.

We are seated, and the President's arrival has been duly announced, but time is being given him to think over what he came for. General McClellan is probably very busy over some important detail of his vast duties, and he cannot tear himself away from it at once. A minute passes, and then another, and then another, and with every tick of the clock upon the mantel your blood warms nearer and nearer its boiling-point. Your face feels hot and your fingers tingle, as you look at the man, sitting so patiently over there, whom you regard as the Titan and hero of the hour; and you try to master your rebellious consciousness that he is kept in waiting, like an applicant in an ante-room.

Another minute—you are probably in error as to the length of it—and the President arises from his chair at the brisk sound of approaching steps. They are here. They come in with a vigorous firmness and rapidity and precision which suggest the idea of dash, of force, of energetic onslaught—that is, of all sorts of forward movements.

General McClellan is indeed a striking figure, in spite of his shortness. He is the impersonation of health and strength, and he is in the prime of early manhood. His uniform is faultless and his stars are brilliant, especially the middle one on each strap. His face is full of intelligence, of will-power, of self-assertion, and he, too, is in some respects a born leader of men. He has been admirably educated for such duties as are now upon him, and he has studied the science and art of war among European camps and forts and armies and battle-fields. He has vast stores of technical knowledge never to be acquired by any man among the backwoods, or on the prairies, or in law courts, or in political conventions. He can hardly conceal the clearness of his conviction that he ought not to be trammeled by any authority in human form that is by him supposed to be destitute of the essential training which he himself so fully possesses.

Why, then, should he not confine his genius to army matters, and let Constitutional questions and politics and policies alone? He cannot. No American general ever did or could, and therein is the danger of the present situation. Even if he were willing to let politics alone, he is as sure to be seized upon and utilized as was Zachary Taylor. A party without a head is conscious that it cannot organize for effective campaigns without one, without him, or something like him, and its printed journals have with one voice summoned him to a place upon the vacant party shoulders, or, if the figure is better, to a seat in the empty political saddle.

In attendance upon McClellan are a brigadier-general, and, part of the time, a colonel, but they take no part in the conversation beyond a reply when spoken to. There were brief introductions when the military dashed in, and now the two chiefs have it all to themselves.

There they sit, facing each other, in the most cordial and mutually respectful manner, for their personal relations are said to be excellent.

The contrast between the two exteriors is very strong. It would not be easy to find two men who would resemble each other so little at any visible point. How will they ever agree?

They will not; they do not now, as they talk, although they are conferring rather than arguing; for here are two generals widely at variance, not only as to plans of campaign, but also as to the extent and nature of their respective authorities, although nominally and technically in accord. Here are also two political chiefs of two great parties into which the nation is dividing. They are hardly less so now than they will be two years later, when, as opposing candidates for the Presidency, they will formally call upon their voting countrymen to decide between them as to which has been the most sagacious and faithful interpreter of the popular will.

Keep your temper, for the President does not seem to have any to keep, although the brilliant officer before him is less and less able to conceal the fact that he hardly considers himself a subordinate. By keeping cool you will better understand a subtle process which is going on, known or unknown to either of the two remarkable gentlemen who are talking. You can perceive, as the conversational mist clears away, that the President has the deeper, wiser, broader, stronger mind of the two, and that he is utterly assured of his own position and of his own purposes. The great magic of the stonger will, the tougher fiber, the greater moral courage, the untellable power which dwells in an unflinching, unshrinking faith, are with Lincoln and are not with McClellan. The Constitution and the laws are also with him. So will be the unanswerable logic of events, and he will surely win the long wrestling match. Just now he hopes and expects that his splendid young army leader will win in the military campaign upon which he is entering. Men, resources, help of every kind, will be lavished upon the effort to capture Richmond, and there will be lacking only one thing—the inner force which the President possesses, but which he cannot impart to another.

The interview is long, but it ends, and we return to the White House, and with us goes a strange sensation of having been present at a battle, a kind of drawn battle, from which both sides retired with an unsatisfactory consciousness that they must meet again and fight it over.

The President talks more freely on the way home. He seems more cheerful, and he even so far throws off his cloak of gloom as to relate something which happened once to General Marcy. He almost laughs, but not quite, when you respond to his comments upon General McClellan's staff, by telling him that the volunteers have given up trying to pronounce French names, and have reduced the Duc de Chartres to Captain Chatters, and the Comte de Paris to Captain Parry. Perhaps he knew it already, but he does not say so, for he has paused before going into the house, and he is standing by the parapet at the eastern end of the front, gazing silently southward. There is good moonlight, but not enough to see the Potomac. The river is there, however, and in the camps and forts and works beyond it is the great army, which has been so well organized for war under the skilled supervision of General McClellan.

A long-drawn breath and a smothered exclamation terminate the President's long minute of absorbed pondering, and he turns away and strides on across the portico, but the door swings open as he approaches, and there is a serious tone in the voice of Old Edward.

"The doctor has been here, sir."

"What did he say?"

"The Madame would like to see you right away, sir. Soon as you came in."

Any remainder of Mrs. Lincoln's message is cut short, for the President wheels to the right, and seems to vanish up the private stairway.

"Is Willie really sick, Edward?"

"I think he is, indeed; but she told me not to alarm the President. We'll know more in the morning. Good night, sir!"

Morning comes, and there is really nothing unusual in the air, although we are all aware that a tremendous effort is making to urge the Army of the Potomac out of its winter camps and on toward Richmond. It is a splendid army and something should be done with it. It is understood that an advance has been ordered to begin as early as Washington's Birthday. It is not now imagined that it will not be made, or that the President will soon be officially informed that it cannot be made "because the pontoons are not ready." Nevertheless, as the days go on, there is an increasingly gloomy shadow in the house. Work in all the rooms goes on as usual, but now and then the President rises nervously from his chair by the desk and window, walks hastily out of his office and over into the family side of the building. He will not stop to speak to any one by the way, and he is never gone long. He is a bondsman, and he cannot spare many of the moments sacred to the work of saving the life of the Republic, not even to linger over the pallid face of his sick boy. He must look at him and come away. Men and women all over the land have trusted the lives of their soldier boys in his hands, and their own best hopes for themselves and for their other children, and for uncounted multitudes yet unborn. He must not flinch, although the face of little Willie seems to him to come back with him, and the habitual gloom upon his own has assumed a deeper shade of sadness.

Day follows day, and the shadow deepens, and some who understand its meaning go about as if they did not wish to make a noise in walking.

"Is there no hope?" is the question which has to be asked at last.

"Not any. So the doctors say. But the President is in his room over there. You can send your card in, Mr. Senator, if you wish to see him. I've no doubt he will see you."

"See him? Send my card in, at such a time? God help him! Seems to me he had enough to carry without this. I won't add a feather." And the kindly hearted Senator stalks out of the northeast room almost as if he had been insulted.

"So, little Willie is dead! An awful blow to Lincoln! He was fonder of that boy than he was of anything else. I remember, away back in Springfield, I've seen him—well—I don't want to say any more—it's an awful blow to the old man. Good morning. I guess I'll go." And an old Illinois neighbor walks out, with his head bowed, as if he had lost one of his own.

The President at work in his room to-day? Why, the coffin is in the house! So it is; the casket is here, waiting to receive its treasure, while the general now crossing the hall goes into the bereaved father's office to carry to him the information that the army cannot move, and that the plan of the winter campaign is frustrated by the mud. The Confederate commanders have some wonderful secret of their own by means of which they overcome mud. There is magic in it.

The funeral is a very solemn affair, but it cannot be permitted to interfere overmuch with work. The burden is increased rather than laid aside. It was put by for a few hours, on Thursday, February 20th, the day that Willie died. There will be another break next Thursday, and the next almost a breaking-down with grief, and then calmer counsels will prevail, and the voice of Duty will be heard as clearly as ever, and Thursday will become like any other day, but really there will have been no perceptible intermission in the grim routine of the toil which is wearing out the life of Mr. Lincoln.

The Monitor and the Union League

It is somewhat more than a fortnight since the death of little Willie, but we can yet all feel that the White House is a family residence as well as a business office. Everybody under this roof feels, at any time, like a member of a household rather than like a cog in a machine.

There will, of course, be no more receptions this season. Even the Diplomatic Corps will expect that such as are sometimes given it, of a limited and official character, will be dispensed with by the social law of a house in mourning.

Speaking of that kind of formal and perfunctory hospitality, the first reception by this Administration of the diplomatists who represent Europe at the court of this republic, took place on the 9th of March, 1861, and it was, in some respects, an odd affair. Every man and woman among them was imbued with the idea that one of the frequent revolutions to be expected in republics had arrived and was at work, and there was no such thing as telling what it might do. They were deeply interested, and they all came to pay their respects to the revolution. That reception was, in fact, a lot of fine old governments, in professedly robust health and expecting long lives, dropping in to see a young government, which they believed to be mortally sick and soon to pass away. So they all offered what they called their congratulations.

There seems to be something in a diplomatic education which enables a man to be impressively sincere, conversationally. Here is a polished and highly developed example, talking French, for he knows no English, across the table in the northeast room. Part of the reply he obtains is an expression of regret for the secretary's limited vocabulary. Calmly and smilingly he responds:

"You speak French like a native!" just as if the listener did not know that he is adding, inwardly, "of the United States." He will say the same thing to this other gentleman, none of whose French either of us can exactly make out, and will as inwardly add, "of Holland." It is a very, very old joke, but it has rarely been more perfectly acted and spoken. A fine actor, and he bows admirably.

One of the best bows every brought here came last summer, all the way from Asia. It came with a sun-seasoned ex-officer of the British army in India. He was an Anglo-Indian, who had somehow been born in Boston, and he carried the first white umbrella ever seen by the Army of the Potomac, and he proposed to command a regiment, or even a brigade, with that thing among his possibles. He made a temporary sensation, but the weather just then stood by him, and the boys agreed that there was some sense in the shelter-tent that you could carry on a march.

As to his bow? Why, that's the very point of it. He did not bring any with him. His head would balance a pail of milk even when he was being introduced to the President. That is by no means the case with the polite pair who are here to-day, and who are also willing to accept commissions with American pay and rations.

There are not so many applicants this season. There are not many visitors of any sort to-day.

Is it possible to remember all who have been here? Yes, at times; every form and face in the long procession.

The most striking figure? The handsomest face? That of Secretary Chase? Perhaps so. Some would say so, but do you remember how Senator Colonel Baker looked, when first he came through the hall to the door of the President's room, with his flowing white hair, his brilliant eyes and his noble face all aglow with genius and enthusiasm? Came to offer his California regiment and his own true heart and his life? You thought of his dramatic record in the Mexican War; of his early friendship for Lincoln; his eloquent lament for Broderick—soldier, orator, poet, statesman, and knight of romance more than all; but then, the pity of it, he was thrown away at Ball's Bluff!

The house is as full of shadows to-day as if it were haunted by all the ghosts of its long history; but one has just arrived which is altogether new and startling.

The President is vehemently urging an advance upon Richmond, whether by way of the Manassas line, now abandoned by the enemy, or by way of the James, or by any other way; and this piece of news and of black shadow seems to say that the banks of the James are closed against the Union troops, and also that river to the Union fleet. Some of our best ships have been shattered and sunk near its mouth by an iron-armored monster against whose sides their bullets rattled like so many peas. That monster, the ram

Merrimack-Virginia, it is said, can steam up the Potomac and shell the President out of the White House, Congress out of the Capitol, and the army out of its earthworks, while the Confederate forces march in to occupy the city of Washington.

A few moments of thoughtful consideration of the channel of the Potomac do much to dispel that black illusion; but the mischief the *Merrimack-Virginia* has already done is terrible, and there is no telling how much more she may do. It feels as if some of her shells had indeed been thrown near enough to the White House for its inmates to hear the explosions, and one of them has blown to pieces the plans which were under discussion for the capture of Richmond by way of "the Peninsula." Have similar sea-monsters been building in the other rivers and harbors of the Confederacy? Is it, or can it be, true that one or more of them will quickly steam into the harbor of New York and carry into effect Fernando Wood's idea of severing that municipality from the fortunes of the Union? Of making it as free as one of the Hanse Towns? The air and the minds of men teem with panicky imaginations hatched out into rumors.

Night comes, after a long, long day, and it is an uncommonly dark night, for it is to be spent in waiting to hear that the *Virginia* is again in sight, coming out of her lair in the James.

There is no sleep had worth mentioning, and when morning comes there seems to be no morning at all until late in the day.

The hours go by at the White House under the pressure of a constant stream of dispatches, sent over from the War and Navy Departments, except when the President is there himself to read them as they come.

It is a very bright and pleasant kind of wintry day after all. There was at no time any danger that the Confederate ram could or would ram down the Capitol or the Washington intrenchments. The President has been reading, with keen enjoyment, an all but continuous telegraphic account of the remarkable encounter between the *Monitor* and the *Merrimack-Virginia*. The monster which was destroying our ships has been met and beaten by another monster, Bushnell's and Ericsson's and the President's own, and the story of the fight sounds as nearly like a story of a miracle as one could expect to hear in these degenerate days. It is a costly day for Europe. Probably it is the costliest sea-fight ever fought, for it compels all the old nations to put away their existing navies and build new ones, and each of the new ships will be a worse drain upon depleted treasuries than would a squadron of the old. We shall at least have peace with France and England until their armored rams and monitors can be built and launched, and that is worth something.

A very important part of our shadow has vanished, or rather it seems to have retreated up the James under a bond that it will not come out again to meet the *Monitor*. By a species of jubilant reaction, moreover, its retreat has sealed the matter and the manner of the proposed advance upon Richmond. There is to be a Peninsular campaign, and the Army of the Potomac is in splendid condition to make it.

It is said, and probably with correctness, that one of the most important improvements made by General McClellan in the organism of that noble body of men, in his thorough processes for turning raw troops into soldiers, has been the weeding out of incompetent officers. There are now, indeed, some regiments which have hardly any officers left, and not by reason of deaths in battle. They all are State regiments until mustered into the National service, and even after that the President has no appointing power over them. He can manufacture a general, but not a colonel nor an officer of a lower grade, except in the staff, or in the regular army.

To show how the division of the appointing power works, read this letter just arrived. It is from a patriotic gentleman in Central New York, inclosing one from his son, serving in the Army of the Potomac:

"It is remarkable, you say? He is only an orderly sergeant, and he has no commission, but he is actually in command of all there is left, several companies, of a fine regiment of cavalry.

"They are tip-top letters, his and his father's? You have known them from your childhood? Well, Mr. Lincoln will give him his shoulder-straps, beyond a doubt. He will be out of his difficulties right away, and so will his regiment."

We will go over into the President's room, at all events, and state the case to him.

It is easy to get his attention to it, of course, and he listens, and he takes the letters and reads them, and he seems to be pondering important matters suggested to him.

"It's of no use. I cannot promote that man. His appointment must come from the Governor of the State of New York. You had better sit down and write to him."

"May I say that I do so by your direction, Mr. Lincoln?"

"Yes; tell Morgan I told you to send the matter to him."

The several State Governors have sent many requests to the President, relating to the affairs of their regiments and their officers; but this, perhaps, is the first petition of the kind sent by the President to a Governor. Write the letter, put in the letters of the sergeant and his father, and see how it will work.

There are not many days to wait, and it looks half-way as if Mr. Lincoln had some power. The return mail announces a commission to the sergeant as second lieutenant, but almost the next mail from Albany to this camp lifts him another step, and he hardly has time to turn around before he is made a captain. He is a competent officer, and he will draw his pay in that grade but once or twice before commanding his thin regiment as its major; but his consecutive commissions are signed by Governor Morgan, and not by President Lincoln.

There is a kind of relief to be obtained, now and then, by getting up and going to the door of this northeast room and taking notes of those who come and go through the hall; but there is generally small time for that, or any other mere amusement. It is not often, however, that any visitor, great or small, can arouse any active feeling of curiosity in a mind that is hackneyed or surfeited or hardened with so much meeting of great men and startling events. Nobody's heart can now be made to beat quickly so easily as it could a few months ago. Still, it is curious that the President should have so much to do with the Land Office, when he does not buy or sell any land, and when all his land patents, few enough, nowadays, are signed for him, and when he will not so much as appoint a Land Office clerk. That is Judge Edmunds, nevertheless, that tall, stooping, sagacious-faced, humorous-looking, tobacco-chewing, carelessly dressed, elderly man, and he is Commissioner of the General Land Office. He has been up here again and again of late. To be sure, he is a personal friend of the President, and is supposed to be much trusted by him. He has just held a long conference with him, and now he is coming over into the northeast room, for he is a great friend of ours also, and a shrewder, keener political manager has not been found alive since the burial of Martin Van Buren.

The condition of political parties is not easy to understand. A vast number of the voters who unreservedly sustain the Lincoln Administration are doing army and navy duty, and not only their votes but their personal influence will be absent through this current season, and at the polls next November. The shattered and scattered elements of the Opposition are finding each other out, and are organizing. Nobody knows how large a part of the old-time Democracy, Douglas or Breckinridge, is now Republican. We know where Dix and Stanton and Logan and Grant and Butler and many another Democrat has landed, but they are not at home just now, and the aspect of things is dark. From every corner of the country comes up the many-voiced report: "The Republican party is disorganized, and is on the way to a disastrous defeat."

The Opposition will be a Union party, moreover, with a brilliant Union general at its head, and it may obtain control of both the military and the civil powers of the Union, and it may make peace at any sacrifice. Nobody can guess what changes it might make in the present attitude and future life of the nation. Something must be done, for it is well known that the wise and energetic chiefs of the Confederacy are tirelessly at work upon the political field of the North. The secret lodges of the Knights of the Golden Circle, and of other knightly orders, are established more widely than you might see fit to believe. Baker's detectives have attended hundreds of them.

"Good morning, Judge Edmunds."

"Good morning. Come down to my room in the Land Office at about seven o'clock this evening. Don't tell anybody you are coming—not even Mr. Lincoln."

"All right; I'll be there."

So the day goes by in its usual routine and evening comes, and you saunter down the avenue and up Seventh Street to the Interior Department building, containing the room-ranges of the Land Office. The office of the Commissioner is a trifle disorderly and musty, but it is large, and it is exceedingly retired at this hour of the day. Nobody, without a special permit, or a latch-key, can obtain admission to the building, and evidently less than a score of names have been left with the doorkeeper. The gentlemen whose names were on his list arrive rapidly, and there is a great deal of informal discussion going on among them before they are called to order by Judge Edmunds.

They are men who do not need to be minutely instructed as to the political situation, or as to the reason why they are here. Knowing what they have come for, they go to work in a dry, practical, business-like way, and not a single flash of oratory breaks in upon the busy conference. They have a pretty important job on hand, too, for they are planning, and at the close they have planned and are prepared to create and to organize the Union League of America, the most perfect party skeleton ever put together for utter efficiency of political machine work. They have determined to form a dozen subordinate councils in the city of Washington to begin with, and they have chosen a president, vice-president, secretary and corresponding secretary, each with a prefix of "Grand," and a permanent Grand Council of Twelve. The entire business wears a look of having been prearranged, and your latch-key fits the door of the Grand Council, as belonging to a member of it, and will continue to do so; and you are grand corresponding secretary, in addition to your other mail duties, and have a council of your own to preside over, consisting mainly of Members of Congress, Department clerks, and a Cabinet officer, and a lot of army men. There is no trouble about the finances of the young organization, and it can send out its missionaries by the score to spread its work. Money? Why, as an instance of patriotism, one prominent contractor for army supplies was informed at one of the Departments of the pressing needs of the League, and he at once sent in a check for $10,000. The Department always did like that man, and it liked him all the better for his prompt and patriotic munificence. There were innumerable instances of liberality, large and small, and the missionaries were sent, and in every city and town and village of the North they set a-going a rigidly spontaneous local organization, well known by its organizers, except in a few cases, to have sprung up like a mushroom, without the help of outside hands to plant or to cultivate it.

Under nearly all previous Administrations, the White House has been the centre of a vast spider-web of political machinery and party operations. Its present occupant has another kind of war upon his hands and he would gladly attend to that altogether, but he cannot. There is no Confederate army in the field that is so dangerous as is the political army now assailing the Administration, and the Commander-in-Chief must watch every foe at every point of the wide and stormy horizon. The Union League is to be the rearguard of the Boys in Blue, and its numberless "councils" are to be as camp-fires. All that the loyal voting elements required was to be mustered in and drilled and disciplined, and the coming political battle-fields are now to be securely won beforehand.

The Capitol and the Future

There is a wearisome degree of sameness in White House days, although no two of them are alike, any more than are the men who come. Just such a descriptive rule applies to the press reporters. There is a limited list who privilege themselves to come here whenever they see fit. They come when news is scarce, with a hope of having some found or invented for them. They come when news is plentiful, for they intensely represent the excited and hungry public mind, and they are anxious to assure themselves that they have learned all there is to be learned. The President himself likes to have them come, and meets them cordially. Among them are a number of remarkable men, young or old. Probably they have no idea how much they tell him, or how through them, as if through so many human magnetic wires, he receives message after message from the current thought and purpose of the popular masses whom he understands so much better than they do.

That wiry, sallow, silent-stepping gentleman, who has just come over here after a visit to the President's rooms, is Mr. Gobright, the agent and representative of the Associated Press, the censor of all war rumors, and the condenser of all unofficial news dispatches. He knows a great deal, and he looks as if he knew everything and wished only to ascertain whether or not your own knowledge and understanding are accurate. That is all he came for, and he may have found the President fairly well advised of the condition of things. If not, he has set him right, as a duty, but he will rarely tell you or any other mere private citizen of any news-error he may find you falling into. He will hear what you have to say, however, with extreme courtesy. His entire face is critical, but confidential and trustworthy and secret-keeping, and he is an epitome of the entire reporting science and art. When you have conversed with him analytically, you have no need to study any of the other reporters, except as interesting individual characters. As for that, the widening system of press correspondence is drawing into its service a remarkable variety and amount of capacity and of culture. That young-looking woman out yonder, for instance, whose face and form were modeled in Athens, is not exactly a reporter, but she is an enthusiastic war correspondent, and she, and others more or less like her, come up here frequently to gather materials for present and future letter-writing. She is a genius, and so, of a widely different type, is the lady who passes her without speaking, and gazes out of the eastern window of the hall.

This lady, so tall, so handsome, though neither pretty nor beautiful, with such fine black eyes, such luxuriant black hair, so liberal a display of white teeth when she so often smiles, she is neither reporter nor correspondent. You should not say "woman" when you speak of her, for the essence of her position is that she is a lady, descended from the first families. She is careful of her social position, whatever it is. She has a house, and she is said to keep boarders, but she by no means keeps a boarding-house. She is a singularly regular attendant upon the sessions of Congress, and she knows its members well, of both Houses. She has endless rounds of visits to make, upon varied business or pleasure at the several Departments, but if she is at all a lobbyist, she would not have it said so. She dresses well, for her shapely and graceful figure is always covered by much-trimmed black silk. She may be thirty, and she may be five or ten years more, but you cannot always tell. She has excellent tact, and her business visits here to the White House have been well managed. They have been mainly with reference to pardons and the like, or else—and somewhat more frequently—she comes merely to show the White House to distinguished friends or guests from a distance. She shows them the Capitol also, and they learn that she knows all things and everybody, and that she has influence, and the *entrée*, and somehow or other her field of operations is made profitable.

If you can consent to play the prophet for a moment, and come up here again in the days of President Cleveland, only a quarter of a century later, we will sit down in an ante-room that is now the sleeping-room of Nicolay and Hay. While you are waiting to be called into the President's room, you will see a tall, dark-eyed, dark-haired woman walking around, and gracefully explaining to a party of friends some interesting points of the history of the White House. It may be by accident, a mere slip, that she speaks of actually meeting somebody here in Polk's time, for she cannot be over thirty or thirty-five—you cannot always tell, but she corrects her remark, and erases the expression of her personal presence then, just as you remember something. You will remember the smile and the teeth, and the black silk, and it will be of no use to rub your eyes and say to yourself, "Sometimes a daughter is the very image of her mother," for she slips again with, "That was Lincoln's room. He said to me once—"

The rest you do not hear, but a picture steps down and out of its place in your memory, and comes into the northeast room to say, winningly,

"I do so wish to give my friends a look at the conservatory."

There sometimes comes a curious, vague, not altogether pleasant impression that the spreading, rambling, half village, half fortified post, into which the city of Washington has grown, contains but two buildings, to which all the other structures serve as one and another kind of outbuilding. They are a mile apart, but they reach out into everything else, and, in several ways, they reach into each other, for they are the Capitol and the Executive Mansion.

Always and every day, when the President is here, Congress is well represented at these headquarters. The Committee upon the Conduct of the War does its duty nobly, and so do all its self-appointed assistants. No men in Congress are more frequent visitors here, or are more cordially welcomed than are the very important squad of War Democrats. They are a capable set of men, and they are not found voting on the wrong side half so often as are some nominal Republicans. In fact, the old party lines are disappearing and new ones are forming, and some of the symptoms of the change are almost comical. That robust and jolly-looking Congressman yonder, for instance, an old antislavery man, puts on an injured air as soon as he draws near the portico, for he has not yet recovered from his original idea that he and Lincoln were elected President at the same time—Lincoln to carry on the business as his agent, but he to direct how it is to be carried on. Such an understanding as that should have been reduced to writing in the first place, so as to bind both parties, for the nominal President has forgotten it.

Perhaps he has no time to think of it, with so many other Congressmen and Senators coming up to see him with fully developed perceptions of their own rights of every kind. A splendid lot of men they are, too, in spite of the stupid abuse heaped upon them by the critical press. They are honest, able, patriotic, and they are beginning to really understand Mr. Lincoln.

If the Capitol reaches over into the White House, it is partly because now more than ever before—excepting during the days when Jackson ruled one House through Martin Van Buren and the other through James K. Polk—the Executive branch of the Government powerfully influences and, at times, all but controls the Legislative branch. Thad. Stevens is here very, very often.

There are many public messages going, almost daily, it seems, from this end of the avenue to the other, but they carry only part of the electric current of influence which travels the same road all the time.

It is Nicolay's business, or Hay's, or that of both, to carry those messages, as a rule, and they have a two-horse cab in which to ride to the Capitol. When those horses were first procured, the two younger secretaries were seized with the idea of perfecting their horsemanship by taking early morning saddle exercise, but in less than a fortnight they gave it up. Gallops before breakfast were too much like cavalry service without pay or rations.

There is an uncommonly severe pressure in the other room to-day, and we have to take our turn in bearing a message from the White House to the Capitol. We need no carriage and go by the street-cars.

There is remarkable company to be had, at times, in a Washington City street-car. Stand here on the rear platform and look in, for it is not necessary to go in and sit down. In the far corner is the Governor of a Northern State, conversing with a Senator sitting opposite, and ignorant of the character of the pickpocket sitting next him, as he probably is of the character of these overdressed females in the centre. The pale-faced volunteer, yonder, is chatting freely with the major-general, who may some day lead him in the field. It is not easy to guess why that dashing paymaster should be laughing so familiarly with the witty fellow at his side. He may, or he may not—perhaps not, on the whole—be acquainted with the faces of all of Baker's detectives. That is a witty friend of Baker, as well as of the dashing paymaster. The very quiet gentleman, this side of them, is a member of the Cabinet, undergoing a course of instruction from a war correspondent.

The Capitol is a superb building, in spite of its unfinished look. There are massive stones and other materials scattered over the ground beyond it, but we do not see them as we approach from the west. Not until we are carried away around the north side and up the hill. The flags are floating upon both wings to show that Senate and House are in session, but you hardly notice them in the daytime. At night, however, there is an arrangement by which a brilliant gleam of light shoots up across their stripes and stars, and makes them beautiful. In the dark nights at the close of the Buchanan term, it sometimes seemed, especially toward morning of the long and stormy night sessions, as you came out before an adjournment for a look at them, as if the light upon those banners was about all the cheerfulness left in the country, and you believed it was a kind of prophecy. One custom, correspondent to this, has never been adopted, and, with or without a reason for it, the flag of the United States does not float over the headquarters of the Commander-in-Chief, even in time of war. Perhaps his tent does not need any flag.

Near the corner of the vacant space before the eastern front of the Capitol, the space the crowd stands upon to hear Inauguration addresses, there is a small, unpainted pine cabin, with a sign over its door: Superintendent of the Dome.

There is a queer superstition that the dome is never to be finished, and that the coming crash of the Republic will leave the Capitol in the hands of those who will tear it down, even if they do not convey its stones to Richmond. So strongly has this idea been expressed that it has greatly stimulated economical Congressmen in the matter of appropriations for this and other public buildings, and work upon them is pressed with greater, costlier energy, than it was before the outbreak of the war.

Up the steps to the eastern portico and into the building, not at all as a private individual, a citizen, but as something from the White House, reaching into this other side of the National Government. Both Houses must be visited, but both will receive you in the same manner. We will visit the House of Representatives after having looked in at the Senate.

You are carrying something in the nature of a paper latch-key, and the door before you seems to open of itself, so prompt is the ready doorkeeper to recognize the presence of an errand from the Executive. He walks into the Chamber of Representatives with you, just as an eloquent member is denouncing some feature of the misconduct of the war, and his eloquence is suddenly interrupted.

"The President's Private Secretary!"

Down comes the Speaker's hammer, and he announces, loudly:

"A message from the President of the United States!"

Forward marches the Sergeant-at-Arms to your side, and in a moment more your paper latch-key is before the Speaker, and with its further treatment by the House you have nothing to do. The doorkeepers have made you free of the legislative chambers heretofore, but from this day forward you are legally entitled to "the privilege of the floor," to come and to go at will, except when the Senate is in executive session, the theory being that you are supposed to be always on business for the President and cannot be questioned as to its nature. Your latch-key will fit at any time, but it may wear out, or the lock may be changed.

After all, there is something like smoothness in the way the Legislative and Executive horses pull together at the national load. It is so very heavy, and both are in such patriotic earnest, that it shall be pulled through all this varied mud to the high and dry ground of a final victory. It is terribly deep mud, however, and it is said now that the road up the James is as bad as anything ever discovered over here, across the Potomac, toward Manassas Gap. The current reports from the Peninsula tell of much camping and of comparatively little forward marching, and it is well understood that the Confederate leader is concentrating his forces to resist the Union advance. He ought to be shot by his own soldiers if he did not, and the fact that the opportunity is given him is calling out a terrific storm of angry comment from every corner of the North. Never before did such letters of wild reproach come pouring through the mails. They come by the hundred; and they come now, largely, from even mothers whose sons are in the army. The President cannot take time to read them, but it is not true that he does not hear and understand the vast and thrilling volume of these voices. He will have their tone and meaning in his mind and memory a few months later, when he takes action which will seem to some timid people to be perilously beyond the prudences of his authority.

Read! read! read! and hear also what is said to one another by the Senators and Congressmen who drift into this northeast room for little conferences and conversations before going in to lay their views before the President. If they talk to him as they do here, his ears must tingle at times. Your own tingle, and your cheeks burn as your eyes glance over the letters before putting them into the waste-baskets. It is almost a relief to find that every other commander in the field has as bitter commentators as has General Mc-Clellan himself. According to a mass of testimony daily consigned to these wicker-work oblivions, Halleck is a pedantic fool; Grant is a blundering drunkard; Burnside is a sluggard; Pope is a windmill; Buel is a traitor; Schofield is a tyrant; and a score of other more or less prominent generals are mere thieves, feathering their own nests, with the assistance of corrupt quartermasters and commissaries. Every assignment to duty yet made by the President is a pernicious mistake, and every campaign is a failure, in spite of the fact that the army lines are moving steadily southward, that the Atlantic coast is ours, and the Gulf and the mouth of the Mississippi, and that McClellan is confidently expected to win some victories, very soon, upon the James.

Mr. Lincoln is alone in his room this morning, and you have good cause to go in and show him something, and it seems as if the fermentation within you blows out its cork. He is sometimes a very patient listener, and he hears more than some men think he does. You have a keen sensation that he is just now not exactly listening to you—that is, not to you only—but his reply is of a sort which you will not at once repeat. It is given very thoughtfully, slowly, with wrinkled brows and with eyes that turn toward your own from a long, dreamy stare through the window southward:

"Well, well, I will say it: for organizing an army, for preparing an army for the field, for fighting a defensive campaign, I will back General Mc-

Clellan against any general of modern times. I don't know but of ancient times, either. But I begin to believe that he will never get ready to go forward."

He turns from you to a pile of dispatches, and a few months later you will think you are listening to almost a repetition of the same mournful commentary, and then the Army of the Potomac will pass rapidly into the hands of chief after chief, until one is found under whom it can do no other thing than go forward, through blood and fire, to the very end.

Sentries and Passes

A somewhat remarkable order has been issued by the military chief in command of the city of Washington. The way he came to issue it is this. Over in the western part of the city there was an extensive cavalry corral, with stables and sheds and piles of baled hay and other forage. One night it was all burned up, with a loss also of many horses, and the fire was said to have been lighted by a cigar. Another saying put the blame upon Confederate spies or sympathizers, but the angry general has sent out a decree rigidly prohibiting smoking "in or near any Government building." His order was intended only for army use, of course, but its phrases are somewhat broad, and he has zealous and intelligent subordinates. There is, moreover, an immense amount of smoking going on, and there are a number of Government buildings, of one sort and another.

It is getting dark early this evening. We have dined, but we must look in at the White House once more. It is a pretty carefully guarded headquarters in these days, for some unexplained reason. They post foot-sentries at the foot-gates of the grounds, and mounted sentries in the carriage-gates, and there is a regular guard-mounting, so that things begin to look more like war. They don't require a countersign yet.

"Put out dot cigar-r-r!"

"What?" But the pathway through the eastern gate is barred by a rifle and a sabre-bayonet, and the command is sternly repeated, in an accent that tells of the Rhine:

"Put out dot cigar-r-r!"

There is no help for it. Out it goes. We will walk on into the house.

"Mr. Secretary! Wait a moment! Best joke you ever heard!"

It is the voice of the mounted guard, who sat in his saddle in the carriage-way and chuckled over your discomfiture, and he has galloped alongside of you.

"It wasn't an hour ago that Germany halted Stanton right there, just as he did you!"

"Did he make him throw away his cigar?"

"Well, he did! Stanton all but ran against him in the dark, and Germany shouted at him: 'You puts out dot cigar!' till he gave it up. But that wasn't all. Stanton laughed, but he hadn't more'n got out of sight before old Seward, he came along, and he's 'most always a-smoking."

"Did he halt Seward?"

"You bet! He pointed his frog-sticker at him and yelled: 'You put out dot cigar!' 'Oh, I guess not,' said Seward, and he was going right along, but he had to halt and stand still, and no kind of explanation was worth a cent. Out it had to go before he could pass the gate."

"Stanton and Seward both!"

"That isn't all, though! Seward got away without being prodded, but a few minutes later along came old Ben Butler, as large as life, and he was swinging right in. 'Halt! You put out dot cigar!' shouts Germany, and Ben halted. 'Are those your orders?' he asked. 'Dose is my orters! Put out dot cigar!' 'Orders are orders,' said Ben, as he threw his cigar over the fence, 'and they must be obeyed. There it goes.' You'd ought to have seen it and heard it!"

The cavalryman makes his account as vivid as he can, and then he wheels laughingly back to his post; but the joke is a little too good to keep, and Mr. Lincoln is at work in his room. Perhaps he never did laugh harder.

"Seward! And Stanton! And old Ben! Well, well! I reckon I'd better send for the officer on duty and tell him to let up a little. The orders against smoking don't include this part of the camp."

There is nothing more severe than a bit of good-humored sarcasm in the admonition given to the officer, and orders of a general nature will go out tomorrow that will allow posted men to discriminate among buildings. Perhaps no three men could have been picked out who would have made the over-strictness more grotesque. As for Ben Butler, he is a kind of favorite with the President, but he may never again wear quite so much uniform as he did when he paid his first formal visit of military ceremony. He was then in command of Massachusetts militia, and he wore a militia parade uniform—cocked hat, scythe sword, boots and all. He looked very large when he swept across the hall to the door of the President's room, and he was a peculiarly welcome arrival. As for Seward, the cavalryman was right about his smoking, and he is even reckless about matters of uniform, except upon State occasions. He went into the President's room the other day with the knot of his cravat nearly under his left ear, and carrying an unlighted cigar in his hand; but then he carried in the other hand highly important dispatches relating to the attitude of France and England. The other Cabinet officers are somewhat particular, as a rule; but the President's wardrobe always requires the watchful supervision of Mrs. Lincoln. He simply will not pay special attention to his personal appearance, and he cares very little how other men dress.

Spring often turns rapidly into something like midsummer in this latitude. Weather such as this must be felt severely by men who have long marches to make, such as have recently been performed by some of our fellows away out West. The Army of the Potomac is not being forced to wear itself out in marching just now; but then the sun is bringing out in full force the pestilential vapors of all the marshes around its camps. It is said that no army ever had better camp regulations, or better supplies, but there is a great deal of murmuring. The President himself is murmuring, mainly because of so much camp and so little marching; and he has gone down the river on a steamer to see the other general, and to talk with him about the capture of Richmond. That is a result which ought to be very near just now, unless the costly war is to be dragged out year after year.

It is very warm, this Sunday morning, if it is Sunday. It must be, for all the larger business places on the avenue were closed when we came by. There were no flags floating upon the wings of the Capitol, and so Congress is not sitting to-day. The calendar on the mantel in the northeast room says that it is Sunday, but somehow there is less and less of a religious or sacred idea connecting itself with that seventh part of our weekly time. The mail has been brought in—nearly a bushel of it—a larger mail than common, and it will not do to let it lie there until another bushel shall be landed on top of it to-morrow morning.

"Can it be finished in time for church? It is yet very early, and it might be done?"

No, there is too much of it, and, besides, you have half lost the old habit of attending church on Sunday. So much the worse for you and for hundreds of thousands of others, to whom, as to all the occupants of the White House, the war has come to break up or to break down all their accustomed ways of living and of thinking. Everything has to give up to a fever and its deliriums. Even human life itself does not seem to have the sacredness it once had, while you habitually count men as food for powder, and expect, hourly, to hear how many more of them have been expended.

It is very warm, and all the windows that are open seem to let in heat instead of coolness. There is very little valuable matter in this heap of penwork when you tear open its envelopes and sift it out. It is worth while, nevertheless, to note that fully half of the epistles which of necessity go into the waste-basket, are patriotic denunciations of General McClellan for lack of vigor, and of the President for not driving him forward. It is almost a pity that he cannot read them to the general. He has entire confidence in Mc-Clellan's ability and in his patriotism, but these angry letter-writers hold different views. They aver that the general is a traitor, in league with Jefferson Davis, that he is an Arnold in heart, and that he will sacrifice the army to his ambition, by seeming to fight and yet not fighting, or even by worse military misconduct. They are as unjust to him as they and others are to Mr. Lincoln, and they express themselves with furious vehemence. On the whole, it is not unpleasant reading, for here, at the national headquarters, there is a strong anti-McClellan feeling, and with it something of the other feeling voiced in these letters, that the President is too confiding, too conciliatory, too indulgent, too much disposed to almost make a pet of his brilliant army leader. It is a piece of ignorant household presumption, but it breaks out frequently, when there are no outsiders around.

There are no outsiders here to-day, nor are there any insiders, apparently. Now that the mail is finished, we can get up and walk around and see what this summery silence means. Every door upon this floor seems to be wide open, as if to let the lazy, heated air drift through; but not a living soul is to be found in any room. We are all alone upon this floor of the White House, and the headquarters of the Commander-in-Chief are about the most peaceful piece of silence that could be found. It is the general's tent, but now that he is gone there is no sight nor sound of war. Even the brace of swords leaning against the mail-table are sheathed, and wear a sleepy look.

The President's own room is just as he left it, and there is a map lying outspread upon his desk. Look at it. There is one pin at Fortress Monroe, and another at Williamsburg. Pin, too, at Yorktown, and he has stuck several in, along the James, all the way to Richmond. He has been studying that map, or somebody else has, for there are blue pencil marks dotting another line, between Washington and Richmond. It may or may not be what is called "the Manassas line," although that position is marked and included, but it is a route which General McClellan will not travel. A new army driver, named Grant, will one day get hold of the reins, and you will watch the road he takes and will be strongly reminded of those blue pencil marks, only that they will seem to turn red—as red as blood.

There are many books in the Executive business office nowadays. They come and they go from this place and that. They litter the tables and they lean against the walls, and they look out from under the sofa, as if they were asking if their turn for consultation had come. Nobody knows when the President finds time for reading, but he does find it, somehow, between times and between days, and he will shortly be able to write to General Mc-Clellan that he gave a certain order, under discussion between them, "on the unanimous opinion of every military man I could get an opinion from, and every modern military book—yourself alone excepted."

That is to be the result of all this litter and this patient study; but even now he finds a need for a more condensed and convenient military library, better arranged for reference. He has found such an epitome of war science in the luminous brain of one of his Western generals, and has sent for him. General Henry Wager Halleck is to be made nominally General-in-Chief of the Armies of the United States, but he is really to supplant all these volumes and many maps, and to act as the scientific military counselor of the Commander-in-Chief. He will become the President's Chief of Staff, and will act as a buffer between him and the other generals in the field. He will, therefore, be as popular among them and elsewhere as is the Secretary of War himself. He and Stanton and Lincoln will be charged with the reverses, and the heroes in front will get the credit of all the successes. That is the process which has been going on from the beginning, and it will require long time and much research, with the help of many tremendous events, to justly balance the great account. Look out southward from the window of Lincoln's room, from his own window, by his chair, just as he looks daily, while he ponders questions relating to the land and the people beyond the Potomac. Even in these days, as he sits here, he is pondering a paper stronger than an army with banners, which he will send across the river in the early fall. A first draft of it is lying now in one of the drawers of this writing-desk, but no other living soul is aware of it, for there is nobody living, with any right or power to enter this room, who would presume to meddle with anything guarded by the frail wood of this unguarded piece of furniture.

There are children strolling around under the trees and over the grass of the White House grounds. The flowers are doing uncommonly well this season. The grass of the lawn is newly shaven and is softly green. So very peaceful it all is! and we turn away from the window to the war maps as if they must belong to some feverish unreality, some dream of a disordered mind, soon to pass away and leave only peace behind it. Nevertheless, as we turn away and pass out of the President's room, and call to mind where he is and what he is doing, the oppressive, magical glamour of the place and of the time loads more heavily than ever every breath you draw of this dense, frontier-post atmosphere.

Tar, turpentine, resin, pitch, pine, cotton—these were the staples of the old North State, and our navy is in great need of them, and its harbors are of vast importance to the Confederacy; and Burnside has captured the sand-bars and Albemarle Sound, and the other sounds, and a long strip of coast, forest and swamp and sand-hills, north and south of New Berne. It is one of the bright, blue bits of successful sky to be seen peeping through the clouds that hang over the national cause.

Would you like to see North Carolina, and get a breath of sea-air, and a smell of the piney woods?

Yes, after so many long months of close confinement, day and night; and we will go over and tell the President, and we will tell him we will not be gone long.

"Well, yes; I'd like to have you run down to North Carolina. See Burnside, and come back and tell me how it looks. I'll write a letter for you to take to him, and some passes and orders for transportation. Stanton will give you whatever else is necessary, and so will Welles. I reckon I wouldn't carry much baggage, if I were you."

That really seems to be good advice, and your outfit consists mainly of a bright, span new suit of a new kind of military blue flannel, put on the day you leave Washington.

There are barriers in the path of every undertaking, and the first obstacle looms up in the office of the New York quartermaster in charge of coast-wise transportation.

There never was a larger major, for his size, with more uniform and straps and swell and importance. When you quietly and respectfully enter his office, he is intensely occupied with his morning newspaper.

"May I ask when the next steamer leaves for New Berne?"

"No, sir. There is no steamer going to New Berne."

"But I really must go. When is there a steamer to sail?"

One not accustomed to meeting great men cannot help feeling humble in the presence of military power, combined with some that is naval.

"You can't go! There have been too many (epithet) civilians permitted to travel on Government vessels. There's no more to be said, sir. Get out! I can't be bothered with any more applications."

"I think you will read that, sir. Tell me, instantly, when the next steamer sails for New Berne! Read it!"

Down comes the newspaper. Down comes an astonished pair of feet from the chair they rested upon. Down falls a long cigar from the now wide-open mouth which had held it.

"What?" and that word contains a fair steamer-load of utter amazement. Insolence to an army officer? From a civilian? Insubordination from a quiet, subdued-voiced party, with neither straps nor spurs nor sword nor feathers? But he reads automatically:

"Officers of the army and navy are commanded to furnish transportation" . . . . (epithet, four or five of them).

"EDWIN M. STANTON,
"Secretary of War."

You next hear only a confused mixture of syllables of various kinds, ending with the audible words:

"WELLES,
"Secretary of the Navy."

There is now a major, quartermaster, commissary, or what not, on his feet, reading another paper, and gurgling something or other, out of which you pick the words "officers," "army," "navy," "commanded," "my private secretary" (epithet, heavy-laden), "Lincoln," and a ghastly gush of long-winded astonishment that resembles "Presidential States."

Absolutely, the White House has fallen upon that man, and it has all but killed him. So have the War Office and the Navy Department, and he crawls out of his ruins to gasp:

"There's a steamer going this afternoon. No other passengers. Give you a cabin state-room to yourself. I'll send an orderly to the captain right away. Took you for a civilian. Have a cigar?"—and there seems to be a sudden rush of determination to do all the duty called for by such a heap of—well, of official ruins.

It seems to be so: the White House can travel on a card, by sea and land, going and coming, but the North Carolina trip contains no more pleasant picture than that of bright-faced, hearty, hospitable General Burnside, receiving you in a loose white flannel suit, a shilling straw hat, slippers, and no visible sign of major-generalship. You like him, but you do not like your own blue flannel so well as you did. A storm off Hatteras; a drenching night in a bivouac; another drench; much rain of a smaller kind; much sunshine as you go from camp to camp and see all there is to be seen; and all the while, as your stock of information enlarges, your blue flannel shrinks, your Panama curls both ways, your skin tans and burns and peels, and you get back to Washington once more, ready for a change of raiment before returning to the desk in the northeast room.

A Battle Summer

Georgetown is a kind of western suburb of the Capital. It is the sleep-iest old village to be found, and when the war broke out it was dying of re-spectability. Since then it has been in a semi-comatose state, but it may re-vive some day. No other streets are paved with such cobble-stones. Every third stone is as large as a peck measure, with two-quart measures between, and it is an awful pavement to drive over, but it is worse to camp on. When you once lay down upon it, beside your rifle, those larger cobble-stones were a trial. Whatever led us to make so long an early morning stroll all over Georgetown, we are back again, and as short a way as any to get into the White House grounds from the avenue is the walk that runs midway be-tween the War and Navy buildings toward the narrow gate near the conser-vatory. It is a warm morning. It was very warm in Georgetown, and all the way back, but the heat increases as you approach the White House. The air is denser, and the sun strikes down through it with peculiar power. It is tell-ing upon Mr. Lincoln, this August weather, and there he is now, just be-yond the gate, with his high silk hat in his hand, mopping his forehead with his pocket-handkerchief. He has been stopped by somebody on his way back from the War Office. She is an uncommonly black black woman! she is, and she stands right in his path, looking up into his face. She is not in a starved condition, by any means. She might weigh three hundred, and ev-ery pound of her is aware that she is looking into the face of the greatest man in the world. Perhaps she was never before sure that Abraham Lincoln was a reality, a human being—that is, apparently human, but he is now holding out a hand to her, and he is actually laughing. So is she, but she has not ut-tered a word. Her eyes roll wonderfully, and her smile is all over her face, and it takes elsewhere the semblance of an embodied chuckle; but all the words she ever knew have gone a wool-gathering.

"You look happy. Reckon you must be."

Gurgle—chuckle—all over the big black woman, as her hand timidly meets his, but he does the shaking and lets go, and she turns away without an articulate syllable, and so almost bursting with pride and delight that she stuffs the corners of her check apron into her mouth.

He does not have to hold out a hand to the fellow-citizen who was waiting just behind her, but the brawny, long-limbed volunteer is at first as silent as she was. He does not chuckle, but his arm and hand go out, straight, stiff, as if he means to run the President right through.

"I'm from Indianny!"

"So am I," replied Mr. Lincoln. "I almost wish I was back there again."

"That's jest what I was a-wishin' myself, but instid of that I've got to go back to camp. Aint they a workin' of ye pretty hard, Mr. Lincoln?"

"I reckon they are."

"Well, now, some of us boys was a-sayin' so. You'd better take right smart good keer of yerself. There isn't anybody else, lyin' round loose, that'd fit into your boots jest now."

The handshaking he gets is very hearty, but his only other answer is a long, silent, very singular kind of a laugh. It is a morning when the President needs a laugh as much as he needs anything else in the wide world, except news of a crashing victory somewhere along the line.

The Peninsular campaign is ended. General Pope and the Army of Virginia have received and have apparently absorbed the returning sections of the Army of the Potomac, and a sharp, terrible summer campaign is going forward. Pope is a good officer; able, brave, enterprising, patriotic; but he has had upon his hands a great task to perform, under circumstances which will be matters of research and inquiry and bitter discussion through many a long year to come.

It is really the heat of the campaign which makes the furnace air of the White House so all but insupportable this morning after Lincoln goes into his room, and Louis, the messenger, is informed that he does not wish to see anybody. Mr. Nicolay will know to whom, if anybody, that order of exclusion does not apply. Of course Halleck is omitted, for there he goes into and across the hall, in evident haste, with a yellow telegram open in his hand, and he does not wait for any doorkeeper. He has the air of a man who has been hit hard by something or other.

Everybody knows that the Second Battle of Bull Run has been fought, and that it has gone against us, although General Pope is as confident as ever. He has done well, and so has the army, but the reports going out to the country are black with the smoke of a lost battle. He says that the troops under his command are in good spirits and in good condition, ready for further work, but a host of tongues and pens are busy with the assertion that the officers and men of the Army of the Potomac half-way refuse to serve under any other commander than McClellan, under whom, by the way, only a part of Pope's present army ever did serve. Of course, it is a false imputation upon the soldiers and their leaders; but the fact that it is made is full of evil omen, especially on the heels of this severe check to our arms.

General McClellan has not been removed, yet he is not in command, and it is not easy to say where or what he is, as a general, but he is here in Washington, at his own house, as a physical fact.

It is very, very warm, and Halleck comes out of the President's room wiping his broad, intellectual forehead and studying the floor, as he walks, as if he were searching among the carpet patterns for the plan of a successful campaign.

"Bill, I want to see the President!"

You look up from the letters with a start and a shiver of astonishment, for there, at the end of the table, sounds the voice of one of the very few men who remember a time when the other boys used to call you Bill. The face you would not recognize, for perspiration has been wiped from it by hands which had been helping wounded soldiers. Black, red, mud-color, under a broken straw hat, and then the condition of that once nobby suit of clothing! He is a scarecrow from the battle-field of Bull Run, and he insists upon seeing the President. He has been sitting, by special request, in the tent of a corps commander, an old friend, while other corps and division and brigade commanders were induced to utter frankly and fully their military views of the situation, and then he has been requested to hasten to the White House, and to repeat to Mr. Lincoln what he had heard, for he is a civilian and not restricted by army regulations. Swift transportation was furnished him, including a horse from a disabled ammunition wagon and an Alexandria quartermaster's steamer, and here he is, refusing to give particulars to anybody but the one man who should know them. In a moment more the scarecrow is alone with Mr. Lincoln, and it is an apparent age before the bell up there jangles a summons.

The President writes upon a card and hands it to you:

"Take him to Stanton and then to Halleck. They must see him at once," and as you lead the scarecrow out of the room he remarks:

"Then I want to go and get something to eat, and take a bath, and change my clothes. I've had the worst kind of time."

He is willing to relate battle-field experiences as he goes along, but his mouth is closed by his original trust and by Lincoln's orders as to anything he heard in the tent of the corps commander. He is closeted quickly with

Stanton, and then the Secretary himself comes out with him and they cross the hall of the War Office together to Halleck's room, and you have to wait a long time before they come out, and then Stanton and Halleck walk over to the White House, while the scarecrow goes away to eat and bathe and sleep. It seems as if the weather grew all the while warmer, but when, not a great many hours later, you learn that General McClellan is once more in command, you cannot help wondering if the change has anything to do with the verbal "round robin" transmitted to the President from that informal council of war, through the scarecrow.

The army will fight well under McClellan? Of course they will. They fight well enough all the while.

Why, then, do they get beaten?

Well, the Confederates also fight very well, and they get beaten now and then. The Greeks and Romans got beaten, and so has every other nation, and all the great generals have been beaten, and some things must be endured until the tide turns.

There is one tide, however, which never turns, and that is the tide of criticism and advice which sets toward and into the White House. Here is a fine wave of it this morning, sitting in solemn dignity at the end of the table, waiting for Louis to come and tell him that the President is waiting to see him. There is no doubt but that he is an eminent theologian, and he is even now heavily burdened with a religious duty. So heavy is his load that he is willing to land a part of it right here, or at least to get it into order for delivery at the President's desk. He is a delegate, a representative of a conclave of eminent religious men, and they are doctrinally the soundest knot of patriotic pieties to be found any-where.

He comes right out with it. Too many battles have been fought on Sunday, and the feelings of all good people have been terribly outraged thereby. The President is to be appealed to, and the pernicious habit into which the armies are falling must be corrected unless the war is to be a failure. He is a good man, and he is eloquent, and he has no doubt of the effect he is to produce upon the President, but he can lose his temper.

"Do you not really see, sir, where the bottom drops out of your argument?"

Doctors of divinity are accustomed to have more respect than that paid to their arguments, especially from very young men, and the reply you get is a severe commentary upon your own moral condition and religious needs, but you are not at once converted.

"Do you not think you are in the wrong office, doctor? Should you not rather be appealing to Mr. Davis and General Lee and General Jackson, and the rest of those fellows? All the attacking, recently, has come from them. We haven't attacked anybody, on Sunday or any other day. They are a Sabbath-breaking, unruly, mischievous lot of irreligious ruffians, and they do not give our boys time to go to church."

"H'm! I'll see what Mr. Lincoln will say about it." But then the doctor of divinity has melted a little and can all but smile, for he is a man who has talked a great deal of "on to Richmond" in his day, and the pin pricked him.

Curiously enough, while the President is willing to issue special orders relating to Sunday quiet in camp, and as to profane swearing in the army, almost his first response to the doctor is:

"I think you had better consult the Confederate commanders a little."

It is not true that Sunday has entirely disappeared from the White House. It still returns with a faint suggestion that it was meant to be a day of rest. This part of the house grows even peaceful while the few bells left in Washington are supposed to ring for church. They are not allowed to actually ring nowadays, for all of them are too near some hospital or other, or, at all events, there is peril that waves of sound might carry too painful a vibration to the sensitive nerves of some sick or wounded soldier. The whole city is more or less a hospital, and there is no real need of bells. Sitting here, some Sunday mornings, you think you can hear them, but you are really listening to the village church bells of long ago, away up North, because you know that at this hour they are sounding across the greens and along the grassy streets, summoning the people to come to the meeting-houses, and think of and pray for the village boys camped around here and elsewhere, or the other village boys over whom the grass of this horrible summer is already beginning to grow.

Can there be anything hysterical in the absolute need that there now and then seems to be for something like fun? Mr. Lincoln says that he must laugh sometimes, or he would surely die. He laughed right here, a few Sundays ago. The letters were about done, when in came John Hay, all one bubble. He is sober enough most of the time, but he had heard something funny, and he was good-natured about dividing it. Generally he can tell a story better than most boys of his age, but he broke down on that one before he got well into it. The door was open and so was Nicolay's, and he heard the peal of laughter when the story proved too much for its narrator, and over he came, with a pen in one hand and a long paper in the other, and he sat right down to listen. Hay began at the beginning, and went on very well until the first good point was reached. It was nothing so wonderful for another time than this, but it was a first-class excuse for a laugh, and all three of us exploded as one.

The whole floor had been as silent as a graveyard or a hospital, until this uproar broke up its Sunday stillness, and we did not know, or had forgotten, that anybody else was within hearing until:

"Now, John, just tell that thing again."

His feet had made no sound in coming over from his room, or our own racket had drowned any foot-fall, but here was the President, and down he sank into Andrew Jackson's chair, facing the table, with Nicolay seated by him, and Hay still standing by the mantel.

The story was as fresh, and was even better told that third time up to its first explosive place, but right there a quartette explosion went off. Down came the President's foot from across his knee, with a heavy stamp on the floor, and out through the hall went an uproarious peal of fun. It was dying away, and Hay was about to go head, when:

"Mr. President, if you please, sir, Mr. Stanton is in your room."

There stood Old Edward in the doorway, washing his hands and looking penitent, as if he hated to break in upon the apparently untimely, if not unseemly merriment. Senator Trumbull, of Illinois, is also out there, on some special errand or other.

There was something all but ghastly in the manner of the death of that story. Through all the sunny, laughter-filled chambers of the Executive office poured thick and fast the gloom and glamour of the death in life that belonged to them. The shadow came back to Lincoln's face, and he arose, slowly, painfully, like a man lifting some enormous burden. He even seemed to stagger as he walked out, for not only are each day's burdens heavy, but the worst news of the war has thus far been its Sunday news, and such as brings over Stanton in person.

What was the point of the story—the thing so irresistibly funny?

Nobody can tell now. I don't remember anything about it that seems funny.

But the rest of it, that Hay told after the President went away?

He did not tell any more. There was no more laugh nor story in him, and he and Nicolay went over to their room. Sunday will come back again, some time, but the record of this war tallies curiously with the record of other wars. Even Waterloo was fought on Sunday.

Weeks pass rapidly in this White House life, and it is uncommonly quiet today, but there is a restless feeling, nevertheless, for McClellan has led the Army of the Potomac up into western Maryland, to meet the Army of Northern Virginia, under Lee, and there has been a series of terrific collisions. According to the tenor of the dispatches, the struggle shapes itself into a pair of battles, one called the Battle of South Mountain, and one called the Battle of the Antietam, which are really parts of one long match between the armies which have so often been pitted against each other. Confederate sympathizers here assert that their side claims a drawn battle, if not a second-rate victory, but it is growing clearer that Lee is beaten, and that he must give up the re-conquest of Maryland. He will advance no foot further into the North, and it is even fairly sure that he is already retreating into Virginia.

More than the great world knows of has been depending upon this news from the army under McClellan. All through the hot, oppressive days of this battle summer, that great state paper has been waiting in one of the pigeon-holes of the President's desk. He has taken it out from time to time to ponder over it and to correct it here and there, and to long for such a condition of our military affairs as will, in his opinion, make him strong enough before the people and the world to justify him in sending it out upon its tremendous errand. Some weeks ago, the last of July or the first of August, he called the Cabinet together and read it to them, but they all agreed with him that it must wait for the winning of an important success. Mr. Lincoln says that he has promised God that he would issue that paper if God would give us the victory over Lee's army, and now all the later dispatches from the Antietam seem to call upon him to keep his word.

"What is it, Mr. Nicolay?"

"Make two copies of this as soon as you can; one for the Senate and one for the House. My hands are full."

Here it is. Mr. Lincoln's own hand. His draft of the Proclamation of Emancipation. Read it carefully through before you take up your pen, and think of what it means to the future of your country, and to the future of the bondmen whom it liberates. You try to, but you cannot. You are not nervous, but you spoil a sheet or two of paper in beginning your copy. No wonder, for you cannot but think while writing.

It is done, for it is not so long a job after all. Take the copies to Mr. Nicolay. Put the original in your safest desk-drawer. There it will lie until the day when Hay comes to you to ask for it. He is going to send it to the Sanitary Commission Fair at Chicago, to be there burned up in the great Chicago fire.

The Echoes of the Proclamation

There is a kind of paper used as a detective by the chemists, which will turn of one color when dipped in an alkali, and of another when soaked with an acid. There is probably no kind of paper which would reveal the character of the specters which are making this place populous this rainy morning. The President has gone up the river to have a chat with the Army of the Potomac. He has paid it several visits heretofore, in its other camps, but never one upon which such mighty political and military results must surely hinge. All the possibilities which he has gone to confront or prepare for are trooping into and out of this northeast room. The entire White House, without him in it, is only a shell, a sort of perfunctory headquarters, from which the life has departed.

The city of Washington is still only a frontier post, in spite of the victory on the Antietam; but people who come here from the North seem to labor under the delusion that it is right in the middle of the United States. They might understand the matter a little better after a thoughtful inspection of the fortifications, especially those upon the Virginia side. No castle of these modern times is at all like the castles people used to set up before cannon were constructed to pitch a heavy shell seven miles and have it burst on striking. The walls of the White House seem to be here, where you can touch them and look through their windows; but that is only an appearance. They are really far away and they are not white. Their precise tint depends upon that of the mud they are built or building of, and their windows have eyes of iron staring through them and watching for the very possible approach of a Confederate assailing party. This is only the old, the haunted part of the castle of the Presidents, and now that Mr. Lincoln is in the camps, we and the ghosts have all the eastern wing of it to ourselves, at least for to-day. It has temporarily lost its charm for most other visitors. It loses it as they cross the portico and learn at the door that there is no dictator here.

That is what the Opposition press and orators of all sizes are calling him. Witness, also, the litter on the floor and the heaped-up waste-baskets. There is no telling how many editors and how many other penmen within these past few days have undertaken to assure him that this is a war for the Union only, and that they never gave him any authority to run it as an Abolition war. They never, never told him that he might set the negroes free, and, now that he has done so, or futilely pretended to do so, he is a more unconstitutional tyrant and a more odious dictator than ever he was before. They tell him, however, that his edict, his ukase, his decree, his firman, his venomous blow at the sacred liberty of white men to own black men is mere *brutum fulmen*, and a dead letter and a poison which will not work. They tell him many other things, and, among them, they tell him that the army will fight no more, and that the hosts of the Union will indignantly disband rather than be sacrificed upon the bloody altar of fanatical Abolitionism. Precisely what they do not tell him, if he knew what they are doing, it would be hard to say; but there are the baskets, and he is up yonder with General McClellan, congratulating the boys in blue upon the good work they did at South Mountain and the Antietam, and urging their commander to at once push forward and give them an opportunity for doing more as good as that.

What do the soldiers think of the Emancipation Proclamation?

They are mostly a little out of politics, just now, but perhaps one of them spoke for the others when he remarked:

"The Proclimashin? Well! Yes! I'm an old Hunker myself. Hardest kind of Hardshell Democrat. I ain't no Abolitionist. But then, if Old Abe kin git the niggers to quit work, it 'd cut off the supplies of Lee's army, sharpest kind. I'd thought of it myself, but I didn't reckon Linken 'd hev the grit to up and do it. It's an all-fired good move, so far's the army's consarned."

What does McClellan think of it?

There is no doubt or question that he disapproves of it, both on grounds of policy and of constitutional law; but his course has proved that some hotheaded people have been more than a little unjust to him. He is a better citizen and a wiser man than they said he was. Still, the little he has said, and the much more which he has refused to say, fixes his position as the leader of the political opposition, and forbids that he should long remain in command of so important an army, unless he will use it with such energy that no power in this country could presume to remove him. It was said a few months ago that no such power existed, or could or would be exercised; but the position he was allowed to slip into at the close of the Peninsular campaign familiarized the army and the nation with the idea that the President could remove him as easily as he could any other commander—for a declared cause.

Such a cause exists, and enough of it can safely be declared, and among the ghosts which haunt the White House to-day, not one is the ghost of a doubt that McClellan will shortly be superseded, while many of the others are shadows of the possible consequences.

There never was so long a week, but the President is back again, and all that anybody yet knows is that the army received him well, and that he left behind him very positive orders for an immediate and rapid advance.

The tide of official and all other kinds of visitors has set in again, and the White House is as busy as ever. It is understood, moreover, that the remainder of the autumn and the coming winter are to be marked as a society season, and that the city of Washington will be as gay a town as any garrisoned post can expect to be in time of war.

"What is it, Edward?"

"Madame expects you in the Red Room this evening. She's to have a reception. Will you please come down now for a few minutes?"

It is a little early in the season for Mrs. Lincoln's Red Room receptions to begin, but she has good reasons for the announcement she has sent out. She is entirely willing to do her duty and to sit through the evening in her parlor, while her smiling guests pull her in pieces, and she says so, cheerfully, as you chat with her and receive her instructions.

She has gone now, and we may as well linger a moment in the Red Room. It is not large, and it is made smaller by its massive furniture, its heavy curtains, its grand piano, and by the consciousness that it is in the middle corner, so to speak, of an unusually large house.

Put aside the curtains and look out of this window, across the White House grounds. You cannot see far, because of the trees and bushes; but, upon a careful study, you will understand, as you shove up the sash, that this is one of the most important windows in the United States. Mrs. Lincoln is in constant communication with the Confederate Government, betraying the war-plans of the Union generals, and this must be where she does it, for this is sacredly her own room. Even the President himself has never been seen here. The mails are not a channel for treachery, since every letter to Mrs. Lincoln is opened and read upstairs. The telegraphic wires are under War Office censorship, of a peculiarly rigid kind, and there is no private wire to the White House. The servants, downstairs, are known to be intensely loyal, and would neither carry nor bring a communication of the Arnold-André kind. There is, therefore, but one entirely reasonable solution of the problem of how Mr. Jefferson Davis, or his next of kin, can receive army plans from Mrs. Lincoln, after she has obtained them from the President, and Halleck, and Stanton, and McClellan, and General Smith. The Confederate spies work their way through the lines easily enough, fort after fort, till they reach the Potomac down yonder. The Long Bridge is closed to them, and so is the Georgetown Bridge, but they cross at night in rowboats, or by swimming, and they come up through the grounds, like so many ghosts, and they put a ladder up to this window, and Mrs. Lincoln hands them out the plans.

Where do they get the ladder?

Well, now, you tell, if you know. They may borrow it of Jacob. But there is no other way for the alleged treasonable communication to be carried on.

It is a strange thing to get through with White House work early and to have before you nothing but an evening of Executive Mansion sociability.

The Red Room does not look unpleasantly red by gas-light, but the prevailing tint has its effect upon any and all other tints exposed to its influence. For instance, it heightens the deep crimson shade of the silk that Mrs. Lincoln is wearing this evening, and makes it contrast more decidedly with the simple blue worn by the slender young woman who is here to assist her. When good Mrs. Welles comes in—for she is to come, with a party of friends from the North—there will be more and very capable assistance; but there will also be another and even a stronger contrast, for she always wears sober colors.

Mrs. Lincoln's robe was made for her by one of the best dress artists in New York, but you cannot help disliking it, not to speak of the fact that your taste keenly rebels against Queen Victoria's draw-room edicts about low-in-the-neck toilettes. You rebel more vigorously after this bevy of Boston, Concord, Lexington and Bunker Hill women come in, with one or two who are all the way from Plymouth Rock and the deck of the *May Flower*. They, too, evidently agree with you. Not one of them but has deemed it her duty to dress as if the war-taxes had cut down her income but had not clipped the upper part of her wardrobe. The tall, gray-haired, severe-faced lady, in very plain black silk, has two sons in the army. She may own streets in Boston, for all you know, but her dark eyes search the crimson silk and every other item of Mrs. Lincoln's outfit remorselessly, in spite of the warm, hearty cordiality of her greeting. Every woman who has yet arrived has come as a critic, and not one of them will be capable of doing kindly justice; and they will be authorities, hereafter, swelling a miserable tide of misunderstanding. Somehow or other, the best of women make too much of dress, and there is no more patriotism in their plainness than there is in the tint of this Red Room, which has not been changed because of the war. Still, it is something of a relief to welcome a different bevy, now sweeping in; for the Knickerbockers are almost a distinct race from the Puritans. There are vivid colors now to help the situation, and you can be thankful to Manhattan Island, and to Staten Island, and to Long Island, and to Hell Gate, Spuyten Duyvil, the Dunderberg and Anthony's Nose. Red, blue, and other tints which you do not know the correct name of, and a fine glitter of diamonds. It is all right now, for the entire Bunker Hill party disapproves of the Hudson party, and there is sincere reciprocity, and the recent victories give a fine excuse for exuberant good spirits in the Red Room. Nevertheless, the honors are largely with Bunker Hill; for the gray critic with the severe eyes comes out in all but fiercely enthusiastic approval of the Emancipation Proclamation, and it is not taken up very audibly by the echoes between the Dunderberg and Anthony's Nose. Long Island and Staten Island do better, and make you glad of being yourself a sort of Bunker Hill Knickerbocker. On the whole, these women, queens of society in their own parishes, should have perceptive faculties capable of telling them, and others through them, that Mrs. Lincoln—a Kentucky girl whose years have been passed, for the greater part, in a growing village on Grand Prairie, among prairie villagers and settlers—is doing the honors of the White House remarkably well. Not one woman in a hundred would do any better; but then these women, the visitors of this evening, consider themselves, not as one in a hundred, but each as one in a thousand, with nine hundred and ninety-nine ranged below her. So they will show no mercy.

Other guests arrive, and some of the earlier arrivals depart, and new groups form and re-form and separate, and there is no end of mutual criticism among them. The various elements do not take the trouble to melt together and assimilate. It is almost as if the severe gray lady, so admirable every way and so well aware of it, set a pattern which cannot be departed from by any lesser light, and she did not stir from the chair in which she first sat down. That kind of woman has been here before, and she never by any chance walks around the room.

The evening passes, and at the end of it not one visitor can be recalled who did not offer a good reason for being at the Capital at this out-of-season season, or who did not express a purpose of coming again some day, during what is supposed to be "the social season" at this fortified post upon the Confederate frontier.

Day after day goes by with an increasing sense that this Administration is fighting a double battle, and that it has by no means too large a force in either field. Even in Mrs. Lincoln's parlor the guests who come leave behind them very plain expressions of the disturbed state of the public mind; but that is a zephyr among flowers compared to the gusts which are rising among the busy politicians and the many disappointed patriots of the North. It was a foregone conclusion that General McClellan would not abandon the cautious deliberation which marks his military nature, and that he would be superseded by Mr. Lincoln's equally cautious but predetermined search for a forward movement embodied in a living general. The Army of the Potomac, the representative force, in one sense, of the whole army of the Republic, has passed under another commander, for good or evil; but the autumnal elections have been held, and State after State has given warning that Mr. Lincoln's hold upon the men who are near enough to the polls to cast ballots has been strained almost to breaking. The voices which come through the mails are simply terrific in their volume and vehemence, and we are in great need of victories in the eastern battle-fields as well as in the Valley of the Mississippi.

The shadows have been deepening, day by day, but this morning there seems to be a peculiar smell about the White House. If at any time you go down into the basement, even in cold weather like this, you will be reminded of old country taverns, if not of something you have smelled in the edge of some swamp. But this is quite another matter. It is more like a suggestion of much waste of gunpowder. And the wind comes up across the Mall with a plaintive, moaning whisper, as if it bore a story it could not find the heart to tell.

Yes, that was General Burnside himself, coming out of the President's room. This odor of gunpower and this whisper of grief have been here, floating around the house, ever since the battle of Fredericksburg was fought and was not won. Its cost was mournfully heavy. We lost fifty per cent more men than did the enemy, and yet there is sense in the awful arithmetic propounded by Mr. Lincoln. He says that if the same battle were to be fought over again, every day, through a week of days, with the same relative results, the army under Lee would be wiped out to its last man, the Army of the Potomac would still be a mighty host, the war would be over, the Confederacy gone, and peace would be won at a smaller cost of life than it will be if the week of lost battles must be dragged out through yet another year of camps and marches, and of deaths in hospitals rather than upon the field. No general yet found can face the arithmetic, but the end of the war will be at hand when he shall be discovered. Such a gift of Providence to the Union armies at this present hour would be a Grant that would hardly be appreciated by the nation; but Mr. Lincoln is searching for him.

That was Burnside, and a fine man he is, a good officer, but not quite up in his battle-field arithmetic. The breech-loading carbine he invented before the war was a very nice weapon, but it was a small bore and did not equal some of these later patterns. He will cease to command the Army of the Potomac, but he has lost no part of the confidence and esteem felt for him by the President. He will have another first-class command, and his future will be as honorable as is his past; but hardly anything in it will be more a credit to his memory than is the way he has borne himself in this his darkened hour. His interview with the President is supposed to have had no witnesses, but a young man who all but accidentally knew something about it says that it gave him a higher idea of human nature, manliness, generosity, unselfishness, and all that sort of thing, to hear Lincoln and Burnside trying each to relieve the other of the excessive burden of the Fredericksburg responsibility and to carry it himself. It will not do to say anything about it, for fear of fatal results. If such an example of generosity were held too closely before some men it would kill them. Their meanness would strike in, and they would die.

Realities and the Drama

"If you can do anything for the passage of the National Bank Act you ought not to fail of doing it. There seems to be no other way for placing four hundred millions more of government bonds."

The other features of the Act, as a vital part of the policy of the Administration, are briefly rehearsed by the speaker, very much as you already understand them.

"Beyond a doubt," he says, "a decisive vote will be reached to-morrow, and the bill will surely be defeated, unless —— in the Senate, and —— in the House can be induced to support it. They are good enough Republicans, but they are going the other way, some of them for one reason, some for another."

"And mostly without reason! Perhaps something can be done!"

Very likely the views of such men as he has indicated cannot easily be changed, but there are sometimes curious coincidences nowadays. It happens that the very Senators and Congressmen named, and not any others have been invited to attend a meeting of a committee of the Grand Council of Twelve of the Union League this very evening, to discuss the work of the League in their States and districts. They all are members of the League, and they have gladly agreed to come; for their very seats in either House depend upon the support they receive from the great party machine.

We may as well attend that meeting, for many subjects of interest may come up for discussion.

There is no better place for a caucus than in the room of Grand President Edmunds in the Land Office. The committee of the Grand Council is not large. It is a mere business committee for practical work, but it has facts and figures to present which are intensely interesting, not to say gratifying, to the invited legislators. They are as pleased a lot of patriotic politicians as ever listened to the details of a thorough work of local organization for their own benefit. They avow their determination to coöperate more vigorously than ever before with the League, and it seems only natural for them to drift off, as they do, into a discussion of the National Bank Act. Here, too, in this secure privacy, they are quite willing to set forth the nature and degree of their opposition, and to say why the bill is to be defeated, as it surely will be. At the same time, they are in the state of mind which listens courteously and kindly to the other side of any question, and they frankly admit, point after point, the force of the arguments set before them by Judge Edmunds and other members of the committee.

"Well, now, I did not so understand it. If I could be assured that the President felt so deeply about it, personally. I did not know."

"The President, Mr. Senator, is always cautious, and rightly so, about saying or doing anything which can be construed as Executive interference with the independence of the legislative."

"Of course he is. But then! I had no idea! Do you mean to say, of your own knowledge, that he regards—that he has said—or that he would look upon any man who voted against that bill as a public enemy?"

"By no means, Mr. Senator! Do not misunderstand me! I have said nothing of the kind! He has said nothing whatever, nor would he assume such an attitude. He would only feel that the men who defeat that bill are cutting off pay and supplies to the army in the field; starving the soldiers; forcing the abandonment of campaigns; acting as reinforcements to Lee, and as supporters of Jeff Davis. Of course he would not influence in any way."

"That'll do, sir! I don't want to hear any more. He can have his bill! Is there any more business, Judge?"

"No, I guess not. I'm glad you take so favorable a view of the Bank Act. We all do here. Now, if there is anything in the way of coöperation that you require—"

"Oh, of course we will call on you. Certainly. I'm going up to see Lincoln, after Congress adjourns, to-morrow. The army needs money! All right!"

The committee and its legislative guests adjourn in a highly amicable state of mind, and if the Bank Act were here it would leave the Interior Department Building arm in arm with two of its worst enemies, just as each member of the Grand Council Committee is now doing. It was a pretty long but a very pleasant evening, and it ended well, and the future existence of the National Banking System is assured. The right kind of men are always to be reached by argument, but one of those Senators will meet you half crustily always, to his dying day. He will never forget that, after all, it was a kind of pill.

There are a great many things to interfere with routine office work, in a room the door of which must be kept open. To be sure, it is a great place to see the course of events from, this chair behind the mail table. Did you know that this kind of revolving chair was invented by Thomas Jefferson? It was, and it is one of the many good things he did for his country. It is the ideal political chair, for you can turn every way without losing your seat. He also invented the Declaration of Independence; but some of these men here seem to have an idea that they invented Lincoln. When a man invents anything of importance he should take out a patent for it, or it will get away from him. Then he will feel as sour over it as do some of those excellent inventors from the banks of the Sangamon and Vermilion, or that other gentleman yonder, who is so sadly proud of the historical fact that "I set him a-going in New York, sir. I was the first man there to come out for him. Before his Cooper Institute speech. I stuck to him, in spite of his speech, and I'm a-sticking to him now."

So he is, and he is not at all aware that the quizzical-faced artist fellow over by Hay's desk is making a sketch of him, and is wishing, behind his grin, that he were a camera. It is not every artist who comes here that can appreciate what he finds. Good figure painters or character sketchers, with a gift for the grotesque and for caricature, are rare birds; but, take them all as they come, the men of the pencil and brush are as interesting as are the reporters themselves. There's one of the quill remarkables now, and he should be a favorite with the artists. He is the editor of a Washington paper, and he is an old favorite of William Shakespeare the play-writer. He goes under a modern *nom de plume* at present, but his real name, as every Shakespeare reader knows, is Falstaff—a thin man, and modest and truthful.

They say there is but one living actor who can present Falstaff as he really was known to Shakespeare, and the President has been almost anxious to see Hackett. He needs not to be so, when the original comes up to see him as often as he can find an excuse for doing so. Hackett is to play at Ford's this evening, but we cannot go. Work has been so badly put back to-day that it can hardly be caught up with before bed-time.

There are other of Shakespeare's friends who come up here from time to time, but we cannot stop to name them now—we must go home to dinner.

The evenings are somehow always long in the White House, winter or summer, and this threatens to be as long as any, for everybody else has gone, and it is lonely work. Slash them through! It is curious what a difference there is in mails. Some are almost half wheat, but this is all but solid chaff and rottenness of one sort or another. What sickening insanity!

"You are here? I reckoned I'd find you here. I am going to the theater, to see Hackett play *Falstaff*, and I want you to come with me. I've always wanted to see him in that character. Come to my room. It's about time to go."

There are a few minutes spent in the President's room, while he puts away some papers; but he is not thinking, apparently, of the mess of public business he is thrusting aside. He is making an obvious effort not to think of it, and he has actually been reading over the play that he is to witness the presentation of. It does not seem correct to ask him particular questions, but things can be said which stir him up to make remarks, and the more he says the plainer he makes it that he is a thoughtful student of the great poet. He anticipates an evening of unusual enjoyment, and of mental relief and refreshment, and you are keenly conscious that it is the very thing that he is most in need of, next to a great victory by our army in the field.

There are those who severely criticise the President for his occasional weakness and wickedness of going to the theater, and setting a bad example to all the young men and women of the land. They are excellent people, who always think of the pit when they think of a theater, as if that might be all there is of it—that and a smell of sulphur—and they prophesy awful consequences to Mr. Lincoln and to the nation. If their premonitory warnings shall seem, at a day which is not foreseen, but which is coming, to have a tremendous and blood-stained fulfillment, will there really then be any voice to assert that the lightning of that blow fell upon him and upon the nation because he went to Ford's, and on Good Friday evening? If so, the evidence in the Surratt trial and the other trials will correct that erroneous view of the matter.

There is no premonition of peril to-night, as we sit here in the President's box. There was a storm of applause when he came in, and now it seems as securely safe a corner of the great Washington City fort as any which could be selected. He is incomparably better guarded here, to any critical human eye, than if he were walking through the White House grounds, or to and from the house of one of the secretaries, alone, or with only an unarmed attendant. The house is crowded. There are soldiers, police, citizens—hundreds of them, a bodyguard through which no assassin could force his way. Besides, assassination works in secret and in darkness. Who can imagine a diseased, abnormal vanity, which will commit murder in the face of certain death, in order that the manner of the deed may make its theatrically performed tragedy take the frenzied shape of something hellishly resembling fame? So it will be; but at this moment it can be ascertained how many of those men and women carry opera-glasses, for they are all aiming their binoculars at Mr. Lincoln as he sits so quietly looking at the curtain and waiting for it to rise.

If he is a study to those people, and to hundreds more who carry no glasses, so he is to us, and we wait with a sense of hopeful satisfaction to see his face light up and to hear him laugh.

Hackett is indeed superb. Even when the living Falstaff comes to the White House after news, or to criticise generals and campaigns, and public men, and the measures of the Administration, he is not nearly so much his complete self as he is here upon these boards to-night. The roll in his gait is the same there, but he is near-sighted and has to wear spectacles, and Hackett wisely omits them in representing him. He is playing his very best, and he is well supported. It is a perfect idealization, and the President is studying it intensely. He is enjoying himself. He has forgotten the war. He has forgotten Congress. He is out of politics. He is living in Prince Hal's time. He is studying Shakespeare as intensely as he used to study him between cases and law-books and works upon mathematics in the old law-practice days, when he drove around the Eighth Judicial District of Illinois in a borrowed buggy until he could collect fees enough to buy one.

It is a long performance, but at last the curtain falls. The applause has been frequent, prolonged, sincere, and Hackett has been called out, and has responded, and has retired, and you rise as Mr. Lincoln does. The smile with which he now tells you how thoroughly he has enjoyed it all, how much he has learned, how much better he now understands the poet—well, it is absolutely the first smile you have detected, during the evening, upon his intensely studious, absorbed, abstracted face.

"Have you been vaccinated?"

"Yes, doctor, but it was long ago. Is the small-pox on the increase?"

"Terribly, and everything else is on the increase, and I have been so busy I had been forgetful of my duty. I should have attended to you before. Guess it isn't too late. Bare your arm."

That was early in the season, and the results of the attention you then received, whether late or early, from your own physician, made you about down sick for a week. Ever since then you have understood that the extent of the prevalence of the dreaded disorder is one of those secrets which the Surgeon General's office does not give to the reporters. On the whole, you believe that you are safe and always have been, and you have a natural absence of nervousness about any kind of infection. It is very much as if you were a fatalist, and yet you are somehow startled, almost into a shudder, by precisely the same question, asked of you here, at the mail-table:

"Have you been vaccinated?"

"Yes, doctor, thoroughly—" and you tell him your unpleasant experience, but he says:

"Glad of it! Very glad of it! But it will do no hurt to repeat. I'll shut the door a moment. Take off your coat and bare your arm."

He is the President's own physician, and he is a rapid operator; but he supposes you to know more than you yet do, for he chats along while he punctures:

"Mr. Lincoln's case is not fully developed yet. Varioloid."

"Not the small-pox!" you exclaim, with another shudder, which helps the entrance of the keen point of his feathery flash of steel.

"Oh, no, probably not. I won't say more just now. There, you'll do. I've really no uneasiness about him."

Everybody else has, then, after the doctor has taken his confident and smiling departure. Whoever yet believed that a doctor could read the end of a smallpox case from the beginning?

But the varioloid is not the smallpox.

What is it, if it isn't that? Couldn't he die of it? Of course he could. And where would everything go if he should die?

There has been such an absence of any thought concerning the President's health! The idea of assassination has been held up before us until it is worn out and there is no more scare in it; but the idea of his possible death in any other way never came before, and it is all the more grisly now that it is here.

Nobody is supposed to know it, but the White House has suddenly been turned into a smallpox hospital, with a certain degree of penetrable quarantine.

This is surely a remarkable addition to the other elements of its peculiar character. The loneliness enforced, so far as the ordinary run of visitors is concerned, has in it something that is differently oppressive from the old familiar clamor. It is impossible not to calculate consequences, and to remember all you know about Mr. Hannibal Hamlin. He would be President if Mr. Lincoln should die, and there is no means by which you can form an opinion of his capacity as dictator. No, absolutely; he could not step into Mr. Lincoln's shoes, and something of inestimable value would be lost to the country, even if Mr. Hamlin were twice as large a man as he is believed to be.

Day follows day, and all the reports from the sick-room are favorable, but the whole country is nervous about this case, mild as it is, and so are you.

There are, indeed, some people whose nerves are not at all shaken, especially those belonging to their facial muscles. Here is one of them, who has managed to pass the lower door quarantine. He does not explain how he did it, but he is eager to unfold the fact that he is an important office-seeker, sure of success if he could see the President, his papers of recommendation are so overpoweringly strong.

"But Mr. Lincoln is sick, dangerously sick. He cannot attend to business, except such as is of the utmost national consequence. He cannot receive visitors."

"Oh, that's nothing. I don't mind the smallpox. I am not in the least afraid of infection. You can tell him so. He needn't be afraid I'll catch it. Tell him I'll come right in. I've been vaccinated."

It requires something like engineering to get that fearless adventurer out of the White House, for he really is a man who is of some value, but he is also one who has a right to know that another man, enduring pain and fever and intolerable irritation, ought not to be intruded upon. Perhaps he was thinking less of that, and more of the fact that Mr. Lincoln could appoint him to-day and die to-morrow.

There are many others like him, but the quarantine is usually too much for them. So, if they succeed in passing that, is the impassable Mr. Nicolay, and he has a fine faculty for explaining to some men the view he takes of any untimely persistency. Hay does it equally well, in some cases, but he is even too fine about it, and there are fellows who went away and did not know how much he told them. It is of no use to employ verbal needles upon pachydermatous natures.

"The President wishes to see you. He understands that you are proof against infection."

"I want to see him, then! Is he sitting up, Edward?"

"Indeed he is, and he won't be there long. He's doing finely!"

It will never be possible to forget how this sick-room looks. So bright it is, in the perceived certainty that the peril has passed away! Even the welcoming smile that lights up Mr. Lincoln's face is a half-amused reflection of your own exuberance. He has not been alarmed about himself at any moment, and he combines his instructions concerning the duties he assigns you with a humorous response to your personal inquiries. He almost wishes he could have his office in one of the smallpox hospitals. It would relieve him of one part of his pressure: "Well, no," he adds, "it wouldn't. They'd all go and get vaccinated, and they'd come buzzing back, just the same as they do now—or worse."

A Vigil and a Victory

"Will there not be any dancing?"

"Dancing? Why, no! What room will there be for dancing, even if it were expected? Do you know how many people we've got to stow away? And feed them all, too?"

"I don't know. You say I can't have any ticket, and you've sent them all over the country, or Mrs. Lincoln has."

"No, she hasn't. It's a rigidly official affair—a consolidated reception."

"What makes them call it a ball, then?"

"They're thinking of cannon balls. We're forced to be rigid. The Cabinet, the Supreme Court, the heads of Departments, some lesser judges, the entire Diplomatic Corps, Senators, Congressmen, generals and admirals, Governors of States—have you got that list in your head? Well, now add to each man of it from one to three women, and then come with me. I've procured a tape-line, and I'm to measure all the floors for Mrs. Lincoln, to see if there is going to be standing-room. There won't be a chance for any man or woman to stumble and fall down. Dance? I'd say not!"

You explain it fully to this reporter, as you have to others, but all the Northern journals are crammed with discussions of "Mrs. Lincoln's party," and one illustrated weekly has printed a full column of mournful verses, supposed to be sung by a wounded volunteer in hospital, concerning "My Lady President's Ball."

Much the volunteers care whether she has a party or not! All the boys in blue, we know, would be glad to go to one—the nearer their own homes the better.

The fact is that a kind of established custom, something like a tradition-law of the White House, seems to require of each President, or of his wife, a certain number and routine of official dinners, dull, stately, costly affairs, coming along in a wearisome string through the season.

Jefferson's way of following, or of helping to create, the custom, nearly ruined him; so did Madison's and Monroe's, and John Tyler was tremendously vilified for the niggardly, or wisely prudent, manner in which he pruned it down. It is objected to by Mr. and Mrs. Lincoln upon several grounds. Not the least of the objections are the loss of time and the worry; but these are small compared with the perpetual peril of having some official jollification set down beforehand for the evening after the arrival of stunning news from the army. It was, therefore, deemed well to crowd all into one grand affair, given to about the same complete list of official personages.

"But what about all these invitations," he asks, "to all the great society people all over the country?"

"You mean all the invitations which have been asked for by all the would-be great people of the land, and which could not be given without first enlarging the East Room to include Lafayette Square, and then it would be a tight fit, and no dancing."

Every rejected application for tickets of admission to the "ball" operates, through one channel or another, to swell the storm of absurd disapprobation which has been aroused by this unfortunate "reception with refreshments." Mrs. Lincoln is made the target of all manner of misrepresentation and abuse, but it is well to be polite to the gentlemen of the press.

"Reporters from each of the leading journals will be admitted. Every accommodation they may require—"

"No, sir!" is the proudly indignant rejoinder; "if we cannot come as gentlemen we will not come at all! We are refused cards of invitation."

"It is hard to see how you can have a better claim than Secretary Chase, for instance, or Vice-President Hamlin, or the Chief-Justice."

"They all have invitations!"

"Not one of them is invited simply as a gentleman, or by reason of any social position he has outside of his official character. You have no more right to an invitation than has any hod-carrier on Pennsylvania Avenue. It is strictly an official affair."

"We won't come without cards!"

"Don't come, then. The fact is, you are only stealing a little spent thunder from Charles Dickens. He refused to perform his theatricals before the Queen, at her command, because he was not a gentleman of England, and could not be received at court. This is another run of shad, altogether."

Nevertheless, that was where the storm really began, and the reporters have the ears of the people, and there is such a buzz-making that good people in far-away farm-houses are dreaming o' nights of the wild orgies of waltzing and eating and drinking and general wickedness which the judges and Senators and other reckless old men are about to whirl in around the lurid wastes of the President's house at Washington.

There is difficulty enough to be encountered in preventing kindly Mrs. Lincoln from making matters worse, and breaking the official rule all to slivers in her good-humored desire to oblige a persistent stream of applicants who appeal to her personal friendship for them. She has been compelled to make a kind of scapegoat out of you, and you have been getting black looks from elegant people who blame you as the cause of their disappointment. It has been a relief to inform two or three favorite generals and Congressmen what you thought of them for almost obtaining extra tickets from her.

The reception evening arrives and there is as dense a pack as was expected, but everything goes off reasonably well. There are reporters here, after all, and they seem to be gentlemen; but still there is danger in what they may cause to be printed about "the ball," all because they are invited "officially," as reporters, and not as if they were entitled to come by reason of individual excellence. It is not likely that many of them will ever succeed in seeing the funny side of their position. It is curious, too, considering how bright a lot of fellows they are. It is really the work, mainly, of that English reporter, Dickens, and of the Court rule which defines the word "gentleman" otherwise than it is understood in America. He had no "sixteen quarterings" to show, and so the Yankee reporters will show no quarter to Mrs. Lincoln.

It is a grand affair, but there is a great deal in it that is new to everybody concerned, and you wish from the beginning that you had had a little more practice, or else a more definite plan of campaign and clearer orders.

There are not many better men than Mr. Seward, and you believe it again before the evening is over, for he helps your inexperience out of tight places among his diplomatic mob with a good-nature and dexterity equal to that which he displayed in handling the Russian treaty. To be sure, he called you a Ganymede, whatever he meant, and you think he thought there was something funny in the way you led him through the wrong door when he had the foreign army at his heels and you did not know that fact.

There are several fine mixes, besides any that you have engineered, and some of them did not have any Secretary Seward at hand to mend them. It is a grand good thing, this official reception, when at last it is over; but it is no ball, no party—nothing but a jam.

"Stanton says that this is the darkest day of the whole war. It seems almost as if the bottom had fallen out."

A dark day, and the gloom of it seems to come drifting, fog-like, across the lines of fortifications and over the Potomac and up the Mall, and to settle in a dense black cloud upon the White House headquarters of the Commander-in-Chief. All day long there has been a rain of dispatches to the War Office from the Army of the Potomac, telling of the net results of the battle of Chancellorsville. Mr. Lincoln has been there part of the time, reading them as they came in, and, before and since, they have been sent over here, until it seems now as if the White House were on the battle-field, or as if the wounded had been brought and laid in the East Room, while the dead were heaped up on the Mall. There are burial parties at work there with lanterns; but they are mostly Confederate soldiers, for the enemy won the field and hold it, and our boys were forced back with such losses as will fill the Northland with mourning. All the members of the Cabinet have been here, and some few Senators and Congressmen, and a number of military and naval officers, but the house has been closed to the general run of visitors.

Meals are eaten, perhaps—nobody has a clear idea whether he has or has not eaten—and the perfunctory office work has gone on, after a fashion, very much as things are done in any other family when there is a coffin in the house—the coffin of a sudden death.

Once more, as at Fredericksburg, the Union losses have been fifty per cent greater than those of the Confederates, and yet the old, terrible arithmetic is as hideously true as ever. If they lost 12,000 while we lost 17,000—some say it is worse than that for both sides—we can afford the seventeen better than they can the twelve. Lee has now little more than 50,000 men that he can put in line to-morrow, and we can double that number. We can fight four more Chancellorsvilles, and then march into Richmond, unopposed, with a larger army than that which now defends it.

What will the country say? Will it sustain the Administration in this hour of distress and disaster? Will it understand how this thing came to pass, or will it back down under the blow?

As to a large part of it, read, if you will, two-thirds of this huge mass of correspondence upon the table. Every letter was written before the fight was lost, yet every writer, man or woman, writes as if this day's reports had already been printed. These are the angry or the heart-broken echoes of the old defeats. What echoes will be aroused by the reverberations now going out from the terrible check of Fighting Joe Hooker's splendid army! Will the people lay the blame on Joe Hooker? About as much of it as they have heretofore laid upon other generals; and when they at all blame him they will also curse the President that Hooker was in command.

This stack is from people who demand the reinstatement of McClellan, and it is not large compared to another of the same sort, which will quickly

cram the White House mail-bag. The President is told, in every form of vehement denunciation, that the country will no longer endure his Abolition
fanaticism, and the greedy ambition with which, for his own personal ag-
grandizement, he has shelved the best and most trusted Union general, to
put the Army of the Potomac into the hands of incapable, second-rate men,
fit only, at the best, to carry out such orders as would be given by the hero of
the Peninsula and of the Antietam.

Will he see or read any of these letters? Will he be informed of their contents?

Well, if you feel like going over to his room with half a bushel of them,
you may go. Tell him you have about a bushel more to open and read before
you can go home, and that most of them curse him. There is one, now, that
you might carry with the others. There are blots and blisters on its white envelope. In fact, it is one of quite a handful, and you might do well to show
them all to him first, before he reads the half-bushel.

You are crying over it yourself? Well, such a day as this a cry would be a
grand good thing for Lincoln, if he could get one. You need to read only one
passage:

"He was my only son. He fell at Fredericksburg. It was so hard, so long
before I could feel reconciled. Oh, Mr. Lincoln, God help you in your trial
as he has helped me in mine. I shall pray for you, day and night. Be very
strong and courageous, and He will bring us through."

Are there any more like that?

Plenty of them! Men and women who cry unto God day and night, and
who do not grudge the cost of this great struggle for the life of the nation.
They believe that God's Country, as the soldiers call it, is worth anything
they have to give for it.

These letters must all lie here, for Halleck and Stanton are with the President again.

They have gone at last, and it is getting late in the evening? Well, even if
he is alone in his room, there is quite enough with him, to-night.

Everybody else has gone, and the house grows tenfold more somber and
funereal in this boding, brooding silence, as the heaped-up mail slowly di-
minishes. An unusually large number of the papers accumulated really require careful reading and reference, and the task will not be finished speedily. Look at your watch and see what time it is. Nine o'clock of the night
after Chancellorsville; but the moans of the wounded cannot be heard so far
as this, and the silence is so deep that you can hear your watch tick as you
hold it up.

And now you are suddenly aware of another sound, slower than the tick-ing of the watch, but almost as regular and as painfully unbroken. It is a dull, muffled sound, which at any other hour could hardly be heard across the hall. It comes from Mr. Lincoln's room, and Stanton must have left the door ajar when he came out. Every man who has left that room to-day came out stepping softly, as men will step in homes where the undertaker is known to be quickly coming. Such faces! and the strongest and the sternest were the saddest. There have been stories told, too, of the groups around the bulletin boards in the city, and your heart goes out to the volunteer on crutches who stood and read and wept, and said to the black bulletin:

"I wish I'd ha' been there! They could ha' had the other leg! The boys fit well, anyhow, or there wouldn't ha' been so many of 'em killed."

But that sound, the slow, heavy, regular tread of the President's feet, pacing up and down in his room, and thinking of Chancellorsville! A man's tread may well be heavy when there is such a load upon his shoulders as Lincoln is carrying. Add to it the load upon his heart, and—well, there is no need for him to read any of these letters. He knows beforehand all that there is in them, of every kind, and he can hear already the voices which are to come, as plainly as he can hear, in his heart, the thunder of the Union and Confederate guns, and the shrieks and the groans that arise on the lost battle-field. It has been a costly victory for the Confederates. Whether men will believe it or not, it has been a severe blow to Lee's army. As his resources are to be rightly counted, every battle he fights brings him nearer his final defeat. His only hope is in a defensive policy, keeping in the field as few men as may be, and at as small an outlay; for the Confederacy is bleeding to death, while the North is growing in wealth and population day by day. The President thoroughly understands that. Can he be dwelling upon it now, as he strides so unrestingly up and down his room? Is there anything in his past, or in his present, or in his future, which he can possibly fail to think of, in this his furnace, heated seven times hotter than usual?

Ten o'clock—and now and then there have been momentary breaks, as if he paused in turning at the wall; but no pause has lasted longer than for a few heart-beats.

It is well that there is enough in these papers to keep one busy, with that muffled thud, crunch, creak, thud, falling upon his ears, like waves upon a beach after a shipwreck.

Eleven o'clock—and it is as if a more silent kind of silence had been obtained and supplied, for the tread can be heard more distinctly, and a sort of thrill comes with it now and then.

Twelve? Why, it is midnight, and there is yet a pile of work on the table. Some of it lay over from yesterday, but it must all be finished now, before another mail shall bring the tidal wave of objurgation which must surely follow this Chancellorsville hurricane.

There has been no sound from the President's room for a number of minutes, and he may be resting in his chair or writing. No; there it comes again, that mournfully monotonous tread, with its turnings at the wall.

One o'clock, and you have become so accustomed to it that you hear it only when you lift your head from your work to listen; but you hear it, then.

Two o'clock comes, without another break in the steady tramp of Mr. Lincoln's lonely vigil.

Three o'clock arrives, and your task is done, and you pass out almost stealthily; but you turn at the head of the stairs to hearken, and then the last sound in your ears, as you go down, is the muffled beat of that foot-fall.

You go to your home, to lie down for awhile, but not to sleep, and you are up again for an early bath and breakfast. Before eight o'clock of the morning you are once more in the White House.

We will look in at the President's room as we go by. He is there still, and there is nothing to indicate that he has been out of it. He has had his breakfast brought in, as he sometimes does, and it has been placed upon the long table. He is eating heartily, and he seems unexpectedly bright and cheerful. Did his watch last until his prophetic eyes could see the dawn, and until the rising sun at last looked in upon him?

There is no doubt of it; for there, upon the table, beside his cup of coffee lies the draft of his fresh instructions to General Hooker, bidding him to push forward without any reference to Chancellorsville. They are orders, moreover, which must be vigorously obeyed, or some other general, Meade, for instance, will be put in command of the Army of the Potomac for their fulfillment.

There has been a memorable all-night vigil; a battle for the national life; a terrible struggle with discouragement and despair; but God has been with the President, and he has gained a victory. His face and voice, as he returns your greeting, declare that, in some inscrutable manner, the load has been lightened from his heart and brain.

The world will never know, nor would it acknowledge the fact, but the victory gained for the Union cause, last night, will soon be known in history as the battle of Gettysburg.

July 4th, 1863

He is a statesman and an orator, and his response emphasizes a request already brought you by a committee from a public meeting of dispirited citizens, that the celebration should be given up. It was a more hopeful assembly which in the first place determined to have one, and made you chairman of the general Fourth of July Committee. You now repeat to the despondent statesman the reply you made to the representative of the wet-blanket meeting:

"Sir, there will be a Fourth of July celebration in Washington this year, if we can hear Lee's cannon all the while, and if we adjourn from the speaker's stand to the trenches!"

The Mall below the White House is a capital place for a speaker's stand, and the Commissioner of Public Buildings gives you permission to do anything you please with it. So does the President. You have secured the Marine Band, of course. It is accustomed to play upon the White House grounds and does not care what day it may be. General Martindale, in command of the city, is an old friend, and he is full of Fourth of July.

"My dear boy! Certainly! I've a lot of batteries and cavalry and infantry to move up the river. I'll fix you. Give you another band, too. Go ahead! Going to have it on the White House grounds? Best place in the world for Fourth of July this year. Meade's going to whip Lee out of his boots!"

Other preparations go on apace, but the summer days grow lurid with intense heat and the pressure of terrible suspense. The White House seems a furnace, and the entire city takes on more perfectly than ever before the air belonging to its real character of a frontier post in peril of capture by the enemy.

"If Meade is defeated, he will strike at Baltimore and we shall be cut off?"

"No, Mrs. Lincoln, all that's left of him after beating Meade will be too lame to march as far as Baltimore."

"Mr. Lincoln is positive that Lee will be defeated. He says the crisis has come and that all the chances are on our side. This move of Lee's is all he could ask for. How does your Fourth of July come on?"

"All we could ask for, but another committee has requested me to stop till some time when they are not so badly scared."

"Don't you stop!"

"We won't, Mrs. Lincoln. I want more flowers, though."

"I'll speak to the gardener! You can have all he can find for you. Anything else I can do?"

"No, unless you can speak to Grant and Meade and have them win their victories on the third so we can have a bigger Fourth."

She wishes she could, but her power stops at the flower point.

There was never before such a Fourth of July in Washington! The stand on the Mall is just where it should be, this hot, bright, zenith day of the year 1863.

Twelve councils of the Union League? Masons? Odd Fellows? Turners? Other societies? Citizens? Distinguished men? What a procession! The Marine Band and the marines. Regiment after regiment sweeps down the avenue, between the long files of the division which has been halted at parade rest along the curbstones on either side. How well the cavalry look, and the artillery! It is brilliant!

So it is, and the really local Washington City part of the procession is large enough to throng the Mall, but the cavalry and infantry and artillery marching with, or before, or forming behind, the civil show, march on up the river, for they are a part of the second army which the President has been gathering to confront Lee with, in case the first should prove insufficient to stem his crazy invasion.

Insufficient? Can anybody measure the fierce intoxication of this Fourth of July celebration, with the news from Vicksburg and from Gettysburg thundering in the ears and thrilling the hearts of men? All the cannon here seem to sound like so many fire-crackers, and yet they all seem to roar with joy to hear what the other Union cannon have been doing.

Very decidedly it was a good thing to have a celebration of the Fourth this year, and to hold it in Washington, and to have it concentrate upon the grounds of the President's house.

As for us, we shall be so entirely used up that in a few days we shall take a vacation and go North. We do not actually travel on Sunday, but a Sunday-night train from Washington lands a passenger in New York City very early on Monday morning. A strange collection of passengers there is sure to be, moreover, upon any train, by day or night, running along this main pathway between the North and the Capital and the army. It is not only all the United States but almost all the earth that is represented in these human car-loads from time to time. The cars are hot and uncomfortable, and there is a keen sense of relief in getting out of them to smell the salt air brought up from the Bay by the light wind that is blowing.

The Astor House is the best and nearest place to go to for an early break-fast, and we can read the morning papers while we sip our coffee. There has been an idea floating around the White House that if there is to be any out-burst in connection with the enforcement of the draft, it will be more likely to take place in New York than anywhere else. It is pleasant, therefore, to open your favorite journal and to learn that the draft began here on Satur-day, and went on to the close of the day without any disturbance whatever.

"What did you say, Colonel?"

"Say? Why, there will be a rising of the mob to-day, beyond a question! There have been caucuses on Sunday, too, of army officers in and out of ser-vice, and preparations are making for calling upon all the militia who did not go on the Gettysburg campaign excursion, and all the disbanded volun-teers in the city, to come out to the assistance of the police. Every man of them will be needed. So will all the troops in all the forts, and all the seamen and marines who can be spared from the ships in the harbor."

"If that's the case, Colonel, I must join the first company of volunteers that gets together."

"Come right along, but street fighting is likely to be hard fighting."

The truth of the soldier's remark is manifested, hour after hour, through all of this terrible Monday. One alarm of fire rings out after another, a fresh conflagration every hour by the clock. The police are reported beaten and driven in many places. So are the hastily gathered soldiery. The pit itself seems to have broken up and out into the streets of New York. Is this what General Lee counted upon when he led his splendid army across the Poto-mac? If so, his movement was none the less a military and political blunder. If he had beaten Meade he would still have been confronted by fresh forces exceeding his own, and while his diminished numbers, even in victory after victory, would surely have melted away, the report of this carnival of riot, murder, arson, inconceivable depravity and cruelty and destructiveness would but have aroused to a more fierce and furious energy the fighting blood of all the indignant North.

General Lee may have looked forward to important help and coöperation from Northern discontent and sedition, but here, in the midst of these hot days of wrath and riot, he or any other honorable soldier may well be acquitted of an intentional alliance with the savages who are going down so fast before the clubs of the Metropolitans, the rifles of the volunteers, militia, marines and regulars, and the storms of grape and canister which have pitilessly torn through more than one of these seething, surging avenues, for the mob also is utterly defeated.

The Contrabands and the New Captain

The colored people are not citizens yet, and they have no idea that they are, or that they are ever to become full-fledged human beings. If you talk with one of them, the more intelligent your selection may be the more quickly you will probably discover a peculiarly dazed, uncertain, half-frightened mental condition. It is the state of unfortunates who cannot formulate any defined idea of the life upon which they have so wonderfully and unexpectedly been forced to enter. Your next catch, after that experiment, should be a white man, and in him you will discover a strictly correspondent mixed and cloudy conception of the future state, upon this earth, of this race which is now no longer merely "contraband of war." A marked symptom or feature of this indicated bewilderment of the liberated bondmen and bondwomen, is that so very few of them seek an opportunity for a look at, or a word with, the Presidential Moses who has set them free. To most of them he is as a myth, or, at least, as a superior being, a demigod so exalted that they have no business with him in the flesh. They are not afraid of him personally, but they are very much afraid of this new order of things. At all events, there are few black men among the tide of citizens which sets toward and into the White House.

Free, as loosened cattle are free, but not as men and women are free, are these multitudes who can no longer be bought or sold, but who are as yet denied the right to vote, and the right to be killed in battle. There is, at least, one man who perceives clearly that the latter right must precede the former in its acquisition, and there are others in whose minds the perception is growing rapidly. As yet the vast mass of the population supposed to be most deeply concerned in the Emancipation Proclamation dwells south of the army lines, but from the very beginning of this revolution large numbers of them from time to time broke through. So many drifted into Washington City and its vicinity, in a vague search after somebody to care for them, that it was necessary to corral them, and what is termed the "Contraband Camp" grew to its present proportions upon some vacant land northward, just beyond the corporaton limits.

It is a place much visited by the charitable and the curious, and particularly by grim old Abolitionists, of both sexes, from the North. As one of them feelingly remarked, "It beats the Underground Railway all hollow! What could the Fugitive Slave Law do with this here collection?"

It is mainly by the enthusiastic efforts of these triumphantly sincere friends of the African that there is to be a grand celebration at the Contraband Camp, on Thanksgiving Day, this year, 1863. There will be a dinner and speeches, and all the available contrabands of the District of Columbia and of Maryland will come flocking in to promote the jollity of the occasion.

"What do you mean, Mr. Senator? A speech to the contrabands on Thanksgiving Day? To-morrow? And here it is almost supper-time. Don't you think you are giving too long a notice?"

"It can't be helped. I've seen Lincoln, and he can't come, and there's got to be something there from the White House. You must look as much like Lincoln as you can. Talk about anything you please."

"Very well, Mr. Senator. I'll be there!"

Who would have thought that the White House latch-key would open the door of the Contraband Camp, but here we are! After all, is it not almost as truly pitched upon the White House grounds as if they had fenced in the Mall for its accommodation? All those people are really gathered into the President's backyard, and are waiting to see what he will do with them.

There is a pretty wide reach of land fenced in, with a tight barrier of six-foot pine boards to keep out, for instance, any attempt on the part of the Fugitive Slave Law to play wolf with the sheep of this fold. Along the further side is a range of shed-like structures, under cover of which hundreds after hundreds are eating their first Thanksgiving Dinner. We need not go over there, for here, at the right, is a rude plank platform, with seats as rough upon it, and on the seats there are already gathered a score of dignitaries. The colored Methodist Bishop of this charge is there, and with him are the few Senators and Congressmen who even now are proud to call themselves Abolitionists. What a nervous horror of stigma used to attach to that term! It included several of the keenest reproaches which could be heaped upon a politician, and now to these seems to be added: "You are the men who brought on this bloody and disastrous Civil War!"

A few very brave women are also there, but the interest at this point hardly concentrates upon the platform, for before it the ex-contrabands are gathering. What a marvelous multitude it is! Some say 5,000 and some say

10,000, but who shall count them, as they press closer and closer to be sure of hearing! There are brief opening exercises, conducted by a Senator, aided by the Bishop and another colored celebrity, and now—but who can think of anything to say, or say it to this assembly? The Senator did but say "Lincoln," and something else, as you step forward, and from all this sea of black and brown and yellow faces there seems to arise a laugh that is almost a yell. It surely is not articulate, but it ends in "Bress de Lord!" from a shrill, musical, penetrating voice of some excited black woman. It is not worth while to talk to those people about their past—not to any length, at least, when all they or we care about is their future. Let us see how they would greet the idea of becoming soldiers, since two-thirds of them are men capable of service. Lead them on to it, in your talk, and then ask them if, having been given their freedom, they are willing to fight for it and for the hope of manhood. Are they going crazy, as you go on? What is the meaning of the hoarse shouts, the wild laughter, the guttural exclamations, the grating teeth, the frantic gesticulations, the fierce, lurid, gleaming faces?

"Gib us dem guns! Let's have dem bay'nets! We'll show yo', marssa! Gib us dem guns! We's ready! Whar's de guns?"

Are you also going crazy? Or has only the fire in their semi-barbaric veins leaped over into your own, to tell you that you are descended from Norse-Saxon pirates as savage as any from Congo or Ashantee?

It is over, and it is time to go back into the White House, but have we really been out of it? Is not this a part of the work that has been going on at the littered old desk, by the south window, over in Lincoln's room?

Perhaps, but there will not be many days to wait before the pen busy at that desk will sign the needful orders for the organization of many regiments of just such men as went mad over the offer of weapons on Thanksgiving Day at the Contraband Camp. Not long afterward, truly, it must once more be busied with an indignant defense of its first action—with more than one defense of the plain common sense which decides that if so many men must die in any battle, he is not precisely the best friend of white fathers and mothers who shall demand that the boys to die must all be of pure Caucasian blood.

Nobody knows what malaria is, but there has always been a great deal of it in and around the White House. Some of it has been social; more of it has been moral, according to some accounts; and the amount of political malaria, of all sorts, has been beyond calculation, from the roofing of the house until now. It is said that great parties have sickened and died of the poisonous atmosphere they breathed when they came to Washington, and that their worst fevers were contracted at and about this place—chills, too. As for any other malaria, the causes of it are not difficult to find. When the first attempt was made to bridge the Potomac, where the Long Bridge is at present, the builders economically began by running out a solid causeway from each bank so as to diminish the number of piles and piers to be employed for the remainder of the viaduct. They thereby engineered a pair of bars, the longest on this side, against which the muddy waters of the Potomac might deposit any stuff, floating or in solution, which came down-stream with them.

We are not above tide-water here, and there is no current to speak of at high tide, while at low tide the flats are bared for wide reaches. One of those flats begins on the Mall, down there, at the line of shrubbery, and its other border is in the middle of the river. They selected the site for the Washington Monument upon that very gentle slope, because it was a better place for an ideal graveyard than it could ever become for the residences of the living. Upon the part of that flat which is under water, the Potomac continually deposits such material as any decent river might wish to be relieved of, and in course of time an ooze has been developed which can testify its peculiar qualities to the best advantage when the river is low and the tide is out, and there is a gentle, balmy south wind blowing. Then, sometimes, you do not imagine that some careless person has left open the door of the conservatory. Everybody who spends much time in the White House is certain to suffer more or less. To be sure, the President has had only the smallpox, but he was well seasoned before he came, and he is too full of anxiety, all the while, for a different kind of fever to get into him. Mrs. Lincoln has suffered in ways which have no chronicle, and little Tad has undoubtedly been injured so that his constitution will not recover. Willie Wallace Lincoln died of it. The private secretaries were all tough, healthy fellows, pretty well seasoned, but they have had sharp down-turns to wrestle with.

"Did you say that this is the typhoid fever, doctor? Why, that's worse than last year's business."

"It can't be helped. It comes from the flats along the Potomac, below the White House."

"Do you think I can get well?"

"You lie still, and I'll tell you what I think when I see you up again."

He is a capital physician. He is a Russian-German, of high professional standing, and you have an idea that he is in doubt about your case. Not until he sees you out again will he tell you that you must get away from Washington, and that you will probably never get the poison entirely out of you— not if you live a hundred years. It is the only part of your Washington earnings which will stick, that and your latch-key, and you have nothing to do but to lie as still as you can, through these long, delirious, wearisome spring days of 1864, while General Grant is getting settled as commander, under the President, of all the armies, and particularly as commander of the Army of the Potomac. Sherman is taking charge in the West, and is preparing to leave Thomas behind him to care for Hood, while he and some of his men walk across Georgia to the seashore.

"You are up at last—"

"I can walk, doctor, and I'm going to walk as far as the White House."

It is Sunday, and we can visit the headquarters with a better chance for a chat with the Commander-in-Chief.

Walk right in, and take your time in getting upstairs.

Nobody in the northeast room? Reckon Hay or somebody had the care of the mail. It isn't more than a third as large as it used to be. All these victories have knocked the wind out of the abusive letter-writers; and the self-appointed critics and advisers are either tired of it, or they are satisfied, or they are dead, and as for the office-seekers—the offices are mostly full. There is nobody in Nicolay's room. He and Hay may have gone to church. I heard them say, once, that they meant to go, some day. Hope they haven't caught any typhoid. Mr. Lincoln's door is shut, but he may be there; that's so, he is lying on the lounge, just as if he were resting.

He is one of the kindliest and most cordial of men. He seems genuinely glad to see a fellow up and out again. It is as good as medicine, too, to find him so cheerful this morning. One topic follows another, rapidly.

"Now, Mr. Lincoln, what sort of a man is Grant? I've never even seen him. He has taken hold here while I have been laid up. What do you think of him?"

The President half lay down again, after you were stretched out in your chair, comfortably, for a talk, but now he very nearly sits up, laughing silently.

"Well, I hardly know what to think of him, altogether. I never saw him, myself, till he came here to take the command. He's the quietest little fellow you ever saw."

"How is that, Mr. Lincoln? I'd another kind of idea about him."

"Why, he makes the least fuss of any man you ever knew. I believe two or three times he has been in this room a minute or so before I knew he was here. It's about so, all around. The only evidence you have that he's in any place is that he makes things *git!* Wherever he is, things move!"

Can it be that at this last Mr. Lincoln has found the very man he has been searching for? The general who can comprehend the stern arithmetic of the battles of this war? The leader who will be unconscious of defeat, and who will rally his forces behind the heaps of their own dead and charge again? If so, there is no wonder that he can lie here upon his lounge, this sunny Sunday afternoon, with such a look of almost relief upon his worn and wrinkled face.

"But how about Grant's generalship, Mr. Lincoln? Is he going to be *the* man, as commander of the Army of the Potomac?"

Once more the half-reclining form comes up to a sitting posture and a long, bony forefinger is aimed at you.

"Grant is the first general I've had! He's a general!"

That is a curious remark for him to make, when you know how high has been his opinion of McClellan, and Burnside, and Hooker, and Meade.

"How do you mean, Mr. Lincoln?"

"Well, I'll tell you what I mean. You know how it's been with all the rest. As soon as I put a man in command of the army, he'd come to me with a plan of campaign and about as much as say, 'Now, I don't believe I can do it, but if you say so I'll try it on'; and so put the responsibility of success or failure on me. They all wanted me to be the general. Now it isn't so with Grant. He hasn't told me what his plans are. I don't know, and I don't want to know. I'm glad to find a man who can go ahead without me."

"He took his own gait in the West, Mr. Lincoln, and he came out pretty well, that's a fact; but he hasn't proved, yet, that he can handle the Army of the Potomac, or beat Lee on his own ground."

The President is sitting straight up, now, and the look is on his face that he used to begin a story with:

"You see, when any of the rest set out on a campaign, they'd look over matters and pick out some one thing they were short of and they knew I couldn't give 'em, and tell me they couldn't hope to win unless they had it, and it was most generally cavalry," and the long, quiet laugh which interrupts his humorous commentary convinces you that he is, indeed, feeling vastly relieved. "Now, when Grant took hold, I was waiting to see what his pet impossibility would be, and I reckoned it would be cavalry, as a matter of course, for we hadn't horses enough to mount even what men we had. There were 15,000 or thereabouts, up near Harper's Ferry, and no horses to put them on. Well, the other day, just as I expected, Grant sent to me about those very men; but what he wanted to know was whether he should disband 'em or turn 'em into infantry. He doesn't ask me to do impossibilities for him, and he's the first general I've had that didn't."

Long years afterward Grant himself will listen to a report of this very conversation, and will say:

"Well, it gives about my idea of the truth of what they call Lincoln's interference with military plans. He never interfered with me from the beginning to the end."

Pictures and Reports

Pictures, did you say? Memory pictures of things which took place here? What are some of the prettiest? It is not very easy to say. There are something like a million of them. There was one that came to mind, just now, from a year ago last winter. There has been, from the beginning, such a rush and crowding and grasping after appointments and promotions, and it is all but swinish, just now!

The picture? It is in the middle reception-room, below, and it is an evening brilliant with uniforms. A slender, pleasant-faced gentleman, in full uniform as a naval officer, is chatting for a moment with Mrs. Lincoln, and then he turns, with the hearty freedom of something like old personal friendship, but before he can speak, your own hand goes out to him.

"Good evening, Admiral Dahlgren. How do you do?"

"What! Is that so? I had not expected it. I had not thought—"

"The nomination went in late to-day, but it is all right, Admiral!"

"The President did it out of his own head," he says, with a face flushed with pride and surprise.

"You are thinking of the way the boy made the fiddle, and he had wood enough left to make another?"

"You are not respectful to either the admiral or Mr. Lincoln—"

"Oh, yes, I am, Mrs. Lincoln. He has chosen the best kind of timber this time—real live-oak!"

The newly made admiral is really so affected that he bows and walks away, for he has been bitterly abused and misrepresented in some quarters, and this is the President's verdict in his favor, closing the mouths of the detractors under whose attacks the gallant but sensitive sailor was writhing. You are especially pleased about it, for in the days when he commanded at the Navy Yard your visits there always carried you to the quarters for luncheon, and for a chat about guns and ships.

The other picture? Well, it is suggested, somehow, by the memory of the admiral who had not expected his promotion. It is not in the White House, but in a parlor of the National Hotel, made into a private drawing-room for an evening. There are a score or more of young women here, and some of them are hardly out of girlhood. There is not one of them who does not represent one of the best-known names of the country—of statesmen, jurists, generals, admirals,—for these are the young princesses and duchesses and countesses of America.

It is a dancing party; but there is one handsome young fellow who will not dance. He came in on crutches, and, young as he is, he wears the uniform of a colonel of cavalry. He is decorated forever with the costly prize-mark of valor in battle. No, he will not dance; but he is not to be left alone for one moment. You heard what that sweet-faced young woman said: "He used to be such a beautiful waltzer! Poor fellow! We must not let him feel neglected;" and the reply from another voice as sympathetic as her own is:

"Is it not cruel! He is splendid!"

There they go, and one of them will be forever associated with the story of the White House; but she does not know it yet. They cluster around him merrily, as if they were trying to keep him from thinking of his lost leg and his vanished dancing days. Only one is left at this moment, and one of the young gentleman ornaments of society, who is not in uniform, is bending before her. You wonder at him, but can barely catch the words, "This set with you?"

There is an indignant flush upon her face, and something in her surprised eyes remarks: "You ought to know better, sir;" but her tongue says only: "Thank you; I'm engaged."

It is none the less a pretty manifest snub for his stupidity, and he is compelled to look elsewhere for a partner. It was a very pretty picture.

"But what became of him? Of Ulric Dahlgren?"

Why, the surgeons were even then fitting him with an artificial leg so perfectly that he could rejoin his regiment. It was only a few days before he mounted and rode again. He rode away toward Richmond, and he did not return; but a sort of vision of spendid, generous youth, bright young manhood and brilliant young womanhood, will always come up in company with your memory of the hero who could not dance.

Andrew Jackson's chair is a pleasant seat, especially when one is too tired to go home or anywhere else, and there does not seem to be any more office work to do. It is a sultry evening, and it is quite likely that the soldiers in their camps are fighting sharp battles with mosquitoes. The few that are humming around in the northeast room have suggested the idea, and one feels half ashamed that he is not himself in camp, instead of sitting here.

That feeling comes powerfully at times; but then, if you were by some camp-fire, another possible soldier would of necessity be doing this work, unless Mr. Lincoln could find a lame man, or a one-armed man to whom he could entrust it. There was a fellow eagerly applying for it at the beginning—a young man who had been acquainted with Mr. Lincoln in Illinois, who believed that he had such personal claims, therefore, that he had a right to be wrathful when it was not given him. He was not of the kind they make soldiers of, and one of the reasons he urged for his appointment here was that he was all but stone-deaf, and so the duties and pay were exactly suited to him. That part of his qualifications now and then turns up, in memory, when this northeast room is in full blast and the visitors know each other.

If it is a good place to loaf in, it is also a good place to read in, and we will go over to the library and get a book.

It is a fairly well selected library, largely from the fact that only part of it was in any manner selected, and all the rest simply gathered from time to time. It is an evening for novel-reading. Something tame and quiet, like Bulwer, to grow still and rested over, after the thrilling realities of the long life-romance of these White House days.

Why not read in the library? Nobody can tell; but it does not seem to be the right place to read in, and then Mr. Lincoln is still at work in his own rooms and you might as well be here.

One can really become interested in Bulwer's *Strange Story*, but if he could have spent a few months in Andrew Jackson's chair, what wonderful things he might have written!

"Ah! I'm glad you're here. I was thinking everybody had gone. Come over into my room."

"Certainly, Mr. Lincoln!"

Down come your feet from the mantel, the *Strange Story* shoots across the table, and you follow him back across the hall into the room where he and so many other Presidents before him have sat, alone or in company, and have pondered or discussed the condition of parties and the country and all the world, if not the other world.

Mr. Lincoln has evidently been sitting at the end of the Cabinet table, and he has been writing something. He has in hand a number of sheets of closely written foolscap paper.

"Sit down. I can always tell more about a thing after I've heard it read aloud, and know how it sounds. Just the reading of it to myself doesn't answer as well, either."

"Do you wish me to read it to you?"

"No, no; I'll read it myself. What I want is an audience. Nothing sounds the same when there isn't anybody to hear it and find fault with it."

"I don't know, Mr. President, that I'd care to criticise anything you'd written."

"Yes, you will. Everybody else will. It's just what I want you to do. Sit still now, and you'll make as much of an audience as I call for."

He has been punctuating his manuscript with a pen, while speaking, and he has drawn the pen across it, through something that is to come out.

If you are indeed an audience, you believe he has forgotten you are there for a moment, but that is only while he is beginning. He is more an orator than a writer, and he is quickly warmed up to the place where his voice rises and his long right arm goes out, and he speaks to you somewhat as if you were a hundred thousand people of an audience, and as if he believes that something like fifty thousand of you do not at all agree with him. He will convince that half of you, if he can, before he has done with it.

The manuscript is long. It is a letter nominally addressed to some gentlemen in Illinois, but really to the country and to the world. He is satisfied that it is about what he intended it should be, and he laughs silently when at last he puts it down on the table.

"Now! Is there any criticism that you wanted to make?"

"Well, I was thinking—of course, it's as nearly beyond criticism as it well could be, but there's one place—"

"What's that? Take the paper and show it to me."

"Why, Mr. Lincoln, some people will find fault with this: 'Nor must Uncle Sam's web-feet be forgotten. At all the watery margins they have been present, not only on the deep sea, the broad bay, the rapid river, but also up the narrow, muddy bayou, and wherever the ground was a little damp, they have been and made their tracks.'"

The silent laugh of the President becomes heartily audible, as he listens to that bit of criticism.

"I reckoned it would be some such place as that. I'll leave it in just as it is. I reckon the people'll know what it means."

"That's about the only fault I can find, but I never saw a web-footed gunboat in all my life. They're a queer kind of duck."

"Some of 'em did get ashore, though," and the silent laugh comes again this time. "I'll leave it in, now I know how it's going to sound. That'll do. I sha'n't want you any more to-night."

There was more than that said, by both the orator-writer and his audience, but the real object was attained, for if one thing was clearer than another, it was the suggested idea that a great deal can be seen by some eyes through a very small pinhole. We will go back to the northeast room, but not to loaf over the *Strange Story*, in Andrew Jackson's chair. Rather to ponder the "web-feet" question, and to study whether a pinhole can set up in business as an audience.

Yes, it can. Lincoln knows now just how that thing will sound in the ears of millions on millions all over the country, and he doesn't care a corn-husk for the literary critics here or in Europe.

The days and weeks go by, and you have had some remarkable experiences since last you found your way into the room where Lincoln wrote and read the "web-feet" letter. Now, however, you are once more here, and he is sitting opposite you with an expectant look upon his face, as if it were his turn to listen this time.

"So you've been all through the Southwest? What do you think of it?"

"Well, Mr. President, I've been down as far as Memphis, and up the White River, and across to Little Rock, and down the Arkansas, and up to St. Louis."

"But about the stealing?"

"There's a great deal going on, there's no doubt of that, but General Washburn's an honest man, honest as the day, and so is General Steele."

"I'm glad to hear that! Glad of it. I like Washburn. I never saw Fred Steele, but I've always liked him, and I like his brother here in Congress. I'm glad the charges are false. How about that corn?"

"Well, there's almost a joke, there, but Steele had nothing to do with it. He doesn't know what became of that corn. When our army marched in, the Arkansas River bottom plantations were mostly in corn instead of cotton. Finest standing crops you ever saw. Sixty—seventy bushels to the acre. It was put in to feed the Confederate army with, but it's been fed out to ours, all the way down to New Orleans."

Mr. Lincoln hated thieving, but there is a look of humor on his face, and he is willing to hear the rest of it.

"Go ahead. How did they get it?"

"Through the contractors. You see, the contracts called for so much corn, to be delivered so and so, up and down the rivers, the Mississippi, Cumberland and so on, and the contractors lived up to their agreement to the letter. It did not specify where they were to get it from. The corn they harvested in the Arkansas valley was good corn, and it cost them something. They had to pay the boys a dollar a day for husking it out, just as if they had been in Illinois or Ohio, instead of in the army. Nobody knows what they paid for the use of army wagons and mules to haul it to the landings and deliver it on board the steamers. There was a heap of it. Some people would call it stealing, but it's a puzzle whom they stole it from, and the boys won't say a word. They took their dollar a day and called it all right."

"The guerrillas would have got it or destroyed it, if it hadn't been stolen."

"Well, about them. There are not so many guerrillas as there used to be. You can see that from the army reports. When any are taken nowadays, either they get away or the boys let 'em go."

"What's that? Just tell me what you mean."

"Well, I got it from the boys. There was about a dozen taken, red-handed, over on the White, while I was there, by a squad of Clayton's cavalry, and I asked a sergeant of that squad what became of them, and he said they happened to have plenty of rope on hand, and so they let them all go. Didn't report them to Clayton or anybody else. You see, if a man with his hands tied behind him is sitting on a mule, and if one end of the rope that is noosed around his neck is drawn a little taut to a limb of the tree he is under, then when the mule—or if it's a horse it's the same—gets a cut and runs away somewhere else, it lets the man go. He needn't be reported. Now, if he is left entirely free, and is ordered to clear out, and nobody says anything till he reaches the line at fifty yards regular starting distance, why, then, if nobody makes out to hit him, at fifty yards and over, he gets away, and there is no use in reporting him, to make trouble for the general or for the War Department, if there are charges of murder or arson against him. That is one reason so few guerrillas are heard of here, nowadays, but there is no doubt of Steele's honesty, or Washburn's, or of—"

"That will quiet all that matter. I'm glad to hear it. Yes, if you really wish to settle in Arkansas, you can have the marshalship as soon as the organization is made. But I want Stanton to hear your report, just as you've given it to me. He'll be as glad as I am to dismiss those charges. Go right over to the War Office and see him."

"The difficulty is that he won't see me. There's a perfect jam outside of his room, and inside, too."

"Yes, he will. Take that. He'll see you at once. Go right over."

A few words written on a card, and when you reach the War Office and send that bit of pasteboard to Secretary Stanton, there is no delay. In half a minute more he has led you into the little cupboard of a room back of his end of the hall, and he sits down by you on its fubsy sofa to hear your story. It is as the President said it would be, and the War Minister is as pleased to hear of honesty—but the report is barely ended, and he is thanking you cordially, when an officer steps in as if in hot haste, and interrupts by handing him a yellow tissue-paper telegraphic dispatch. Mr. Stanton's eyes glance quickly over the lines, and his countenance undergoes a change. It glows with sudden flushes of triumphant red, and he turns to you, handing you the paper:

"Read that! Read that, Mr. Secretary! Hurrah! Take it to the President! Show it to Lincoln! It's the turning-point of the war! It's the beginning of the end! No more work in this office, to-day! This is enough!"

It is Sheridan's first announcement of his victory over Early, in West Virginia, where he sent him "whirling up the valley," and it is the one thing needful at this hour.

Up jumps Stanton, and out he dashes into the hall. There is a swarm there of generals and other officers, of Senators and Congressmen, and among them the grim Secretary absolutely dances up and down, swinging his dispatch, and shouting the glorious good news. He needs the traditional bricks in his pockets just now, but who would have thought there was so much boy in him!

He jostles you hard as you squeeze past him with the dispatch he hands you after his wild publication of its contents, and you actually run a part of the way to the White House. You are out of breath when you get there, and somebody or other—you cannot distinctly remember who afterward, but dimly believe that it was Nicolay and Hay and a Cabinet officer to help them—seizes the yellow missive and carries it into the President's room. You are aware of an idea, however, that he read it through, slowly, thoughtfully, and looked up and said:

"Boys, I reckon that'll do. I feel as Stanton does. We'll shut up shop for the rest of to-day."

It is a day to eat a big dinner in and to be happy. There have been greater battles, and there have been victories seemingly more important, but they were all parts and incidents of the war itself, while this victory is distinctly a part and incident of the finishing up of the war. Stanton is very nearly correct in declaring it "the beginning of the end."

There Is an End of All Things

It is with reference to national affairs of administration, and not to party politics or political movements, that the city of Washington can be called the political centre of the United States. It has been said that the city of New York has a much better title to that rank, as had Philadelphia in the long ago. The truth is that the loose-jointed systems of party organizations in this country forbid the establishment of an American political hub, such as London is for England or Paris for France.

Even the political laws of peace times, however, are subject to temporary suspension in time of war, and just now there is an exceptional concentration of the national blood and brains at the Capital. Ill-natured people say there is something like congestion threatened, and that it is dangerous. The centre of power is more than ever here, at all events, and the party which designs to effect an escape from the pressure of that power must hold its National Convention as far away from it as possible; for instance as far away as Chicago.

The Democratic National Committee are altogether too wise in their generation to gather their chiefs of their many clans under the drippings of the eaves of the Capitol and of its White House wing, or of the White House and its Capitol wing, whichever way one may prefer to arrange that expression of the situation. No national committee of any party would think of assembling its convention in Washington, but there are many hotels and other important conveniences in Baltimore, and experience has proved that that town is much nearer the bank of the Potomac, politically, than it appears to be upon any map. Both houses of Congress and all the Department forces have on several past occasions found it possible to go over and spend the day in Baltimore and get home again upon late night trains, to go over again after breakfast next morning.

With or without any especial reason suggestive of the game of chess, the Republican National Convention is this year to be held in Baltimore, and there was never before such a shaking of wise, prophetic heads over any future event as there is over the prospect of a second nomination for Abraham Lincoln. All the opposition forces outside of his party are rallying under General McClellan, with a great shout that is composite in its sonorousness. One can hear in it the deep growl of dissatisfied patriotism, the angry snarl of ancient party prejudices, and it is only needful to hearken a little to detect the half-smothered fierceness of the Confederate charging yell. The opposition elements inside of the Republican party are many, and it would be shallow stupidity to question the patriotic sincerity of many of them. Good men, as good as any in the land, fail to appreciate Lincoln, and honestly disapprove his methods and his management. It is not easy for his immediate supporters to put aside their hot partisanship just now, and to hear him abused without loss of temper, but he is keeping his own temper very well. So well that no man you know, among even his personal advisers, can repeat to you a dangerous word which has fallen from his prudent lips.

They are assailing him terrifically. Every check of the national arms; every seeming laxity of military or civil management; the ravages of Confederate cruisers; the cost and duration of the great contest; the defects of territorial administration; the draft; the Emancipation policy; the Bank Act; all manner of slanders, falsehoods, and evil imaginations, are stirring up in the heated minds of men to increase the feverish, natural longing for a change.

This state of things, they say, has gone on long enough, and it is time that the nation should decide that it contains more than one man fit to be President. Some brilliant general or eminent legislator or accomplished jurist must be put into the place of power, so long abused by willful incompetence and frivolous ignorance. Lincoln must go!

Under such circumstances it is as easy to ride over to Baltimore this afternoon as to go home to dinner. The convention will assemble to-morrow, and we will see how it looks from a White House point of view.

We cannot see it to-night? It will be scattered among the hotels? Of course it is, and it is worth while to stroll around from one hotel to another, and to listen to what these throngs of our over-excited fellow-citizens are saying.

Your heart is not lifted up as you listen, and you are making a serious mistake over what you hear. The silent part of every group, the men who are listening as anxiously as you are, you do not count or comprehend, while the noisy, argumentative, vituperative part seem to be having it their own way. The delegates are all here, and they are a great mob, and there is also a great mob of outsiders, who are carrying air-guns as delegates until to-morrow.

As we pass from one place to another, the groups are melting, and a part of each moves away in a kind of loose and straggling procession, as if a common errand led them. Come along with the procession through this wide doorway and upstairs. Is this a masonic anteroom? Hardly, but no man can get through any more easily than he could get into a first-class theatre. No ticket is asked for, but you are spoken to, and you answer, and are checked off upon a written list, as you pass on into a large hall.

Is this the Republican National Convention?

It is and it is not. The men upon these benches are the majority in number, and the overwhelming preponderance in power of the body of delegates which will gather in the Wigwam to-morrow. All the debating for the National Convention is to be transacted here this evening, for the good of the party, to secure an appearance of unanimity before the country, in any decision which it then may seem to come to. The Presidential nomination is to be fought over, and practically made beforehand, and the action of this Grand Council of the Union League will surely be ratified. It is the place where all the anti-Lincoln steam is to be let off, so that it will not scald the work in the Wigwam. There was never a wiser provision made for the escape of dangerous vapors.

A very dignified and orderly assembly. We are entitled to an official seat upon the platform; let us go up and take a chair at the left of Grand President Edmunds, and look out over the long rows of keenly intelligent faces. No other nation can call together more intellect and capacity in such a gathering, than the great parties of the United States habitually send to their national conventions. Never mind the habitual chatter which derides and belittles them. This assembly itself is a sufficient rebuke of all that nonsense, for these men are worthy of their trust.

As for their capacity, listen to the eloquent, powerful arraignment of Abraham Lincoln's administration, by the Senator who is speaking in opposition to the formal resolution proposing to nominate him for a second term. Hear his story of malfeasance, of tyranny, of corruption, of illegal acts, of abused power, of misused advantages, of favoritism, fraud, timidity, sluggish inertness, local wrong and oppression, willful neglect of suffering and willful refusal to hear the cry of the down-trodden. Mark the keenness of his personal thrusts, and the subtlety with which he keeps in the foreground the President's alleged frivolity and unfeeling jocoseness, in close companionship with a suggestion of selfish ambition instead of devotion to duty.

He is an able speaker, and so is this Congressman who follows him in the same path, repeating, adding to and enforcing the counts of the long and shameful indictment.

Another and another, all on the same side! Has Lincoln no friends left?

Or are they too bowed with shame to speak? Surely the resolution of approval and renomination is hopelessly lost, so far as can be judged from the platform. Beyond a doubt it is, and if a vote were called for at this moment it would be adverse to Mr. Lincoln.

"Mr. President—Gentlemen of the Grand Council."

That is Jim Lane, who assailed the President so bitterly in the Grand Council a year ago at Washington. You saw him at the White House yesterday. He had quite a talk with Mr. Lincoln, and then he came over and talked with you, but he did not tell you exactly what he meant to do here.

He is making an uncommonly long pause, and he seems to be looking all along the benches, as if he peered into face after face, studying its meaning. His own glance is peculiarly searching at any time, and his voice as he begins would go through a wall.

"For a man to stir up sore and wounded hearts to bitterness requires no skill, no power of oratory. For a man to address the minds of men sickened by disaster, wearied by long trial, heated by passion, bewildered by uncertainty, heavy with grief, and cunningly to turn them into one vindictive channel, into one blind rush of senseless fury—that requires no great power of oratory. It may be the mere trick of a charlatan."

Jim Lane has a peculiar faculty for saying an offensive, insolent thing in the most gallingly offensive and insolent manner, and he has rehearsed his first point with so positively brutal a harshness that a hundred faces blaze with wrath.

"For a man to address himself to an assembly like this, goaded almost to madness by long suffering, sorrow, disaster, humiliation, perplexity, and now aroused by venomous art to an all but unanimous condemnation of the innocent, and to turn them in their tracks and force them to go the other way—that would indeed be a feat of transcendent oratorical power. I am no orator at all, but that is the very thing I am now about to do."

Whether it is oratory, or the power of faith, or the hidden force of inspiration—he is doing it, sentence after sentence, as he pulls to pieces the indictment, and paints in many-colored fire the truth concerning Lincoln's work and that of his assailants. Men lean forward and listen, while they more or less rapidly are swept into the tide of conviction and are made to believe, with him, that any other nomination than that of Lincoln to-morrow is equivalent to the nomination of McClellan by the Republican Convention and his election by the Repubican party; that it would sunder the Union, make permanent the Confederacy, reshackle the slaves, dishonor the dead and disgrace the living.

There is no need for another speech on our side of the question, and in the tempest which follows Jim Lane's fierce closing shout, the resolution is adopted, with a mere handful of dissenting votes, and Abraham Lincoln is renominated. The gathering in the Wigwam to-morrow will seem all unanimity and enthusiasm. There is hardly steam left in the opposition boiler to blow one last, hoarse whistle of a perfunctory vote for a candidate named Grant, who is, however, thereby put on the list as the first name to be considered by the next National Convention of the Republican party.

The war is pressed with terribly energy under the management of General Grant. He is an embodiment of the idea which President Lincoln grasped at the outset, and there can now be no manner of doubt as to the result.

The Confederacy is everywhere losing ground, in spite of the ability of its leaders and the self-sacrificing courage and fortitude of its people.

It is a horrible pity that any more of them have got to be killed before they will give the matter up. There is no bitterness against them here in the White House. At all events Mr. Lincoln has no malice in his nature, and they will be entirely safe in his hands when the war is over.

Will they be in his hands?

Of course they will. All the reports from every corner of the land unite in assuring the success of the Lincoln electoral tickets in November. He will be President for another four years from the 4th of March next, and he will have incomparably less difficulty than would another man in managing the state of affairs which will surely exist after the restoration of peace.

That seems to be the feeling among the Senators and Congressmen you have been talking with to-day at the Capitol, but it will probably be a long time before you again stroll around the floor of either House. It was a kind of farewell visit, but it was not easy to make it appear so. Year after year the Capitol has seemed a place wherein you were almost as much at home as in the White House itself.

"The President is waiting to see you, sir. He is in the room beyond the library. I'll shake hands with you now, sir. I'm going out and I'll not be at the door."

"All right, Edward. I'll go in and see him."

You shake hands with Old Edward, and then you walk slowly on through the shadowy hall to the room where you are to say good-bye to Abraham Lincoln. It is just the place for a quiet, farewell talk. He is looking cheerful enough, but you may as well look into his face pretty closely, for you will never see it again.

You intend taking away your latch-key when you go, but you have been all over the house, for a last glimpse of every room. You have said good-bye to Mrs. Lincoln. You have finished your last arrangements with the other secretaries. There is nothing left undone but this one duty, and then you are to leave all this behind you, for this is the time for the fall of the leaves in the year 1864.

"Yes, Mr. Lincoln, all my arrangements are made, and I'm off to-night."

"Take these things with you, then"—passes, letters, orders for transportation are in your hand—"and now there's just one thing I want to say. The war is nearly over. Just when it will end, I can't say, but it won't be a great while. Then the Government forces must be withdrawn from all the Southern States. Sooner or later, we must take them all away. Now what I want you to do is this: do all you can, in any and every way you can, to get the ballot into the hands of the freedmen! We must make voters of them before we take away the troops. The ballot will be their only protection after the bayonet is gone, and they will be sure to need all they can get. I can see just how it will be. Will you?"

You can hardly tell him how keenly you sympathize with his own earnestness. He is, to your perception, a kind of political prophet. He speaks of the Southern people, as he goes on, in the friendliest and most hopeful manner. They have no better friend than he is, nor wiser. He is without a shadow of doubt as to what the end will be, or but that the Union is utterly and forever safe.

You may as well go now, for you feel something swelling, swelling within you, and it is getting somewhat difficult to talk. He, too, has arisen, and the parting grasp of his iron hand all but crushes your own, while the deep, mournful eyes beam down upon you warmly, full of good-will.

"Good-bye," and the White House days have become as a dream of the night, when it is ended.

THE END.

2

White House Sketches

Sketch 1

My Dear General—I have decided to comply with your request, and to furnish for *The Citizen* a few brief sketches of life in the White House, as it was in the memorable days when I had my green-covered desk in the historical Northeast Room. Many of your readers are doubtless already familiar with much that I may say or describe; but, if you will permit me, I will write only for those who have never visited Washington, or explored the Mecca of American political devotions.

After a not very long residence in Illinois, it was my fortune in 1861 to receive from President Lincoln an appointment to a subordinate position on his personal staff. I obtained permission to serve out my term as a private soldier in the "three months' service," during which time I was only occasionally at the White House, and it was not until after that that I was ordered there for permanent duty.

On reporting, I was assigned to the room aforesaid, in companionship with the versatile and brilliant Hay, and remained until late in the summer of 1864.[1] During that time my duties were as diversified as they well could be, including all that belong to a "secretary," and many others that led me into the various military departments. Among other things, during nearly all that time, the private correspondence of the President was almost exclusively in my charge. You will see from this that it is almost impossible for me to write for you aught that could be of historical value. Much that I know came to me in such a way that it cannot be recorded. If, however, a few gossipy sheets can be of any value to you, here they are.

It seems to me that I am writing of events that occurred centuries ago. Those terrible four years are like a dream. I remember talking with Ellsworth the day before he was murdered.[2] I remember seeing the President standing by his coffin. I remember the panic-rout from Bull Run, the fearful night when the record of Ball's Bluff came in, and Mr. Lincoln mourned over Baker.[3] I remember the advent of Butler, in full militia uniform, cocked hat, epaulettes, big sword and all, and a host of other things;[4] but such was the hot excitement of the period, that all seem like the figures in some fleeting panorama, seen long ago, and almost, if not quite, unreal.

Washington itself is a great, straggling, country town, miserably laid out, and, except [for] the public buildings, miserably built. There are few private residences that would attract attention in a second class inland town at the North, and no business establishment worth mentioning to the readers of *The Citizen*. The hotels are so crowded with "memories" that are national in their interest, that each is an "historical romance;" and though any one has a right to growl at them, he has to do it with a sort of reserve of respect for institutions under whose portals have passed so long a procession of the men who have made the country what we see it to-day.

Socially, in the spring of 1861, Washington was "secesh" to the back bone. The working men, and a portion of the "trades people"—as the proud F.F.V.'s [members of the First Families of Virginia] called them—were "Union," and raised three thousand men for the army; but the rich men, the bankers,—except the loyal firm of L. Johnson & Co., *half* of Riggs & Co., and some others,—the old social leaders, including many who afterwards served the Government for their bread and butter, were bitterly disloyal. They seemed to have an insane idea that all the gentlemen and ladies were for the rebellion, and that it was decidedly low to come out for the Union and the Stars and Stripes. Some of them have not recovered their senses yet. A little more pounding in the mortar, among wheat, with a pestle, as good old Solomon has it, might bring the folly out of them.

But at the time written of—go up any street, past almost any house, and from the open windows you could hear the unwearied piano, in tune or out of tune, dinging away at "Maryland, my Maryland," "The Bonny Blue Flag," or "Dixie," until the days when the Twelfth New York marched down Pennsylvania avenue with a full brass band, expressing the wish of the regiment that they were "in Dixie," and the Second and Fourth New Jersey, or Rhode Island, I forget which [the Twelfth New York], broke out into "Maryland," in the same place, with the new words of loyalty.[5]

Then the pretty rebels declared that the Yankees had stolen their music. They took sundry other things before they got through. It took a whole year to redeem Washington society, and then we did it as the man got rid of the wild onions, by "raising another crop." The same policy might work elsewhere. Morally, Washington was and is very much what the reporters for the daily press say it is,—and I know of no class of men, as a general thing, more thoroughly qualified to report on that subject.

The White House itself is a very respectable building of brick and stone, painted white, built in the form of a parallelogram, two stories high fronting north; but, owing to the declivity, three stories fronting south toward the Potomac. The lower, or basement story, contains the kitchen, lumber rooms and other domestic offices, and is perennially overrun with rats, mildew and foul smells.

The Congressmen who object to an appropriation for a new Executive mansion should be assigned the rooms in the lower story during the hot months. They would then, perhaps, ascertain the cause of the well-known mortality in the upper part of the building. The first floor fronting on Pennsylvania avenue may be divided into three equal sections. The eastern third contains the Congressional and private dining-rooms, and adjacent apartments; the centre is made up of a respectable vestibule in front, where the hat and cloak racks are set up on reception nights, and in the rear of this are three moderate-sized parlors, known as the red room, the blue room or "oval," and the green room—the first of these being used by Mrs. Lincoln as a private parlor. The third section is the famous "East Room," gaudily and tastefully furnished, and unadorned with works of art, except at levees. The upper story of the eastern section is used by the family of the occupant; the library, really a delightful retreat, and several sleeping rooms, are in the centre; while all the space over the East Room is devoted to the business purposes of the Executive—his public reception room, council chamber and the offices of his various secretaries.

That is, the President of the United States has no private residence, and less space for the transaction of the business of his office than a well-to-do New York lawyer. The President's own office is a very well furnished room, hung around with maps, &c., looking toward the South. Too many of its former occupants have been led to do the same. The mantel in 1861 was lined with an arch of brick, on which were plainly visible the marks left by Andrew Jackson's "stocking feet," while sitting in what Dickens calls "the American position." An effort was made to preserve those bricks when the present marble affair was put in, but by the irreverent carelessness of an Irish bricklayer's clerk they were mislaid. I wish we had kept those footprints of the old hero, and could persuade some of our would-be leaders to walk in them. In my room was a queer, wide, crooked, leather bottomed institution, on rollers, known as Andrew Jackson's chair—since stolen, I am told—said to be the counterpiece to the footprints. The frame, though light, was of solid mahogany, and there was a legend that it came from Mexico. I remember once when our poor friend Preston King—of whom let no man dare to speak unkindly—came in to rest himself while waiting for his turn for an audience.[6] He was out of breath, lifting his ponderous form up the long stairway, and was mopping his face with his bandanna: "My—puff—dear boy—puff—it's a long climb—puff—for a fat old—puff—man like me." Then, spying the chair, he added, "Now this is just the thing—just about wide enough," and essayed to let himself gently down into it; but, alas! it was on rollers, and, as his weight bore upon its edge, it shot away across the room, letting the ponderous Senator upon the floor with a jar that shook the room. No one laughed more heartily than the victim. Many a man who thought less of him than I did would give much to shake him by the hand again.

But, to begin my story at the beginning, few at the North—not all even in Washington,[—] knew how deadly was the danger of the Capital during the first two months of the first Presidential term of Abraham Lincoln. I stood within a few feet of him while he delivered his inaugural, and it seemed that all who listened must be willing to trust the man who uttered those solemn appeals and as solemn warnings. A dark cloud seemed to overshadow the city. Treason, treachery, cowardice and folly seemed to rule the hour. The great question was—not "who is the best man?" but "whom, in God's name, can we trust?" A large crowd of us young men from the West went one night to serenade General [Winfield] Scott, at his rooms on Seventh street, afterwards occupied for a long time by Owen Lovejoy.[7] The grand old gentleman came out on the stoop and spoke to us. Taking into account the man and the circumstances, few speeches ever were ever so eloquent, and we went away deeply affected. It was not reported, but I think I remember it sufficiently well to attempt a rude synopsis, and in some places even the exact words:

> My young friends, I thank you for the honor you have done me in coming to see me. I fear that our beloved country is on the eve of terrible troubles, and you can aid her, if I cannot. I do not think, as some do, that this trouble will be over soon, or easily; it has been preparing for a long time. I am a worn-out war-horse. I have given my life and my strength to my country, and I can do no more. Some younger and stronger arm must ' lead the armies of the Union in the struggle that is now before us. Whoever he may be, I shall give him my counsels and my prayers. I believe that the nation will be saved, but I fear that it will be at a great cost. God has been very good to me, my friends, and now I only ask of Him that He will let me live until I see the end of this accursed rebellion. Then I shall be ready to say "Now, Lord, lettest Thou Thy servant depart in peace." You and I, my young friends, will never meet again; take, then, the last exhortation of an old soldier who has tried to do his duty—be true to the old flag, to the country, and to the Union.

The prayer of the old General was granted, and he died, too, before the madness of politicians had been able to make it at all doubtful whether or not the end of the war had left us—anything else in particular to be thankful for![8]

The rebels had a force, regularly organized and armed, in the city itself, and another across the Potomac; and many a night I have trod my beat on the north draw of Long Bridge, with a rebel picket in full view on the south draw. We had not got then to real promiscuous shooting, but we soon learned the knack of it thereafter.[9]

Sketch 2

My Dear General—It is with more than a little hesitation that I attempt a description of the occupants of the White House during the first term of Mr. Lincoln's administration. Those who may take the trouble to read these sketches will be likely to obtain clearer ideas of them incidentally than I can hope to convey by a labored portraiture, and propriety forbids me to discuss too fully those who are still living. Different phases of Mr. Lincoln's character have been given with fair correctness by several writers, but none have painted the entire man as he really was. Nor can it now be well done. There are whole books stocked with his sayings and doings, and many living men who knew him intimately and loved him well; but we were and are too near to him, and our memories are crowded too full of the great events through whose eddying dust we saw him, for him to be thoroughly understood or appreciated by the present generation.

For five years Mr. Lincoln was the central figure of our age, and on him were concentrated the love, the faith, the reverence, the hate, the fear, and the calumny, of half the civilized world. The "plain people" understood him better than did the politicians; and he in turn had a wonderful perception of the real condition of the popular heart and will. For newspaper public opinion he cared little. At one time in 1861 he directed me to make a regular synopsis, every morning, of what I might deem the most important utterances of the leading public journals. I kept it up for a fortnight, and gave it up in utter despair of securing his attention to the result of my labors. He knew the people so much better than the editors did, that he could not bring himself to listen with any patience to the tissue of insane contradictions which then made up the staple of the public press.

Most people have a fair idea of his personal appearance, though the various paintings and photographs are open to like criticism with the pen portraits. Of the latter, the best which I have seen by far is the well known one of the President reading the Bible, with "Little Tad" standing by him.¹ It is as nearly perfect as a photograph can be, and gives the habitual expression of Mr. Lincoln's face while reading or writing. His features were strongly marked and plain, yet not unattractive, especially during conversation. At times they possessed a wonderful power of expression, and became so lit up by the great soul, within, that the rugged lineaments took on a sort of grandeur that did not ordinarily belong to them. Such a moment should have been seized by a real artist.

Mr. Lincoln was a man of genius—a man of powerful instincts and keen intuitions—rather than of close and accurate reasoning powers. In the latter, though his natural abilities were great, he yet at times showed the lack of early systematic training. Perhaps this was a loss, but I incline to the opposite opinion. His perceptions guided him well through labyrinths where logic would have been bewildered. His personal attachments were strong, and may at times have blinded him to faults of character in others which would otherwise have met with his earnest condemnation—though he never committed the absurdity of expecting perfection from his fellow men.² His personal habits were of the simplest kind, and there was not a particle of fuss and feathers in his composition. He was not slovenly, but seldom knew or cared whether or not he was well dressed. He used neither tobacco nor intoxicating liquors in any form, though not disposed to quarrel with those who chose to do so. Indeed, once, when a delegation of [Ulysses S.] Grant's enemies (he was then commanding in the West) accused the General of intemperance, he begged them to tell him where Grant got his whiskey, as he would like to purchase a few barrels for some of the Eastern Generals, "if that was what made him [Grant] behave as he did."

The most absurd and criminal stories have been told of Mr. Lincoln's tendency toward buffoonery. I presume that of the stories and jokes which have been fathered upon him, he heard three out of four for the first time when retailed by some friend long after they were current on the streets and in the papers as "Lincoln's last." The truth is, that as the war went on, a perpetual shade of sadness seemed to gather over him, and he more rarely relaxed into the mirthful spirit which had characterized his earlier manhood. During busy times, and when Mrs. Lincoln was away, he would have his breakfast, his lunch, and frequently his dinner, brought to him in his office, where he would work patiently, thoughtfully and untiringly, from early morn until late at night—his whole manner conveying to an observer the idea of a man who carried a load too great for human strength; and, as the years went on and the load grew heavier, it bowed him into premature old age. He was the American Atlas.

Nothing displeased him more than any attempt—and some fools did attempt it—at unseemly or undignified familiarity, for his nature was genuinely dignified and manly. Towards all who held appointments in his household he was to the last degree kind, considerate, and even indulgent; but nothing could be further out of the way than to suppose that his kindness of heart degenerated into what is vulgarly called "good nature." He was at times, when overworked or weary, even petulant—so much so as to be difficult of access; was always singularly firm in the assertion of his own fixed views or will, and if just cause of anger aroused him, his anger was apt to be hot and lasting.[3] He never did forgive a man whom he believed to have deceived him; of all men he hated and despised a liar. His manner at receptions, and other occasions of ceremony or of social or official formality, was that of a man who performs an irksome but unavoidable duty, though he was never lacking in cordial hospitality. Take him all in all, then, his faults and foibles were mainly the result of early association and defective education, nor were they of sufficient prominence to obscure for a moment from those who knew him the simplicity, integrity, and grand strength of the best beloved and most entirely trusted, if not really the greatest, statesman of modern times. Those who are to come after us will be better able to judge of the work he did, and of him by his work.

I do not think that the name of any lady is public property, because that of her husband has become such, and will, therefore, only say of Mrs. Lincoln that she was a lady of good education and manners, kind hearted, true to her friends even to a fault, strongly attached to her husband and children, and—all calumny to the contrary notwithstanding—devoted to the cause for which her husband gave his life.[4] Robert Lincoln, the hearty, whole souled and popular "Prince of Rails," was liked by every one; and by his sincerity of manner, unassuming deportment and general good sense, won a degree of good will and respect that has followed him into private life, and will one day make itself felt in his behalf, if, which I doubt, he should ever choose to emerge from it. His presence, at long intervals, in the White House, was always a pleasant and a welcome visitation.

Little Willie, whose untimely death cast such a shadow over the life of his father, was a child of great promise, and far more quiet and studious than his mercurial younger brother, since so well known by his self-assumed nickname of "Tad." As to the latter, I do not believe in writing a person's biography before they have arrived at the dignity of tail-coats.

The other inmates of the Executive Mansion at that time may be briefly described. Mr. Nicolay, the Private Secretary, and the only *attaché* of the President who had any claim to that specific title, was a man of somewhat

over thirty, a native of Baden Baden in Germany, but from early youth a resi-
dent of Illinois.[5] A fair French and German scholar, with some ability as a
writer and much natural acuteness, he nevertheless—thanks to a dyspeptic
tendency—had developed an artificial manner the reverse of "popular,"
and could say "no" about as disagreeably as any man I ever knew. That,
however, for which we all respected him, which was his chief qualification
for the very important post he occupied, was his devotion to the President
and his incorruptible honesty Lincoln-ward. He measured all things and all
men by their relations to the President, and was of incalculable service in
fending off much that would have been unnecessary labor and exhaustion to
his overworked patron. For this, and more, he deserves the thanks of all
who loved Mr. Lincoln, even if at times they had reason to grumble at "the
bulldog in the ante-room." Mr. Hay was, by courtesy, "Assistant Private
Secretary;" but, as the law recognized no such office, he was first made a
clerk in the Pension Office, and afterward an officer in the army and ordered
to the White House for special duty. He is quite young, and looks younger
than he is; of a fresh and almost boyish complexion; quite a favorite among
the ladies, and with a gift for epigram and repartee. What he will make of
himself, remains to be seen; but he is capable of something far better than he
has done yet, including Florida and the "Peace Commissioners."[6] He and
Nicolay now hold diplomatic appointments at Paris. The remaining Secretary, the writer of this, was "Secretary to sign the President's name to Patents for Land," under the law of 1836; but, as there was little of that to do in
war times, discharged by turns all imaginable duties, for we were short-
handed, and the era was a busy one. More of that will be said hereafter.

The only other personages who need be mentioned are Louis Berger
[Burgdorf], the messenger at the door of the President's room,—German,
crusty, pragmatical and pertinacious; proud of his position and authority,
and little tolerant of interference; but trustworthy, and, on the whole, capable; and his venerable colleague "Edward" [McManus]—he needs no other
name—for four administrations doorkeeper of the White House, and an in-
exhaustible well of incident and anecdote concerning the old worthies and
unworthies. An undersized, neatly dressed, polite, comical old man, with a
world of genuine Irish wit in his white head.[7] He it was who went with [Pres-
ident Millard] Fillmore to look at a carriage which the necessities of some
Southern magnate had thrown upon the market.[8]

"Well, Edward," said the President, "and how will it do for the President
of the United States to buy a second-hand carriage?"

"And sure, yer Excellency, and ye're only a second-hand President, ye
know!"

Mr. Fillmore took the joke, but not the carriage. This anecdote was told me by Mr. Lincoln, and was called up by the following: One dark and rainy evening we had got as far as the door, on our way to Gen. McClellan's headquarters, without an umbrella, and Edward was sent back after one, the President telling him whereabouts he might find it. In a few minutes he came back, announcing a fruitless search, and adding,

"Sure, yer Excellency, and the owner must have come for it!"

The President laughed heartily, and Edward found us another umbrella. He is no longer at his old post, but I cannot see how they do without him.[9] The remaining employees had nothing in particular to distinguish them from persons holding similar positions elsewhere, though they all seemed to have an idea that it was a big thing to work for "Father Abraham."

Sketch 3

My Dear General—To continue my line of narration I should now say something of etiquette and local customs at the seat of government. These are such as have grown up in the course of years under the pressure of the surrounding circumstances, and have been more than a little influenced by the constant presence of the representatives of European powers, bringing with them their old-world notions and habits. There has been slowly developed a set of customs and observances, all of which have their peculiar use and application, some of which appear odd to people fresh from New England villages or the simplicity of the backwoods, but which, as compared with their counterparts at European capitals, are to the last degree republican and unpretending. It is a custom, almost as strong as law, that a new President shall read his inaugural address from the east front of the Capitol, and that his predecessor shall immediately thereupon leave Washington, and abstain from visiting that city for at least four years. The social observances of the White House are more or less at the mercy of the occupants for the time being, but it would be thought a matter for grave comment if something like the following routine were not observed: On New Year's day, after the assembling of Congress, the Executive Mansion is thrown open for a general popular reception, but the Supreme Court, and the representatives of foreign powers, are expected to pay their respects first, and all things are kept clear for them. The latter come in full court dress, or in uniform, and make quite a brilliant display. Officers of the army and navy who come are expected to wear full dress uniforms. The Cabinet generally make their appearance with the Supreme Court and diplomats, but it is no violation of etiquette for them to be absent.

On these and all other public receptions the President takes a position near the entrance of the "Blue Room," and all comers are presented by the Marshal of the District, or a Secretary or Deputy Marshal, except when the crowd renders specific presentations impossible.[1] Diplomatic bodies are introduced by the Secretary of State. The lady of the White House stands a few paces to the right of the President, with suitable official attendance, but only those who especially desire it, or whose official rank makes the courtesy appropriate, can expect more than a passing bow. None of the crowd of comers remain in the blue room except friends of the family, persons especially invited, and those whose official position gives them the right. Soon after the New Year's Day Reception it is the custom for the President to give dinners to the Cabinet, Supreme Court, Diplomatic Corps, and to his political supporters in the two Houses. Sometimes the latter takes the form of a "Congressional Reception" in the evening, at which only invited guests assemble, and all are in full dress.

It was one of these, on a somewhat larger scale than usual, which attracted so much observation as "Mrs. Lincoln's Ball"—a ball at which there was no dancing, and which broke up a little after midnight.[2] From this time forward, until the beginning of Lent, there is a general reception, called a "levee"—for what reason I know not—every Tuesday evening, at which any one has a right to be present, in any sort of dress. Indeed, a student of the great art of dress could do no better thing than to attend a levee. He would see more varieties in one evening than Broadway would furnish him in a week.

The lady of the house receives on Saturday afternoons.

The Diplomatic Corps adopt with ready grace the republican freedom in which they find themselves, and their parties, balls, &c., are very nearly as free from conventionalities as the affairs at the White House. The President "does not go out," nor is it considered the correct thing to invite him to any social gathering; nor, if by any mistake he is invited, is it proper for him to accept. The members of the Cabinet are in no wise restricted.

Washington society is very much cut up into cliques—diplomatic, political, naval, military, west-end, navy yard, hotel, Congressional, Senatorial, &c., and sometimes the rivalry runs high. However, an officer of the army or navy, a department-man of good standing, a Senator or a Congressman, can always obtain admission almost anywhere, if his character as a gentleman will warrant it. The character of some of our Congressmen has been such as to destroy any social prestige that might otherwise have appertained to the position as such. A man may be able to carry the hundred and first ward of Babylon by an overwhelming majority, and yet not be just the person you would like to see dancing with your wife.

The winter is the season in Washington, and a mean season it is, if it were not for the social opportunities. The climate is simply execrable, and the streets are unpaved, dusty or muddy, and all things conspire together to make a social triumph in the City of Magnificent Distances a well-earned and peculiar glory.

Among the centres of social attraction are, generally, the weekly afternoon and evening receptions of the Vice-President, Speaker of the House, members of the Cabinet, Supreme Court Judges, army and navy officers of high rank, and such of the leaders in Senate and House as possess the cash and the accommodations necessary. It is an easy matter to obtain the *entreé* to these receptions, and they are oftentimes exceedingly agreeable and interesting. Prominent citizens frequently enter the lists, and not unfrequently beat the officials on their own ground. Indeed, one source of strength to the "Southern ascendancy" of former days, was the great attention paid by its leaders to social affairs. There is more real political business done in Washington over the dinner table, and in the glare of the gas-lights at these receptions, than ever there is in the more pretentious and noisy halls at the eastern end of Pennsylvania Avenue.

It is a sign of the times, by no means unworthy of notice, that within the last five years the wealth, beauty and fashion of the North has flowed toward Washington in a steady stream, building new residences and repairing old ones, and prepared to fully occupy the social void left by the downfall of the ancient regime. Never before was the city so brilliant and attractive—so well worthy of the high destiny which has been literally forced upon it. This will be more and more so hereafter, by the inevitable working of natural causes.

Apart from the somewhat singular and heterogeneous collection of "works of art," accumulated by the spasmodic and parsimonious "liberality" of successive Congresses, there is little to boast of in that line, and it is to be hoped that something better will be done hereafter. Part of that which has been done has been well done, and with the aid of a little fire and a good deal of money, we might have something worth while to show to foreigners.

Speaking of levees, &c., it is said that in Jackson's time it was customary to have refreshments of the most liberal kind, at the White House, until the old hero was so disgusted by the exhilarating effects produced upon his guests one evening, and their decidedly exhilarated conduct, that he at once broke up the practice, and it has never been revived. The crowd is always large enough any way, and there is no necessity of offering additional attractions.

Sketch 4

My Dear General—I have so frequently heard European gentlemen of great intelligence express their surprise, and often their admiration, at the stern simplicity with which business is transacted by the Chief Magistrate of the Great Republic, that I am inclined to believe that some account thereof may be interesting.

The building popularly known as the White House, is, in legal and official documents, designated as "the Executive Mansion." It is necessarily not only the President's residence, but also his business office, and all official documents bearing his signature must be dated therefrom. In fact, however, as will soon appear, the several Department buildings, and the offices of the members of the Cabinet, are a part of the "Executive" office, and in them the vast preponderance of the business of that branch of the Government is carried on.

Probably no public servant is daily compelled to attend to so much and so great a variety of business as the President, nor did any other President labor under such an accumulation of duties as did Mr. Lincoln; and yet, by the law, the President is allowed but one Private Secretary, with no Assistant, and one Secretary, to sign Land Patents. This is partially remedied by drafting clerks and army officers to the White House to perform special duty, and these frequently take full rank, by courtesy, as Secretaries;[1] but the whole thing should be remodeled by special act, and proper provision made for the performance of the necessary work. The salary of the Private Secretary, a necessarily expensive office, is but $2,500, and of the other but $1,500; these should be largely increased, and the services of the very best men secured. Our legislators cannot be unaware of the vast power for good or evil which is placed in the hands of a man constantly in the President's confidence, able at any time to "obtain his ear," sure to be listened to without suspicion or prejudice, and always in possession of current State secrets.

There are seldom more than two or three members of the Cabinet who equal the Private Secretary in real power, and he must be a man of more than ordinary brains and integrity if he does not at times do mischief. It is especially desirable that he should be devoted to his chief; and in this, at least, Mr. Lincoln's staff was as nearly perfect as possible. Our faith in him was almost blind, nor has the lapse of time at all diminished it. The Private Secretary on duty is supposed to exercise more or less control over the access of business or of individuals to the President, but with Mr. Lincoln this was difficult at times, as strength and time alone was allowed to be the measure of his day's labor, and it was not often that the hours from nine in the morning until three or four in the afternoon were not given up to the business of receiving all comers.

A careful distinction was always made in favor of public rather than private affairs, but no man went away without an interview if the President was really able to see him. The Cabinet met pretty regularly on Tuesday, at 1 P.M., but special meetings were frequent, and the Secretaries of State and War, and the "Commander-in-Chief"—so called—were constantly coming and going between their own offices and the White House.

A vast amount of business—and the reverse—came to the office through the mail, and of this I had charge, "with full power," for about two years and a half. The packages and envelopes, of all sorts and sizes, sometimes numbered hundreds in a day, and sometimes dwindled to a few dozens. They related to all imaginable interests and affairs: applications for office, for contracts, for pardons, for pecuniary aid, for advice, for information, for autographs, voluminous letters of advice, political disquisitions, religious exhortations, the rant and drivel of insanity, bitter abuse, foul obscenity, slanderous charges against public men, police and war information, military reports—there never was on earth such another *omnium gatherum* as the President's mail.

The spiritualists favored him constantly, and I still have in my possession urgent epistles signed with the *fac simile* signatures of half the dead worthies in our history, not to speak of sundry communications from the Apostles and the Angel Gabriel, of the correctness of whose signatures I am not so certain. As a general thing, during the war, we believed that so soon as a man went clean crazy his first absolutely insane act was to open a correspondence, on his side, with the President. As to the letters of advice, I am truly glad that the writers of many bulky and labored documents do not know what became of their precious productions, and in any event cannot accuse me of any dereliction from duty. One more point is, in the light of subsequent events, especially worthy of note, and that is, the large number of threatening letters. It is quite within bounds to say that they averaged one per diem. Most of them were manifestly merely intended to harass and provoke the President, while others but too evidently breathed a spirit that only needed courage and an opportunity to have anticipated Wilkes Booth. It was impossible to secure the attention of Mr. Lincoln to any of these, except as a matter for contemptuous ridicule; and when his friends, especially Mr. [Edwin M.] Stanton, insisted on his permitting himself to be accompanied and surrounded by a guard, he consented finally only under protest. It was hard for a heart like his to comprehend the venomous vindictiveness and cruelty of too many of his opponents.

After a proper examination, almost all business letters were promptly referred to the special office, war, navy, &c., to which their matter related; another large class—indeed, the largest, as a general thing—went into my willow waste-basket, a few were filed in the office for future reference, and a small per centage, three or four in a hundred, properly briefed and remarked upon, were laid on the President's desk. This, though exciting the furious wrath of sundry unthinking people, was unavoidable; for if every day had been a month it would have been impossible for Mr. Lincoln to attend to all these things in person.

Another huge mass of documents was daily transferred from his table to mine—the accumulation of the offerings of the day's caravan of personal petitions—though these were generally of a class to demand and receive careful attention. Any paper of real importance was pretty sure to do its work, and in due time to make its appearance from the proper pigeon-hole.

Again and again have I experienced the liveliest amusement in having local politicians and others boast of the effect their advice has evidently had upon the mind of the President, and describe the course which they had marked out for his future action. More than one has asked me if I had ever heard Mr. Lincoln speak of his letters, and if such and such a one was not read in Cabinet council. Dante should have seen my willow basket before he completed his list of limbos. Its edge was truly a bourne from which no traveler returned.

One day a well-dressed gentleman—a judge, or something of the kind, at home—sat in my room looking on at the performance of my morning job of destruction, twisting uneasily in his chair, and changing from red to pale with indignation, until he could contain his gathered wrath no longer. He had evidently indulged in letter-writing himself.

"Was that the way in which I dared to serve the President's correspondence? Was this the manner in which the people were prevented from reaching Mr. Lincoln? He would complain of me to my master at once! Teach me a thing or two about my duties! See if this was to be allowed! A mere boy in such an important place as that!" And so on for some moments, until I looked up and requested him to be still for a moment, while I read him a few of the precious documents I was destroying.

Of course, I made judicious selections to suit the occasion, for he was evidently intensely respectable and patriotic. I began with an epistle full of vulgar abuse that "riled" the old gentleman fearfully. Next I put in a proclamation "written in blood," and signed by the "Angel Gabriel;" and wound up with a horrible thing from an obscene, idiotic lunatic—a regular correspondent. The last was too much for him, and he begged me to stop. It was, indeed, sickening enough. I told him that if he insisted on the President's giving his time to such things he must take them in himself, as really I was forbidden to do so. The old gentleman, however, thought better of me by that time, and leaned back in his chair to moralize on the total depravity of human nature.

Complaints did frequently get to the President; but as he never interfered with me in any way and refused to reverse my decisions, I concluded he was satisfied even with the willow basket. No doubt they have one there now, and in these times it may well be a large one.

The applications for autographs were innumerable, but received very little encouragement, as the President had other things to attend to.

Colonel Hay imitated the signature of his Excellency very well, and I strongly suspect that some of the autographs distributed by my enterprising friend were very good indeed. On leaving the White House I had a fine collection, but they now adorn the portfolios of other men and women. Perhaps the autograph of F. E. Spinner is as good as any for collection purposes.[2]

Sketch 5

My Dear General—As I stated in my last, the different departments are supposed to be in some way connected with the Executive Office, and the Cabinet Secretaries to be the immediate subordinates and councilors of the President, but this is more the case in some administrations than others, and at all times the members of the Cabinet preserve a certain amount of independence of executive control (of which they are apt to be jealous), and which they all strive to increase. A fair share of them have future political, if not clearly Presidential, aspirations, and are consequently anxious to employ the patronage of their offices, as far as possible, to add strength to their own personal positions. They have friends to reward and enemies to punish, and no President can secure the entire execution of his will in such matters, even if he were able to attend to it, which he cannot be. The truth is, that our method of managing the public offices is simply execrable, and to the last degree detrimental to the public business. "Rotation in office" may be a good doctrine in its place, but when it takes a man years to become a competent government servant, and he is rotated out so soon as he understands his business, the public must not grumble if at times their work is badly done or not done at all.

I doubt if ever before there was so general a displacement as at the beginning of Mr. Lincoln's term. This was owing largely to the fact that the departments fairly swarmed with the family dependents and connections of the Southern political magnates who then, for so long a time, had controlled the dominant party. A "Blue Book" of 1859 is a sight to see, in that respect. Many of the men from the North were strong Southern sympathizers, and so accustomed were they to consider their offices their property that even avowed secessionists considered themselves bitterly injured when required to make way for more loyal men.

Still, a very large number of the old employees were retained, and the vast increase of the public business gave employment to a host of new men, many of whom had better have been in the army.

For weeks—indeed, for months—after the inauguration, the ante-rooms, halls and staircases of the White House swarmed with office-seekers. More important public business was at times impeded by their brazen importunity, and every man who was supposed to have "influence" was besieged day and night. It is true that one of the most important duties before the new administration was to place the machinery of government, as soon as possible, in trustworthy hands, but it was a terrible job to do so. They say that the office-seekers killed [President William Henry] Harrison and [President Zachary] Taylor—it is no fault of Abraham Lincoln that they did not kill him, for he listened to them with a degree of patience and good temper truly astonishing. At times, however, even his equanimity gave way, and more than one public man finally lost the President's good will by his pertinacity in demanding provision for his personal satellites. Some Senators and Congressmen really distinguished themselves in this respect. I remember a saying of Mr. Lincoln's that comes in pretty well here: "Poor ———, he is digging his political grave!"

"Why, how so, Mr. President? He has obtained more offices for his friends than any other man I know of."

"That's just it; no man can stand so much of that sort of thing. You see, every man thinks he deserves a better office than the one he gets, and hates his 'big man' for not securing it, while for every man appointed there are five envious men unappointed, who never forgive him for their want of luck. So there's half a dozen enemies for each success. I like ———, and don't like to see him hurt himself in that way; I guess I won't give him any more."

The last clause had a dry bit of humor in it, for in good truth the honorable gentleman had had quite enough.

The organization of the Washington Departments proceeded rapidly enough, and nearly all the clerks, as fast as appointed, were enrolled into a sort of militia organization for the protection of the city. The public buildings were all garrisoned in this manner, and the "office-seekers' brigade" bivouacked in the East Room of the White House. Some of them could hardly have paid for their lodgings anywhere else, I fear.

Not to dwell on that, however, the next thing was the organization of the military departments, and concerning one of them and its first commander I have a reminiscence.

About the time Gen. John A. Dix was assigned to the command of the Baltimore District, he was telegraphed to Washington to consult as to the policy to be pursued, &c.[1] On that evening at about half past eight, the President summoned me to attend him, with papers, &c., as he was going over to Mr. Seward's house.[2] The conference was protracted—Mr. Lincoln, Mr. Seward and Gen. Dix, all taking an active part—and it was near midnight when we started for home. As we walked along I said:

"Well, Mr. Lincoln, and what do you think of Gen. Dix?"

"Well, Stoddard, I cannot say that I know him very well, but, judging from the counsel he has given to-night, and from all he has said, I should say that Gen. Dix was—I should say that Gen. Dix—was—a very, very wise man."

My impression is that they had not met before, at least that they were not at all acquainted. I do not think that Mr. Lincoln was disposed to form sudden estimates of men, and he was always cautious in declaring his impressions. His dry, hesitating, and yet emphatic reply to my query, fixed it pretty firmly in my memory, and the friends of our now venerable ex-Governor may be pleased to have it recorded.

One of the queer things in those days was the management of the War Department. The circumstances were peculiar, and it was necessary to employ every available means to secure the purchase and manufacture of the necessary arms and other supplies. What piles of trash were bought, of no use to army or navy—and what singular prices were paid in certain cases need not here be rehearsed—but it seemed then, and to some extent afterward, impossible to entirely emancipate the strictly professional men from outside political influence. To do them only justice, they always fought against it, and the result of my daily notes for so long a time, is the deliberate opinion, in spite of all the newspaper indictments, that the officers of the army and navy of the United States are a remarkably high-minded and honorable class of men in business transactions. There were exceptions, no doubt, some few of which were at times exposed, and that was to have been expected, but the nation may well be proud of the honesty of the men who wear its uniform.

You may charge this digression, if it is one, to my intense disgust at sundry slurs which from time to time still disfigure the columns of some public journals.

One universal idea seemed to be that if any given gun, cannon, ship, armor or all-killing or all-saving apparatus chanced to take the eye of the President, it must thereupon speedily be adopted for army use and forced into a grand success by Executive authority. It was in vain that Mr. Lincoln systematically discouraged this notion, and never went further, even with inventions that pleased him most, than to order an examination and trial by the proper professional authorities.[3] Every inventor posted straight to the White House with his "working model." Mr. Lincoln had very good mechanical ability, and a quick appreciation of what was practical in any proposed improvement. Here, as elsewhere, his strong common sense came in play, to the great discomfiture of many a shallow quack and mechanical enthusiast. It was a common thing for the makers of the new rifles, shells, armor-vests, gunboats, breech-loading cannon, and the multitudinous nameless contrivances which came into being in the heat and excitement of the times by a species of spontaneous generation, either to invite him to witness a trial or to send him a specimen—the latter being frequently intended as a "presentation copy." On the grounds near the Potomac, south of the White House, was a huge pile of old lumber, not to be damaged by balls, and a good many mornings I have been out there with the President, by previous appointment, to try such rifles as were sent in. There was no danger of hitting any one, and the President, who was a very good shot, enjoyed the relaxation very much. One morning early we were having a good time—he with his favorite "Spencer,"[4] and I with a villainous kicking nondescript, with a sort of patent backaction breech, that left my shoulder black and blue—when a squad from some regiment which had just been put on guard in that locality pounced on us for what seemed to them a manifest disobedience of all "regulations." I heard the shout of the officer in command and saw them coming, but as the President was busy drawing a very particular bead—for I had been beating him a little—I said nothing until down they came. In response to a decidedly unceremonious hail, the President, in some astonishment, drew back from his stooping posture, and turned upon them the full length six feet four of their beloved "Commander-in-Chief." They stood and looked one moment, and then fairly ran away, leaving his Excellency laughing heartily at their needless discomfiture. He only remarked:

"Well, they might have stayed and seen the shooting."

I see that just above I have inadvertently spoken of the President as "his Excellency"—a title to which the President has no claim, and the use of which Mr. Lincoln always disapproved. It may not be altogether unrepublican, but it certainly is improper, though somehow it has crept into such general use in speaking of our Chief Magistrate. The constitution provides his simple style and title, than which there is not and cannot be any higher in the estimation of all true Americans. Titles "by courtesy," as a general thing, may be more aptly designated "titles by snobbery," and should be suppressed as such.

Speaking of specimen guns puts me in mind of something which happened as far back as when [Col. Elmer] Ellsworth was alive—only interesting as belonging to a memory still dear to young America. Somebody had left a carbine in Mr. Nicolay's office, and the Sunday before that fatal night in Alexandria I happened to meet Ellsworth there, and had a long talk with him. He was in unusual spirits and very communicative. His plans for the future, his military ideas and ambition were all discussed until we were weary, when he caught up the carbine and I put him through the manual of arms. It was always a pleasure to watch him use his favorite weapon, and he went through the motions with mathematical precision; but when he came to "make ready," he had forgotten his proximity to the south window, and the muzzle of the piece went crashing through a pane of glass. There was no help for it, and as no one else was there we concocted and told with masterly gravity a yarn of a man hiding in the shrubbery, who had doubtless taken one of us for the President and tried a shot at him. Of course, the fib was too palpable to stand much questioning. Well, that day week [*sic*] I sat in the same room again, talking with General Leavenworth, of New York, when the latter spoke of our sad loss.[5] One glance at the window, with the fresh marks of the glazier's fingers on the pane, and another showed me that the General was in the same chair so lately occupied by the dead Colonel, and then for the first time I realized that that bright and brave young life, with all its glowing aspirations, had gone out in darkness—the first of all the good blood which has so reddened the Virginian soil. I am not ashamed to say that it was a little too much for me then; we had not become so hardened as we grew to be under the swift calamities that afterward trod so rapidly upon each other's heels. He died upon the very threshold of the war—a sad warning to the nation that it must give its best and brightest to the great sacrifice before it.

Sketch 6

My Dear General—Not at all with any effort to refer to events in regular chronological order, I shall try from time to time to instance the use of what is called "outside pressure" in efforts to influence the policy of the Government. As the President rarely looked into a newspaper, and thus systematically shunned labored leaders or commentaries on his own conduct, this pressure was necessarily applied personally, in conversation and by argument, and the White House being the peculiar theatre of that sort of war, I had a good chance for taking observations. During the whole time there was always some one topic upon which the popular mind was strongly exercised and widely divided, and concerning which popular representatives, self-elected or otherwise, were forcing their views upon Mr. Lincoln's attention. It was curious to observe how invariably each party in every case accused him of being under the undue personal influence of some opposing leader. In one week I culled from leading papers the several assertions, backed up with bitter phrases, that [Secretary of State] Seward, [Postmaster General] Blair, [Secretary of War] Stanton, [General] Halleck, [General] McClellan, [Senator] Trumbull and those terrible but undefined fellows the "radical abolitionists," were severally managing the Presidential machine and had the Chief Magistrate under their separate or collective thumbs. The truth is that history has given us few names of men so ready and willing to listen to all, and patiently to hear and weigh the arguments of every side, and at the same time so steadily firm in forming and following their own conclusions as was Abraham Lincoln.

This was in him the reverse of a disposition to disregard the popular will, but an instinctive consciousness that he himself knew the real popular feeling, as distinguished from the loud assertions of individuals. He was singularly able to discern between the passion and impulse of a heated moment, and that kind of deep conviction in the minds of the masses which may be relied upon as the enduring basis of a great policy.

The "On to Richmond" pressure which preceded and is responsible for the first battle of Bull Run, was so universal, such an utterance of the people as with one voice, that it may be noted as a singular proof of the President's sagacity that he seriously questioned the propriety of yielding to it. One result was, at least, that the editorial community lost somewhat of that confidence in their own military ability with which they commenced the war. They contented themselves thereafter with a wonderful activity as critical observers rather than originators.

The next great pressure—to pass over the minor cases, of men who turned little screws with a very short crank—was brought to bear for the removal of Gen. Cameron, the Secretary of War.[1] It was something tremendous, and the flood of execrations and charges would have turned a gristmill. Secretary Cameron was removed, but his personal reputation carefully guarded. Mr. Lincoln did not lose confidence in the ability, honesty or patriotism of Mr. Cameron, but wisely deemed it best for the service that the post of Secretary of War at such a time should be filled by a man possessing the popular confidence. The opposition to Secretary Stanton which afterward arose, was of a different nature and under different circumstances, and never was of a character to seriously interfere with the usefulness of our "great War Minister." With the resignation of Mr. Cameron and the appointment of Mr. Stanton [in January 1862], the first scene in the great tragedy may be said to have ended. The changes were gradual, but the old order of things passed away, and we passed from a peaceful into a military people, to whom the army was all in all.

I find it hard indeed to keep within the assigned boundaries of these sketches, but hardly think I do so in referring to the first military event of any great importance in the new era of the army. This was the disaster at Ball's Bluff [in October 1861]. The evening when the news came in was a dark one at the White House. Gen. McClellan came over at once, puzzled, astonished, and not a little "stampeded." I did not witness the meeting between him and the President, but was told it was mournful enough.[2] The central figure of that disaster was Col. [Edward D.] Baker. The first I ever heard of the gallant Senator was in reading his wonderfully eloquent and pathetic address at the funeral of the murdered Broderick, and afterward he had seemed to me the handsomest man in the Senate.[3] I well remember his first appearance at Mr. Lincoln's office in uniform, after he had raised his regiment. He was an exceedingly striking figure, with his ample white hair, flashing eyes and graceful person. The President loved him like a brother, and mourned his untimely death bitterly.[4] All that evening, until late in the night, he paced up and down in his room, outwardly, at least, more overcome than I ever saw him afterward. His warm heart was yet to receive many wounds before the end came, but I always thought that, except the death of "little Willie," the loss of Col. Baker touched him most deeply of all.

Speaking of Gen. McClellan, the eyes and hopes of the Administration seem from the first to have been directed toward him, and such strong hints of the probable career before him were allowed to reach his ears as to prepare his mind in advance, and to draw from him the able and somewhat remarkable letters which he wrote prior to his appointment to the command of the Army of the Potomac. He seemed, from the very first, to consider himself in the light of a "General in Chief," and his character and conduct were constantly the subject of anxious discussion among the personal friends of the President. These discussions had always a bearing independent of any criticism on his merely military accomplishments, and no injustice was done the General by those who condemned his manner of speaking of, and of behavior to Mr. Lincoln. Not that he was often wanting in outward tokens of respect, but certainly he seemed unable to appreciate at their right value the character and ability of his official superior.[5] It is possible that he was unconsciously affected more than was good by the very general feeling of jealousy and almost contempt by the regular army for civilians, whether volunteers or not. This feeling had for a while an evil influence, but happily wore away with time, as the experience of the war assigned to one man after another his true position, without reference to his antecedents. President Lincoln himself did not know what it was to be jealous of any man, and cared so little for official punctilio as to be quite as likely at any time to go to a subordinate as to send for him. At one time he esteemed Gen. McClellan very highly, and that esteem might have been easily retained. Indeed, the removal at last, of the General, was in no sense a yielding to popular clamor or political pressure or expediency.

President Lincoln, with a high opinion of McClellan's abilities, at last decided that he was not sufficiently incisive for a great commander; that he lacked the striking power. To illustrate this, one day a committee of some sort called on him to urge their complaints against the General in Chief, and he replied nearly in these words: "Well, gentlemen, for the organization of an army—to prepare it for the field—and for some other things, I will back General McClellan against any general of modern times—I don't know but of ancient times either—but I begin to believe that he will never get ready to fight."

The emphasis on the last few words clearly indicated a strong and growing conviction. I never knew Mr. Lincoln so really angry, so out of all patience, as when it was reported impossible to obey his celebrated order for a general advance of the army on the 22d of February, 1862.[6] I doubt if the impression then made upon his mind was ever afterward removed. It would not have surprised me to have heard of General McClellan's removal at any time thereafter, but I knew that the question of who should be his successor was even more perplexing than that of the propriety of a change. That question, like many another, finally settled itself to general satisfaction.

I have already alluded to the constant attempts, in letters, to influence the mind of Mr. Lincoln by threats of violence. There is no doubt that his friends were affected by these communications, if he was not, and, if we were at times indifferent to the manifest possibilities of the case, some epistle betraying more of malignity than usual was sure to awaken us. Not all of these letters, by any means, came from professed rebels; there was no want of variety in the avowed causes for hatred.

The President was frequently alone in his room evening after evening—the whole East Wing unoccupied except by himself and a sleepy messenger in the ante-room, and ingress and egress entirely unobstructed. We never discussed the subject much, for some reason, but I believe that both Mr. Nicolay and Col. Hay, as well as myself, thought more about it than we ever confessed. At least we spent many an evening in our offices, with a sharp eye and ear open for the footstep in the hall, when we would have been puzzled to give a good reason for our presence, other than that in some vague and unaccountable way we were "on guard." In the latter part of the war a formal guard was kept, both at the White House and when the President was at the Soldiers' Home.[7]

This guard were proud of their duty, and sometimes exerted a degree of zeal that might have been dispensed with. At one time, after several wooden buildings, containing army stores, &c., had been destroyed by fire, a general order was issued by the Commander of the District, forbidding any one to approach any of the public buildings with a lighted cigar. Although the intent of the order was clear enough, the officer in command of the President's Guard decided that it applied to the Executive Mansion and grounds. In consequence, that evening, as I approached the gate, puffing away at my customary after-dinner Havana, I was compelled, by the rifleman on duty, to pitch my luxury into the gutter, in spite of sundry grumbling expostulations. There was, however, a mounted man also on guard, and before I had proceeded many steps he shouted, "Hey! Mr. Secretary, won't you just come here a moment?" and as I approached him, "that wooden-headed cuss has got off a couple of good jokes since he came on, if he only knew it, and I wish you would tell them to Mr. Lincoln. I'll bet he'll laugh well. You see he hadn't been there five minutes, with his head full of his new order, when along comes old [Secretary of State William Henry] Seward, and you know he's always a smokin'. Well, he didn't want to throw his cigar away, a bit, but he was good natured about it, and said something about people having to give up a good many things on account of the war, and he went on. Then, in a minute or so, up comes Ben. Butler, in full military fig, and he was smokin' too. 'You musht put out dat cigar,' says guardy, for he's Dutch as ———. 'Are those your orders, sir?' says Butler, drawing himself up, and trying to look at the fellow with both eyes.[8] 'Well, sir, orders are orders, and they must be obeyed!' And so the General threw his cigar over the fence. It's a humbug, you know, but then it's fun to see cocks like them obeying orders."

The thing was funny, and quite reconciled me to my loss. When I related it to Mr. Lincoln he laughed heartily. "What! did Seward throw his cigar away?"

"Yes, sir."

"And Ben. Butler too?"

"Yes, with appropriate remarks."

"Well, it's a very good joke, but I guess it has gone far enough."

So the zealous captain of the guard was sent for and the prohibition removed, to the great comfort of all the smokers. It was said that the boys caught Mr. Stanton himself before they lifted the embargo, but I do not know how truly.[9]

We had our little "lights," you see, as well as our "shadows," and one of these came to pass in this wise. I think Hanscom, of the *Washington Republican*, is responsible for it.[10] About the time when [Treasury] Secretary [Salmon P.] Chase began to issue Treasury notes, an item appeared in that paper announcing that "the original greenback" would be on exhibition in front of the White House next day, at such an hour, and not a few deluded sight-seers came to the show. Now, in the little enclosure between the house and the avenue there is a green and gloomy looking affair, facing the street, which "sets up" to be a bronze statue of Jefferson, but looks more like a mouldy old Indian, just dug up—and it was to the verdant back of this figure that the curious were directed as they filed across the portico. Is there any fun in making one's fellow-men look like lost sheep?

Sketch 7

My Dear General—In the course of these sketches I have had, and shall have, frequent occasion to refer to various public men by name, in connection with fact or anecdote. I take this opportunity of saying that I shall never intentionally allow any partisan feeling or political bias to influence the tone of such reference. It is my object to draw only from the life, and not to attempt to add to my "effects" by high colors laid on at the expense of others, or to gratify personal prejudice. I presume, however, that you have taken all this for granted.

Applications for pardon, in their various forms, made a very considerable item of the business of the Executive Office, and the papers in such cases frequently formed quite an accumulation upon my desk. The great mass of papers in all criminal cases in the army were, of course, in the custody of the War Office, or rather in the Judge Advocate General's Bureau; but no sooner did any unfortunate, be his misdemeanor large or small, become an applicant for Executive clemency, than petitions, reviews, arguments, &c., began to make their appearance, through the mail or by private hand, at the White House. For a long time it was my duty to examine and make a brief of these documents, so as to be ready to present them for reference when called for, or to report upon them as the circumstances of the case might demand. So many stories have been told of Mr. Lincoln's clement and merciful nature that I do not need to add to the list, and will only say that, especially when the death penalty had been awarded by the court, military or otherwise, he seemed to search anxiously, and to wish me to do so, for some good reason for the exercise of his constitutional power of pardon or commutation. A portion of Friday was set apart with some regularity for the examination of capital cases; but as few weeks passed without the necessity of abandoning at least some one poor fellow to his fate, the President came to look forward to that part of his duty with extreme repugnance, and stigmatized Friday as "butcher's day."[1] It was his opinion that "no man was ever yet improved by killing him," a very doubtful proposition, but fully in accordance with his merciful and kindly nature. Nevertheless, his tendencies to mercy were held in wholesome check by his strong natural sense of justice—justice as distinguished and separate from any thought of vengeance.

Those who wonder what would have been his political course and conduct had he lived, can hardly go far astray if they study the facts with this strong trait of his character in view. It would undoubtedly have furnished the certain key to his action.

I do not now remember that I ever saw Vice President Hamlin at the White House, though he may have been there a few times for all that. It seems that a sort of etiquette has been established, in accordance with which it is not considered good taste for the second officer of the Republic to meddle much with public business, and which, at all events, keeps him away from the Executive Mansion. It would be difficult to give a good reason why he should not be numbered among the "constitutional advisers" of the President; but the contrary custom seems to be pretty firmly established. The most frequent visitors at the White House, among the Cabinet, were, from the circumstances of the case, the Secretaries of State and War; but, perhaps, they paid few visits which were not speedily returned by the President in person. Especially was this true of the War Office; and in times of excitement, when great news was expected, he [Lincoln] would frequently remain in the telegraph room of the War Department until late into the night. More than a few times have we laid in wait for him in the hall, and gathered the purport of the despatches with almost unerring certainty from the expression of his face. In spite of its strongly marked outline, by the way, his countenance was a very mirror of his emotions. Oh! how it was darkened with pain after the Fredericksburg fight!—though even victory, however thoroughly appreciated, seemed for him to have its element of sadness.[2] Speaking of Fredericksburg, I wish it were possible for me to report in full the memorable interview with General Burnside, in which each of the noble hearted men strove for the terrible responsibility which lay upon them.[3] The war has produced no other such picture of unselfish generosity. Much that passed was heard in the Secretaries' room. Perhaps the record already before the public is sufficiently accurate.

From the very first, from before the premature and unauthorized proclamations of Frémont and Hunter, until the end, as a matter of course, the different phases of the everlasting slavery question disturbed not only the White House, but all the official, social and business circles of the Federal capital.[4] Hardly any of the many public utterances of Mr. Lincoln were not thus called out, and it should be said that they were all his own. Good, bad or indifferent no member of his Cabinet or of his circle of personal friends has any responsibility for the published declarations of Abraham Lincoln's policy. I have copied too much of his manuscript not to know well how it was made up, and how rarely any correction was found in another hand than his own.[5] This, of course, does not apply to matter quoted, or reported for use in any message from any department. The greater part of his writing was done when alone by himself in his room. He composed somewhat slowly and with care, making few erasures or corrections, and, indeed, being quite tenacious of forms of expression which he had once adopted. It was then his custom to read his manuscript over aloud, "to see how it sounded, as he could hardly judge of a thing by merely reading it."

But to go back to the pressure on the slavery question—it was perpetual, multiform, clamorous and unreasonable, at times arraying many of the President's staunchest friends and supporters—against their will, perhaps—in bitter opposition to his policy. Not to discuss the better known and more generally familiar forms of this agitation, I shall never forget the sensation produced at a levee by the appearance of two tall and very well dressed Africans among the crowd of those who came to pay their respects. It was a practical assertion of negro citizenship, for which few were prepared. The President received them with marked kindness, and they behaved with strict propriety, not seeming to court attention, but went on their way with great self-possession. It was well done, whatever were their notions in coming; but a universal reporter might have made a good thing out of the remarks volunteered by the brilliant assembly in the parlors and East Room. It was as good as a play.[6]

This puts me in mind of something which happened long afterward. One of the first regiments of black soldiers was raised in the city of Washington. Up to that time, at least, the attempt to make troops of them was regarded very generally as a somewhat doubtful experiment, and some people can hardly yet believe that they ever did any fighting. Their first public parade was a sort of a "go to meeting" affair, and took place on Sunday. It was a fine morning, and as I strolled over from breakfast at the club to the house, I saw the regiment coming down the avenue, and waited in the gateway to have a good look at them. Just then along came Secretary Seward, smoking as usual, and stopped for the same purpose. They were really a fine looking body of men, and marched well for such new recruits. It was indeed a curious and deeply interesting sight, seen for the first time. Mr. Seward seemed to be thinking pretty seriously, and of course I did not presume to interrupt him until after the regiment had passed on and we turned toward the house together, when I asked him:

"Well, Mr. Seward, what do you think of our black troops?"

He took his cigar from his mouth and slowly replied, without looking up: "It grows, it grows."

I could not help feeling that no more questions need be asked just then of that man, and could imagine his thoughts going back through long years of his eventful life to the time when alone in the United States Senate he stood up in defence of freedom, and in opposition to that slave power which was now tottering to its downfall. Little could he then have expected to look upon such a spectacle as the column which had just marched before him. He could hardly have dreamed of circumstances which should set liberated slaves fighting in defence of their new freedom in the uniform of the army of the United States and under the national flag. Well, I went up to my room, which, as I have said, fronted on the avenue. By and by, the regiment came marching back again, and some one told the President of its approach. I was standing in the window when I heard his heavy step behind me. He, too, seemed preoccupied and contented with looking without speaking; but I looked up in his face and asked him:

"Well, Mr. President, what do you think of that?"

For a moment his lips were firmly compressed, and his eyes assumed the half shut expression habitual to him when thinking; but as he turned to go to his own room, he said in a low voice:

"It'll do, it'll do!"

He, too, was busy with old memories, as well as great questions of State policy. I had obtained from the two foremost men of that day just about four words each on the negro troops question; but it somehow seemed to me as if a volume was compressed into the brief utterances. The words of men in power sometimes mean a great deal. I remembered this afterward when Mr. Lincoln read me the manuscript of his famous Springfield letter, as I noted the singular emphasis which he put upon the words: "And there will be some black men who can remember that with silent tongue, and clenched teeth, and steady eye, and well poised bayonet, they have helped mankind on to this great consummation."[7]

It seems strange now that so many of us, even of those opposed to slavery, found it hard to approve of what was doubtless so wise, so necessary a policy as the arming of the blacks.

Of course, in a society so largely made up of the Southern element as that of Washington, not to speak of the fossil remains of former political eras, the omnipresent African had a good deal to do with likes and dislikes. I shall never forget the horror of one good old lady at some heretical expression of my own, as with uplifted hands she exclaimed:

"Why, Mr. Secretary! I always thought that you were a Virginia gentleman!"

Fancy the accent on the last two words. From that moment I recognized the physical fact that spectacles have a power of expression; hers certainly expanded. The old army and navy circles, especially, were slow to awaken to the new light, as was evidenced by more than one general order. Perhaps the worst temporary effect of this was to increase the causeless unpopularity of the regular army and "West Point" at the North. It was unfortunate; but, like many other evils, corrected itself in due time. It was not easy for a people like our own, knowing so little about professional soldiers, to understand a class of men who even refused to know anything about politics, and refused duty to anything but their orders and their flag. By the way, what a load of thinking a man is relieved of by such a military creed as that. As for the President himself, he had too much good sense to expect a sudden crop of "miraculous generals," and from the first seemed to rely for the results of war on men who had made war their study.

I hardly think it would be best to insert here some remarks of his about what we may call our "sensation generals." They were good and pointed, however, I can assure you.

When the negro troops were first organized many of the best officers in the army offered their services in any capacity; but it was astonishing how large a number of second lieutenants of volunteers were willing to sacrifice themselves for the good of the service as majors and colonels. It was really a pity to disappoint such gushing patriotism, but I am sorry to say it was done to a crushing extent. No doubt the unexpected degree of success attained was largely due to the care originally exercised in this process of selection. Not, however, that some blunders were not made.

Speaking of a certain class of applicants for office, reminds me of a fat and ruddy individual, in a swallow-tailed coat, who entered my office one morning with an expression of the most beaming, gushing, greasy and cordial familiarity, and asked "if Old Abe was in?"

"Whom, sir?"

"Why, Old Abe? I want to see him a few minutes. How is the old fellow, anyway?"

"Really, sir, I cannot imagine of whom you can be inquiring, unless, indeed, by any accident you are trying to speak of the President of the United States. If so, he is in, but you can't see him to-day."

"Not see Old Abe! Why not?"

It required several unsatisfactory remarks to explain matters to him. I wonder if some people do not imagine it a smart thing to address even letters to public men by their nick-names; and, if so, how soon they get their answers, on an average.

Sketch 8

Dear General—Sunday at the White House was, even more than elsewhere, a day by itself. No anxious visitors waited in the vacant ante-rooms; no busy committee men promenaded up and down in the halls; no strolling parties of gaping sight-seers peered into the corners and examined their dresses in the mirrors of the parlors and the East Room. It was evident to every eye that this was Sunday, and yet under all the surface of silence and decorum, the great work was uninterrupted even by the Lord's Day. The sentries paced their beats up and down the several entrances, the messengers came and went, and unceasingly the electric click sustained its irregular pulsations in the dingy rooms in the War Office Building, carrying orders to and bringing reports from the countless armies of the Great Republic.

War has no Sunday, no day of rest, no hour that is sacred above the others—and civil war least of all.

President Lincoln was deeply and genuinely religious, without being in any way what may be called a religionist. His religion was in his faith and in his life rather than in any profession.[1] So far as I know, his religious belief or opinions never, at any period of his life, took the shape of a formal profession. His nature was not at all enthusiastic, and his mind was subject to none of the fevers which pass with the weak and shallow for religious fervor, and in this, as in all other things, he was too thoroughly honest to assume that which he did not feel.

In Dr. Gurley's church (Presbyterian), in Washington, there is a pew set apart for the President of the United States, and, as Mrs. Lincoln was a member of that denomination, she attended morning service pretty regularly, and frequently;[2] when affairs of State permitted, Mr. Lincoln accompanied her. He was not, however, a man to pay much attention to or care much about the thin walls of separation between different denominations.

Either his ancestors or some near relatives of his had been Quakers, and he always manifested great respect for and interest in that highly respectable religious community. I always thought, however, that his strong sense of the humorous and appreciation of the quaint and odd, had more than a little to do with this partiality. It would seem, too, that the Quakers, as a rule, have an unusually large amount of quiet humor of their own; and it may be, moreover, that he had not entirely rid himself of the old popular delusion that the Quakers are more inclined to be honest than other men. His early associations with the Methodists, the religious pioneers and missionaries of the West, had impressed him with a high respect for the zeal and energy of that sect.

For all this, however, he was not what I think the controversialists call a "Sabbatarian," and while he preferred greatly to rest his body and mind, if he could, he never scrupled to give his attention to any necessary work on Sunday. This fact was generally well known, and some prominent men, of sufficient official or representative position to warrant them in disregarding the rules about "receiving visitors," were constantly in the habit of availing themselves of the chance offered by Sunday for finding the President disengaged, and this often to his extreme discomfort and dissatisfaction.

Not unfrequently he would lay aside his despatches and papers, and his Presidency, and stroll into one of the secretaries' rooms for a careless chat with "the boys," and I have seen his face cloud up with unconcealed chagrin when the messenger would announce the arrival of some ponderous Senator, important Congressman, or busy Cabinet Minister, as with a sigh of half weariness and whole vexation he would turn to his own room, or we would disperse to other apartments.

It so happened that a large number of engagements in the early part of the war, many of them with ill fortune to our arms, were fought upon Sunday, and the fact aroused the religious feelings—not to say the superstition—of many excellent people at the North. At last, after many letters and not a few edifying "resolutions," a committee of reverend gentlemen was sent on to remonstrate with the President, and urge upon him the propriety of carrying on the war solely upon week days. They were not a very powerful body of men—hardly of the rank of Brigadier Generals in the Church Militant— but they obtained an audience, stated their theological position, secured the appointment of some of their number and next friends as army chaplains, and returned home. This may be regarded as, in one sense, a manifestation of the deep feeling among pious men at the North that the Lord was on our side—which no right-thinking man can doubt—but did not altogether originate so creditably. At all events, Sunday continued to be essentially a fighting day. The fact is that war is a general and fearful violation of all the laws of God and man, and when all the other ordinances of mercy and of religion are cast to the winds, it is hardly to be expected that in such matters as the sanctity of a day the mandates of Christianity will be specially regarded.

Any one who is inclined to question the depth of Mr. Lincoln's religious feeling need only look over his published official utterances since his election in 1860, from the time when he asked his old neighbors to pray for him, when he bade them good-bye, until the day when he called upon the whole people to unite in a solemn Thanksgiving to God for a peril passed and a nation saved.

Speaking of army chaplains, by some peculiarity in the law their appointment rested directly with the President, and the business was a source of great annoyance to him, until at last he turned it all over to the Secretary of War. For a long time I had charge of all papers relating to these appointments, such as recommendations, certificates of ordination, &c., and a queer set of fellows it brought me in contact with. While many worthy and truly pious men were anxious to serve in that capacity, such men did not always seem able to secure the necessary political endorsement and support, while an endless train of broken down "reverends," long since out of the ministry for incompetency or other cause, men who could not induce any respectable church to place itself under their charge, crowded forward, clamorous to be entrusted with the spiritual interests of the grandest of all congregations—men going out to die. To a lamentable extent they brought contempt and derision on their cloth; many, even, who had maintained fair characters at home, succumbing to the temptations and the freedom from all restraint of a life in camp.

"I do believe," said Mr. Lincoln to me one day, as we were discussing a case of more than usual flagrancy, "I do believe that our army chaplains, take them as a class, are the very worst men we have in the service."

So far as my observation goes, taking their high professions into account, the President was undeniably correct.

The number of men who really had influence with the President, or could obtain favors from him by purely personal application, was by no means large, although the contrary statement has been frequently made. I could name them all upon my fingers. They were, moreover, with two or three exceptions, a class of men who seldom troubled him with personal applications, and when they did come, or write, we knew very well that what they came for, if reasonable, was pretty sure of accomplishment.

There were men, whom I can hardly refrain from mentioning by name, who forced themselves into unhealthy prominence in the newspapers as having power at the White House, by sheer dint of persevering attendance at receptions and levees, everlasting presence in the ante-rooms, and a way they had of blowing their own trumpets in the hotels and lobbies. So soon as he found them out (and it rarely took him long), Mr. Lincoln's contemptuous disgust for these men was almost amusing in its completeness. I have seen more than one of them finding his way down stairs for the last time, with an immense flea in his ear, and looking so unutterably "found out" as to tempt one to offer him a handkerchief.

Some people attended "levees," as they were called, with the dim idea that they were about to make the acquaintance of the President and his wife, and prepared themselves for a quiet little chat, with stores of questions about this and advice about that for Father Abraham. Others, not expecting much time to themselves, would prepare patriotic little speeches, which they would launch with sudden fervor and wonderfully rapid utterance at the head of the President. I remember seeing a little wee bit of a fat man, half smothered in the crowd, stretching out a hand through a chink in the procession, as if he was drowning, and while the laughing President shook him almost convulsively thereby, the persistent little orator under difficulties, wheezed out some choked sentences about freedom, glory, emancipation, &c. When Mr. Lincoln let go of him he disappeared.

The President had a genuine giant's liking for little men. He was by no means sensitive as to his own ungainly length, but considered it a fair enough subject for quiet fun, and I fear he sometimes forgot that little men are rarely so careless about their size as large ones. There are countless jokes in circulation, gathered from his old contests with [Stephen A.] Douglas, whose squat, short, heavy figure, formed a striking contrast to the height of Mr. Lincoln. Generally speaking, Mr. Lincoln had a marked stoop in the shoulders, and his head drooped lower and lower under the weight he had to carry; but at times, when speaking, he would draw himself up as straight as an arrow in the excitement of the moment, his motions would become almost graceful, and then the listening people were sure to hear one of those plain but burning sentences which from his mouth have become historic, if not immortal.

Sketch 9

Dear General—The first thing which occurs to me, as I take up my pen for this letter, might well have been brought in as a preface to all these "sketches." People ask me, not unfrequently, "Where did you first meet Mr. Lincoln?"

I hardly remember, exactly, when or how I first fell in with Mr. Lincoln, the prominent lawyer and leading politician. I was then conducting a couple of large country newspapers, in the eastern part of the judicial district in which his practice mostly lay,[1] and I recall a visit of his to my office, when he claimed that the printer's ink with which I was daubed justified him in calling me a "black Republican." He was attending to some political business then, for he was the undisputed leader of our party in Illinois.

My first sight of him as a lawyer was in a murder trial, when he was defending a man whom the evidence presented seemed to condemn beyond all hope. I had expected some grand and absorbing exhibition of oratorical power, intended to overwhelm the jury; but there was nothing of the kind, only an earnest and semi-conversational review of the evidence, dwelling upon points that at first seemed trivial, and I heard many murmurs in the crowd around me. The jury were plain Illinois farmers, but men of good sense, and it was evident that they perfectly understood his train of reasoning. Undoubtedly when he arose they would have declared the man guilty without leaving their box; but, after that quiet and practical talk with the great apostle of common sense, they put their heads together and rendered a verdict of "Not guilty."

If I remember rightly, circumstances afterwards came to light which fully justified the verdict and Mr. Lincoln's line of argument.[2]

My first view of Mr. Lincoln as the great man he really was happened in this wise. Some nine months before the meeting of the Chicago Republican Convention in 1860, my partner and I began to discuss the subject, "Whose name shall we hang out as our candidate?"³ It was still full early in the season, and we were in no hurry for a decision.

Early one morning, just after I had finished my breakfast, I strolled into the office of the hotel where I boarded, for a chat with some one before going to work. The room was empty when I entered, but in a moment the door opened and Mr. Lincoln came in. He seated himself quietly by the fire and took off his hat, which was packed full of letters just taken from the Post-Office. I was about to speak to him, as usual, when I was arrested by something thoughtful and abstracted in his manner, and, as I always had a "strong weakness" for taking observations of remarkable men, I kept my seat in silence. He opened letter after letter, burning some and glancing hastily over others, until he reached one somewhat longer than common, which seemed to affect him profoundly. He was evidently thinking, and thinking deeply; and so few men know by experience what genuine hard thinking is, that I fear that this will hardly convey my meaning.

Leaning forward, with his hands folded across his knee, he gazed abstractedly into the fire, his rugged face gradually lighting up with vivid and changing expressions until it was almost transfigured.

I felt, without knowing how or why, that the gaunt form before me was that of no ordinary man. I had seen, and, as it were, accidentally looked into (through his face) one of the great ones of history. Long as I knew him afterward, I never saw so much of him again.

Without disturbing him, I quietly stole from the room and hurried to my office.

"Doctor, I have made up my mind whom we are going to support for the next Presidency."

"Well, who is it?"

"Abraham Lincoln, of Illinois!"

"What! Old Abe? Nonsense!"

"No nonsense about it, I tell you. He is our man, for certain."

"Pshaw! every one likes him well enough, but we never could get him nominated. For Vice President now, and because we are Illinoisans—"

"Lincoln for President, Doctor, and nobody else. My mind is made up."

And as I generally had my own way, after a brief trip to Springfield to open communication with his friends and collect material for leaders, &c., the name of Abraham Lincoln blazed in broad letters at our editorial masthead.⁴ We were, so far as known, the first in the field, and it had an important result for me, of which, at that time, I never dreamed; it drew Mr. Lincoln's attention to me personally, and procured for me the opportunity I afterwards had, in his own household, of learning a still more profound reverence for the great man I had seen in the light of the fire that chilly prairie morning.

Just now another picture occurs to my mind, more apropos to "White House Sketches." Most people have seen Frank Carpenter's picture of "Lincoln reading the Emancipation Proclamation in Cabinet meeting," or they have seen what purports to be an engraving of it.[5] I was at the house much of the time while that picture was "a building of," and had thus good hopes of a great thing; but since it was finished I have only seen the engraving, and if that fairly represents the picture—well, I have no criticism to make just now, except the following note of what a Cabinet meeting really was.

When that half-dozen of overworked and anxious men did get together, it was not their habit, dignified as they were, and however important their business, to collect in studied stiffness around the table; but several times when I have been called in—to be sent for papers, &c.—I have seen one stretched on the sofa with a cigar his mouth, another with his heels on the table, another nursing his knee abstractedly, the President with his leg over the arm of his chair, and not a man of them all in any wise sitting for his picture.

Perhaps it would have been in violation of the canons of high art to have painted the thing as it really was—not being an artist, I cannot say about that. Carpenter has done an excellent thing in commemorating so great an occasion; but the engraving should be labeled, "Table, surrounded with gentlemen waiting to have their pictures taken." ("Landscape with Cattle," you know.)[6] I hope my good friend, the artist, will forgive me; of course he could not have given us the whole room on canvas, and had to "concentrate his subjects." I only want to say what a Cabinet meeting was as I remember it.

The conservatory was an important feature of the White House, and really contains a fine floral collection. It was always open to that portion of the public who might be presumed to be above stealing flowers, although really the class in good truth proof against floral temptation is somewhat mythical in my mind. After a while few were admitted without some sort of official or servile attendance. It was from this conservatory the flowers came which cut such a figure in newspaper descriptions of the "lavish profusion and extravagance at the Executive Mansion." Economy, as interpreted by some people, would have consisted in allowing the gorgeous exotics to wither on their stems, in the congenial warmth and moisture of the conservatory.

Mrs. Lincoln was fond of flowers, and distributed them around her reception rooms with excellent taste. Every morning, too, sundry bouquets were made up to gladden the senses of her suffering protégés in the several hospitals, and, as often as possible, the kind-hearted lady carried them herself.

Speaking of that "extravagance" business, there never was a more puerile humbug. Large expenditures were absolutely necessary, but all proper economy was always exercised. This remark is made under cover of a protest, that it is nobody's earthly business how the President spends his salary, or whether he chooses not to spend it.[7]

Mr. Lincoln himself was careless of money, rather than extravagant. He never could, under any circumstances, have made or kept a fortune, and I don't believe he ever sued a delinquent debtor in his life.[8] If he ever did so it was not because he cared for the money. Although his practice was always large and lucrative, and his habits simple, so indifferent was he to accumulation that he would have died a poor man but that some of his more prudent friends, Judge Davis of Illinois, for special instance, took the matter in hand and exercised a degree of care and foresight for him which he would never have taken for himself.[9]

If he could have been extravagant in anything, it would have been in horses, for he rode well and liked to be well mounted. Like most western men, he was a fair judge of horseflesh, and yet, so entirely was he absorbed by the cares of his office, that he hardly seemed aware of it when his carriage span became so thin, worn out, and badly groomed, that they were a general subject of remark in the city. By the way, they were a presentation pair, and about up to the showy and non-enduring average of that peculiar breed of horses.

The flowers above spoken of were not the only items which seemed to tempt the cupidity or memento-collecting visitors. All was fish which came to their net, from buttons deftly cloven off from Mrs. Lincoln's dress, or flowers from the vases, to strips rudely severed from the curtains or the carpet. Tassels, fringes and minor ornaments were perpetually disappearing. One relic-worshipping vandal, male or female, cut nearly two feet in length out of a nearly new silk window curtain. All the furniture, vases, &c., were of the heaviest description, or they would have doubtless been carried off piecemeal. It is no matter of wonder that, during the confusion which followed the murder of Mr. Lincoln, this sort of plunder was carried on by wholesale. The wonder, if any, is that the house itself was not split up and carried off for distribution among curious collections of similarly stolen property. The stealing was all done well and successfully.

And now, my dear General, I fear that I am stringing out these sketches unconscionably, and will bring them to a close, almost wishing that I was back in "Andrew Jackson's chair"—the queer, old leather-bottomed Mexican—with my heels on my table, listening once more to the sparring between you and the "boys" in the northeast room, where I lived so long, and saw and felt so many, many things.[10]

Sketch 10

My Dear General—While the ever varying throng which passed in and out of the doors of the White House furnished an almost unlimited field for the student of human nature, I think that the best point of observation was at the very moment of presentation to the President.

Among the daily applicants for an interview with Mr. Lincoln were representatives of every class and grade in the social scale, and from every corner of the vast domains of the Republic, and it would be hardly correct to say that he was less than perfectly "at home" with any and all of them. Even in conversation with men whose superior culture and information he frankly acknowledged, or for whose moral dignity or great achievements he professed the utmost respect, Mr. Lincoln was free from that embarrassment which at times is so painfully manifest in weaker men. Such entire self-possession is sometimes the consequence of overwhelming self-esteem, or an ever present consciousness of the possession of power, but with him it was the result of his utter absence of self-consciousness.[1] His thoughts rarely reverted to any effect or impression which he himself might be making, and he was, therefore, if not at all graceful, at least easy and natural.

He was a most teachable man, and asked questions with a childlike simplicity which would have been too much for the false pride of many a man far less well informed. His fund of knowledge was, as he himself declared, very largely made up of information obtained in conversation, and if not so well arranged and digested as if it had been the accumulation of careful study and exact research, it included a vast amount of valuable matter hardly to be found in books. I may have occasion hereafter to instance the manner in which some such information, and the resulting ideas, was brought into play, not only in his law practice, but in the public service. His early education had not so disciplined his mind as to render hard study, mere book work, either easy or agreeable to him, and his reading was laborious and by no means rapid. It was his custom and preference to have all matter which was brought before him for consideration thoroughly digested and reduced to the smallest practicable space beforehand; and when facts and ideas were thus presented, he was able to grasp them rapidly, and his mind followed out all collateral lines of argument or suggestion with an acuteness and comprehension which rendered elaboration useless, and made him at once the master of the situation. He needed fewer "explanations" than any other man I ever knew.

He was a curious student of what Dean Trench calls "the power of words," and used them for no other purpose than to express his meaning. Herein is the secret of the otherwise inexplicable success of his several notable public declarations, single sentences of which have become, and will continue to be, household words and fireside proverbs not only in this country, but wherever the English language is spoken. There were not in those days many ladies among the applicants at the White House. Perhaps two or three a day would be a very liberal average. I think over rather than under the mark. His manner with the softer sex was kindly and courteous, and he had a great deal of that chivalrous deference for women which is the invariable characteristic of a strong and manly nature, but here his disposition to yield special privileges terminated. In his eyes, a lady who called upon him in the prosecution of business, public or private, was simply "a lady on business," and she was little, if anything, more. Indeed, it seemed an unpleasant and irksome thing to him to have a lady present a petition for any favor when the same duty could as well have been performed by a man; and if there was anything contrary to propriety or policy in the matter presented, or if the petitioner presumed upon her feminine prerogative to press too far upon his good-nature, she was very likely to receive an answer in which there was far more of truth and justice than flattery. To this fact he is probably indebted for a certain degree of freedom from a class of pertinacious and troublesome visitors, to whose undesirable attentions any public man at Washington is liable to be exposed.[2]

It may not be generally known, but the fact is that what may be termed "female influence" is by no means an unemployed agency in political circles at the National Capital; and it is applied in such manner and of such a character as the nature of each case and subject may seem to demand.

The race of pardon brokers and office procuresses existed before this present time, and, although it sent few representatives to the White House, it was sufficiently well known, and at times intolerably troublesome in other quarters, as many a too modest or too gallant public functionary can testify. It is not my business to talk scandal in these sketches, nor would it be a pleasant job to make pen portraits of some "ladies" whose faces were as well known in political circles as the statue of Andrew Jackson. It was considered what is called a "good sell" to see some well known gentleman, from North or South, it might be with stars on his shoulders, convoying to the galleries of the House or Senate, or attending in the boxes of the theatre, the fair but too celebrated heroines whose fortunate acquaintance he had made at his hotel.

Among the female visitors who did come there were from time to time certain exceptional cases to whom Mr. Lincoln never failed to extend cordial welcome, prompt attention and the kindest and most respectful sympathy. A few of them—few because that noble class of our country women rarely required any favor from the Chief Magistrate and had better work on hand than making visits of curiosity or ceremony—were of those ministering angels who went to and fro among our camps and hospitals, carrying blessings in their benevolent faces to our suffering soldier boys. To such women Mr. Lincoln's whole heart opened at once, come when and why they would.

Others there were, sorrowing and broken hearted mothers, wives, or sisters, of suffering or erring men in the army. One would want a pass to visit a wounded man in such or such a portion of the great field of action, or a permission to remove some poor fellow to his home, "so that she might take care of him." Another would beg for the discharge of her soldier, urging often the most purely feminine reasons, but sometimes with arguments which appealed at once to the tenderest feelings of the good President.

Others again, and these were the saddest of all, came in behalf of those whose crimes or errors had brought them into the terrible grasp of martial law. It was mournfully hard at times for these poor creatures to comprehend how that which would have been but a venial peccadillo at home, should be a capital crime in the army.

"Oh, sir, he only fell asleep when he was on guard—that was all—and he must have been very tired, marching all day! Surely you will not let them punish him for a little thing like that?"

"But," said the President, "suppose that in consequence of his neglect the army was surprised, and hundreds or thousands of men killed, don't you think that the wives of those men would say he had been guilty of something of an offence?"

"Oh, but Mr. Lincoln you can't punish him just for falling asleep when he was tired!"

And I believe that the poor woman was very nearly right. I don't believe he could do it, either—at least the cases were so rare in which he did allow the execution of the full sentence of the court in such cases that no little grumbling was occasioned in military circles.

"Oh, sir," pleaded another poor creature, "he did'nt desert, indeed he did'nt! He only wanted to come home for a while to see his wife and children—that was all, sir!"

"But, don't you think the other boys wanted to make a little trip home, too! And where would the army be then?"

I do not think that these petitioners gained their cases much quicker simply because they were women, but they had less trouble in securing an audience, and Mr. Lincoln was always glad enough to find a good reason for the exercise of the pardoning power. The only men whom he seemed to have very little sympathy for were the spies, and such deserters from our ranks as were afterwards taken with arms in their hands fighting their old comrades. Such men got their hanging, or whatever it was, with very little interference on the part of the President, as a general thing.[3]

For my own part, if I had wanted an agent to procure anything like a pardon from Mr. Lincoln, I should have unhesitatingly sent a child rather than a grown woman of any kind. Anything like helplessness appealed to him strongly, and he was very fond of children at all times.[4]

To such an extent did he carry his indulgence for little "Tad," who, by the way, was a very intelligent and affectionate boy, that he allowed him free access to his business office at all hours and under almost any circumstances; and I well remember the dignified expression of disapprobation with which a testy old Senator declared his opinion that "that boy was becoming decidedly more numerous than popular."

Tad had the same weakness for unlucky brutes which his father had for unfortunate men, and always had under his protection one or more ill-conditioned curs of low degree, famished appearance and unimaginable extraction. Somehow they never stayed long, and I do not know whether or not they fattened as well as others at the "public crib."

Nor were there wanting biped petitioners who were quick to seize upon what seemed so vulnerable a point as Mr. Lincoln's affection for his boy, and attempt to bring themselves to the favorable notice of the all powerful President by the assiduity with which they cultivated his little pet. Of course they succeeded with Tad, for a boy's heart is easily fished for, and there were a few of the earlier approaches on this line which were tolerably successful; but only a very few found their way to his knee or table before Mr. Lincoln saw the point, and "Tad's clients" became more a matter for joke than anything else. Otherwise, as a general rule, it was not apt to be to any man's advantage to have his case pressed by a member of the President's family.

In every family, in private or public life, there is of necessity a "kitchen cabinet," but the dimensions of that institution during Mr. Lincoln's administration, were far less formidable, and meddled with a line of subjects more appropriate to its own sphere than is recorded of some others.

I do not know that any one else has recorded the anecdote of the good widow woman from Michigan, who was unable to meet a mortgage of a few hundred dollars on her little home, and determined to get it from the President. In her simple mind she had no doubt of his boundless wealth, or that when once he heard her story he would pay off the mortgage. So she raised some money among her neighbors by subscription, and started for Washington, traveling by all sorts of conveyances, and of course taking the longest road, and bringing her four little children with her. How she did it is a mystery only to be solved by Him who feeds the young ravens, but she actually reached the capital with more money than when she started, and fell into kind and charitable hands when she got there. Of course she saw Mr. Lincoln, and he listened to her story and read her letters with a half humorous, half vexed expression that was irresistible.

He did not say much, only muttering "children and fools, you know," but put his name on a subscription paper for a moderate sum. The subscription so started rapidly swelled to the desired amount, and the poor woman was ticketed homeward over the Government routes, puzzled and yet satisfied. She had spent more money, going and coming, than the whole of her debt twice over. Such is wisdom.

Sketch 11

My Dear General—So much has been said about Mr. Lincoln's theatre going that a great many people have imbibed the idea that his tastes
were dramatic; but this was not so. With the exception of a few of Shakespeare's plays, I do not believe that he ever read a play in his life.

I have heard him say that there were several of even Shakespeare's
dramas at which he had hardly ever looked. "Macbeth" was certainly one of
his prime favorites, and I went with him one night to see Charlotte Cushman
as Lady Macbeth.[1] It was of course a grand impersonation, but it was impossible to get Mr. Lincoln to make many comments upon it. He seemed to
have a poor opinion of his own powers as a dramatic critic.

Another of his favorites was "Othello," and he eagerly embraced the opportunity of seeing it when Davenport and Wallack brought it out in Washington.[2] I was very much struck with the keen interest with which he followed the development of Iago's subtle treachery. One would have thought
that such a character would have had few points of attraction for a man to
whose own nature all its peculiar traits were so utterly foreign. Perhaps he
was fascinated by that very contrast.

He did not lose a word or a motion of Mr. Davenport, who played his part
exceedingly well, and conversed between the acts with, for him, a very near
approach to excitement. He seemed to be studying what sort of soul a born
traitor might have.

His strong love of humor made Falstaff a great favorite with him, and he
expressed a great desire to see Hackett in that character.[3] The correspondence between that gentleman and Mr. Lincoln has been already published.[4] He expressed himself greatly pleased with the representation, and
went more than once during Hackett's engagement. I was with him the first
night, and expected to see him give himself up to the merriment of the hour,

although I knew that his mind was very much preoccupied by other things. To my surprise, however, he appeared even gloomy, although intent upon the play, and it was only a few times during the whole performance that he went so far as to laugh at all, and then not heartily. He seemed for once to be studying the character and its rendering critically, as if to ascertain the correctness of his own conception as compared with that of the professional artist.

He afterwards received a call from Mr. Hackett, and conversed freely, frankly acknowledging his want of acquaintance with dramatic subjects.

Had his earlier education been of a sort to develope [*sic*] more perfectly his literary tastes, his keen insight into human nature, and his appreciation of humorous and other eccentricities of character, would have enabled him to have derived the highest degree of enjoyment from the creations of the great masters. As it was, he probably understood Shakespeare, so far as he had read him, far better than many men who set themselves up for critical authorities. He himself deserves to be depicted by some pen not less graphic than the immortal bard's.

When Mr. Lincoln first came to Washington, as President, there was very little in the way of public amusement to call out him or anybody else, and for a long time he worked away steadily in his official treadmill, hardly caring for or thinking of any such thing as recreation. To such an extent was his absorbed devotion to business carried that the perpetual strain upon his nervous system, with the utter want of all exercise, began to tell seriously upon his health and spirits, and occasioned some alarm among his friends. Mrs. Lincoln particularly remarked frequently upon his gradually changing appearance. Even his temper suffered, and a petulance entirely foreign to his natural disposition was beginning to show itself as a symptom of an overtasked brain.

Gradually, however, under the auspices of new managers of experience and enterprise, the crowded and excited capital was endowed with several highly meritorious places of amusement, theatrical and musical. A good degree of healthy sociability was restored to the various social circles of the city. The very levees at the White House became more brilliant, more conversational, and less insufferably tedious. All other faces put on a more cheerful aspect, and, though Mr. Lincoln never, to the day of his death, entirely recovered the old elasticity of his spirits, he seemed to feel in some degree the general reaction, and was willing to listen to the various plans suggested for relaxation and amusement.

He never could be persuaded to travel any distance from the scene of his immediate duties—never out of close communication with the army,—but readily consented to spend his summers at the Soldier's Home, and was easily drawn into many little excursions down the Potomac, which were planned from time to time for his recreation. He was somewhat fond of attending military reviews, and these always included a good ride on horseback or in his carriage.

His most available resource, however, as least interfering with his official duties, was to spend an hour or so at the theatre or the concert. Perhaps, too, the drama, by drawing his mind into other channels of thought, afforded him the most entire relief, and the most rigid enemy of theatrical representations could hardly have grudged him what was to him at least so harmless and innocent a medicine.

The proprietors of Grover's Theatre fitted up a handsome and commodious box for his especial use, and there was always a similar accommodation ready for him at Ford's. The latter, alas, is destined to a mournful immortality in connection with the last sad tragedy of his career. It matters little, however, where or when the malignity of the assassin succeeded in reaching his victim, whether working or resting, though it is clear enough that the half insane vanity of Booth found a species of barbarian pleasure in the dramatic surroundings of his cowardly deed.

Just here I may as well record an anecdote which furnishes an all sufficient answer to more than one sneering libel upon some of the circumstances attending so sad an event. One of the excellent ladies who gave their sympathizing attention to Mrs. Lincoln at the time of the murder, and who has frequently expressed admiration of her conduct happened to be in company where some individual, whose narrow and bitter soul was unaffected even by such an event, had indulged in strictures as untrue as they were uncalled for, and answered about in these words:

"Suppose, madam, that you were at such a place of amusement, in company with a husband whom you tenderly loved, in the enjoyment of all that earth can give of prosperity and happiness—in the very hour of triumphant success, after long continued sorrow and trouble,—utterly unsuspicious of any coming misfortune, and in one terrible moment found your hopes and your prosperity all crushed, yourself a widow, your very dress sprinkled with the blood and brains of your husband, murdered at your side; if you could preserve your equanimity unruffled and your nerves unshattered, you would be more or less than a woman, and I should say less."

That is the whole story, and the whole argument, and does not require any elaboration.

It was not my fortune to be in Washington at the time Mr. Lincoln was murdered. I learned the terrible story from the booming minute guns away in the Southwest; and it was not until after my return to the North that I ever found a man or woman mean and hard enough to speak lightly of that event or its surroundings. There are such creatures at the South, but in those days they were silent, and all the worth and wisdom of that region joined the loyal men in unaffected regret.

Sketch 12

My Dear General—Everybody knows how strong were Mr. Lincoln's personal attachments, but it was somewhat peculiar how generally his interest in any individual extended itself to all his kith and kin. It was almost enough to have seen or heard of one of his old associates to secure a pleasant greeting, at least, at his hands.

I remember once having a personal report to make about a certain General officer, who had, I was persuaded, been sadly slandered, and whose brother was an active war-Democratic politician at the North, and rather a favorite with Mr. Lincoln. Before he would give me a chance to open my budget, he interrupted me with,

"Well, first, Stoddard, what do you think of Fred. [Steele]? I want to know that first."

"Mr. President, General [Steele] is an honest man, you may rely upon it."

"I am delighted to hear you say so. I rather thought he was, and was afraid they would make out something against him. You see, I don't know him, never saw him in my life; but I like his brother here first-rate. He is one of the best men, for a Democrat, we've got. I like him, and should have been very sorry to hear anything bad of his brother. Go on now, let's hear all about it."[1]

Fortunately I was able to make my position pretty clear by the time I got through, and was promptly ordered to the War Office to tell my story. Before I had completed it, a thing happened which I will put on record here as giving a glimpse of the real character of our great War Secretary.

I was sitting by Mr. Stanton in his private office, when a messenger from the telegraph room brought in a war-telegram and handed it to the Secretary. He read it through and gave it to me, saying:

"What do you think of that, Mr. Stoddard?"

I read it hastily. It was General Sheridan's announcement of his first great victory over Early in the Valley, for this was in September, 1864.[2] As I returned the paper, Mr. Stanton said, in a somewhat excited voice:

"This is the turning point, sir; the turning point!" And, jumping up, rushed out into the crowded ante-room and hall, shouting the news with all the enthusiasm of a newsboy. I never thought before that the somewhat grim and silent War Minister was capable of such an escapade.

He gave me back the telegram in a moment, saying:

"Take that to His Excellency! That's news enough for one day. No more work after that."

And sure enough, there was but little attention paid to routine duty that afternoon, and a part, at least, of the official population of Washington, was as badly demoralized as Early's army, before the celebration was over. Somehow, it was pretty generally felt, without much calculation on the subject, that the victory in the Valley was a sort of sure earnest of better things to come. Nor was the idea an erroneous one; for once our instincts did not deceive us as to the value of our war news.

Mr. Lincoln's attachment to Mr. Stanton arose less from any merely personal feeling, than from a thorough conviction of his patriotism and business efficiency. Great efforts were persistently made to unseat Mr. Stanton from his place in Mr. Lincoln's good opinion; nor were these efforts confined at all times to fair argument, or even to political pressure. Darker accusations than any lack of ability were by no means uncommon; but the President remained to the last firm in support of his unpopular assistant. His reply to a gentleman who was very temperately urging the substitution of General Banks,[3] was somewhat after this fashion:

"General Banks is doubtless a very able man, and a very good man for the place, perhaps; but how do I know that he will do any better than Stanton? You see, I know what Stanton has done, and think he has done pretty well, all things considered. There are not many men who are fit for Stanton's place. I guess we may as well not trade until we know we are making a good bargain."

As time went on, however, the daily habit of sympathizing co-labor and mutual counsel seemed to have built up a really strong personal friendship between the President and the Secretary, stronger than at first seemed at all probable.

It is worthy of remark that the group of men around whose names the great events of the past five years will be clustered in the history of these times, were, almost without exception, singularly undemonstrative in manner, though for the most part of warm and genial natures.

They were men of plain though striking exterior, barely sufficiently careful about matters of dress, not in the least prone to display, and to the last degree chary of expressing publicly any emotion aroused by the circumstances of the hour. Whether they met to repair the injuries of defeat, or to grasp more strongly the consequences of success, they were the same grave and self-respecting gentlemen.

America need be in no manner ashamed of her leaders, either for their ability or their unspotted private character.

Whatever may be set down concerning them by contemporary prejudice or partisan malice, the verdict of the future must be that Mr. Lincoln and his immediate supporters, including his Cabinet, leading generals, heads of departments, the foremost men in Congress, and the patriotic Northern Governors, presented an array of strength, wisdom and executive ability, rarely to be found in the history of any country or any era. They were strong men, made strong for a great work.

It is curiously illustrative of the "practical" turn of the American character, that almost the whole nation was ready to take advantage of the opportunities offered by the times, for what is so well expressed by the word "speculation." Not altogether in a trading or avaricious spirit, but seemingly as much for excitement as for anything else, the very men who were willing to give their all, and themselves with it, to secure the success of the cause, were ready to move heaven and earth to get hold of a paying contract, or a hint for a stock transaction.[4]

I have seen men jubilant over the award of a contract which involved an almost dead certainty of pecuniary loss, and gambling madly on the result of military operations in which their dearest hopes and most cherished convictions were at stake. We used to say that "everybody gambled except the President." This was a little too strong, for it is a matter of honorable record that most of our public men are comparatively poor, although numberless opportunities for questionable gain have been long within their reach. Corruption exists, no doubt; but it does not seem to find its way into the upper stories of American statesmanship. After all [is] said and done, our politicians are better and purer men than the opposing journals of either party are in the habit of painting them.

While Mr. Lincoln was careless of moneymaking himself, he nevertheless, true to his Western training, could see no harm in a good "speculation," provided it was an honest one, and not at the expense of the country. From time to time he was badgered for assistance in this direction by some of his old friends and acquaintances; but, with few exceptions, very little was obtained from him.

The prevailing rage was for "cotton permits," and I believe the President is responsible for a few of those queer affairs, given before the business of collecting cotton was reduced to a system, and the "cotton-thieves," as they were not inaptly called, became salaried officers of Government. He afterwards expressed his regret that he had ever meddled with it, at the same time that he admitted the force of the arguments on the cotton side of the question. There were, of course, two sides, and both sustained by plausible arguments, effective accordingly as you viewed the subject from a military or a commercial point of view. Of all questions which could be presented, however, a financial one was the least suited to Mr. Lincoln's turn of mind. Contracts, as such, he never meddled with, except so far as ordering the purchase of a few indescribable new guns which seemed to him worthy [of] a trial in the army.

Next to cotton, gold was the great speculative agency, and more than one gallant soldier, as well as patriotic civilian, watched the ups and downs of the Wall street fever with anxious eyes, glorying in his luck or cursing his "burnt fingers," according as he hit it right or not. In all times of great excitement people search for or create additional stimulus for the mind as well as the body, and it may be a sort of sanitary precaution, harmless if not beneficial, to administer it in reasonable doses.

The correctness of my view of the nature of this speculation may perhaps be gathered from the fact that a man's political status could generally be gathered with fair correctness by ascertaining whether he was a gold "bull" or "bear." If a loyal man operated for a rise he was not apt to say much about it, and when, in 1863, gold took its great tumble, the "lame ducks" on the street were almost exclusively secessionists, Jews and Englishmen, while the Union men were almost universally on the winning side. It was vice versa a while afterwards.

Speaking of Mr. Lincoln and his guns puts me in mind of the balloon men. Mr. Lincoln himself had for years been decidedly interested in the science of aerostation (is that the right word?), and I have a suspicion that at some time or other he had meddled with it practically in a small way. When the army began to employ balloons for military reconnoissances, a host of ingenious fellows all over the country turned their attention to the art of aerial navigation, and, as a matter of course, every man of them was sure that he had the right machine, if he could only get [the] Government to build one of sufficient size to prove it.

It would, indeed, have required a big balloon to have proved the value of some of the inventions whose "drawings and specifications," often accompanied by a small and rude model, from time to time cumbered my table. A good share of these inventors began by a modest request for a few hundred dollars to bring them to Washington. One fellow proposed an iron-clad balloon to carry heavy guns. He succeeded in raising a good laugh, if nothing else.

The most pertinacious of all was a chap who rigged up a sort of wooden model in the basement of the White House—an upright stick with a long arm on a pivot, to which his air-boat was attached. His clockwork and propeller did certainly work until it ran down, and Mr. Lincoln spent an odd hour or so in examining the arrangement. I believe that he voted it "curious but not useful."

Sketch 13

My Dear General—Although I am well aware that in your late gallantly contested and triumphantly successful struggle with the powerful organizations opposed to you, you were actuated by better motives than the mere itch for office, or even a laudable desire to win for the winning's sake, yet somehow the late struggle has brought back the old office-seeking and office-giving times at Washington more vividly than they have been brought to my memory for many a day.[1]

I did not myself know when I went to Washington, although I had some idea, of course, just in what capacity I was to be employed; but went because Mr. Lincoln sent for me, glad enough to exchange the treadmill life of a newspaper editor in a Western village for the keen excitement promised me by a life in Washington. It has always been my understanding that the President had given comparatively few promises or pledges, all of which he more than redeemed in due time, and I was quite unprepared for the Egyptian locust swarm which crowded every hotel and boardinghouse, before the inauguration was fairly *un fait accomplit.*

From that time forward, for two years, the stream poured on with [a] steady flow, diminishing after the first few months only from a freshet into a well sustained river.

There was a reason for this in the fact that the tremendous convulsion caused by the war in all industrial occupations had thrown so large a number of effective men out of their customary avocations; but there was little or no reason in most of the applicants themselves. I do not know whether you or any other of the lately elected have or have not many offices to give away—my impression is that you have not—but in either case "I feel to pity you." Where there were offices everybody seemed to want the same one—the best one, of course—and where there were none, the President was expected to make them, by some inscrutable necromancy supposed to be inherent in his high prerogative. The circumstances of the case helped him somewhat, though many a man found himself, somehow, in the field, who would much rather have settled down to salaried fatness in Washington or at home.

And such a swarm! Mingled with men of worth, energy, efficiency and highly meritorious political services, were the broken-down, used-up, bankrupt, creditless, worthless, the lame, the halt and the blind, from all the highways and byways of the North.

To judge by the claims set forth, there were a thousand men at least upon whose individual labors and prowess had turned the fate of that eventful canvass.

Men there were who had never been known to pay an honest debt in their lives, but who, nevertheless, "expended their entire fortunes to secure Mr. Lincoln's election," and who deemed it only fair that their immense expenditures should somehow be reimbursed from the overflowing coffers of Uncle Sam.

This was a style of argument so foreign to all Mr. Lincoln's habits of thought, that it rarely seemed to make much impression upon him. It was hard indeed for him to estimate very highly such a thing as pecuniary outlay. I have little doubt, however, that if the after course of such of these gentlemen as were successful could be traced accurately, it would be found that in most cases they had at least repaid themselves. Is not the laborer worthy of his hire? At least, does he not generally think so?

Somehow an incident occurs to my mind which at the time occasioned no little merriment. An appointment to the Naval School or to West Point was a thing eagerly sought after, and a "vacancy" was a sort of godsend to the White House records at any time, as affording an opportunity to gratify one more of the countless clamorous applicants, who would not believe that "everything was filled." There were always enough "promises" out in advance to render a visit of the cholera to either of these institutions comparatively in[n]ocuous, so far as keeping their numbers up was concerned. I do not say this scoffingly, for we had and have only too few thoroughly educated men in either branch of the service, and those "graduates" who are scattered among the people at large are doing no manner of discredit to themselves or the country.

Well, in the course of human events an item got into the newspapers foreboding some objectionable change of regulations at the Naval Academy—I have forgotten what; it might have been a decrease in the number of beans in their soup, or it might have been a proposed appointment of colored cadets, but nothing of any vital importance. At all events, the pride of the youngsters took fire, and they held a meeting somewhere—it may be in the cockpit (is there such a place?) of the practice ship, and solemnly voted it down unanimously. They seem to have chosen one of their number, by lot or otherwise, to bell the Presidential cat, and straightway there appeared at my desk one morning a solemn document, elaborately got up and tolerably correctly spelled, detailing the views of the entire crew of Admirals *in petto*, and announcing that, unless the plan disapproved of was at once abandoned, they would—they would, indeed—one and all resign!

What would, in that case, become of the American Navy, was a question which their desperate indignation cast aside with reckless indifference.

By good rights of red tape the precious epistle should have been forwarded to the Navy Department; but, after a hearty laugh over its contents, the President directed it to be protected by fire from the disciplinary eyes of senior officers. Nothing more came of it; but some day when these unfledged Farraguts and Porters are old enough to make fun of it themselves, they may join in Mr. Lincoln's almost uproarious merriment over their "Indignation Meeting."

There were, on an average, about fifty strongly backed and apparently meritorious applicants for each and every one of the President's appointments at West Point. Of those less prominent the number was positively out of all possibility of estimate. No mail failed to bring several of them. The Navy hardly seemed to be as popular.

Somebody has sent me, clipped from some miserable sheet or other, a resuscitation of the often-refuted slander as to Mr. Lincoln's personal temperance—not that I intend to stultify myself by seeming to fear that any sensible man believes it, but it puts me in mind of the liberal-souled gentlemen who at different times forwarded cases of choice liquors to the White House "for the President's own use." Some of the specimens were, indeed, excellent in their way, and ought to have secured offices in the Custom House or Revenue Department for the men who sent them. I know that if Mr. Lincoln did not feel grateful there were others who did, and no small allowance found its way into the stores of the Washington hospitals.

At the table, when his attention was especially called to some rare wine, I have seen Mr. Lincoln barely touch his lips to his glass, "just to see what it was," but there was no perceptible diminution of its contents. I never once saw him drink a glass of any such thing. He may at some time have done so, for he was not a bigot in anything, but if he did I did not happen to know of it.

Among the many presents sent by various admirers, I remember several good lots of turkeys—wonderful birds, all the way from some distant State, and which did not all arrive in cookable condition—beef, apples, pumpkins, potatoes, game, slippers, bookmarks, neckties, photographs (with a request for an exchange), and an endless medley of queer contrivances, whose exact purpose was not exactly so clear.

Mr. Lincoln was quite fond of fruit, and presents of choice varieties were by no means unfrequent. I remember a peculiarly luscious-looking basket of pears, on the strength of which we boys formed a sort of procession into the Executive Chamber one afternoon, and managed to get business suspended while a circle of distinguished gentlemen gathered round the fire and discussed the last slice, amid an amount of fun and anecdotes which at that time was becoming only too rare in that sombre apartment. It is sad enough to know that I shall never hear him laugh again.

Notes

Editor's Introduction

1. William O. Stoddard, *Abraham Lincoln: The True Story of a Great Life* (New York: Fords, Howard, & Hulbert, 1884). John G. Nicolay and John Hay, *Abraham Lincoln: A History*, 10 vols. (New York: Century, 1890). Stoddard wrote other books about Lincoln as well, including *Abraham Lincoln and Andrew Johnson* (New York: F. A. Stokes, 1888); *The Boy Lincoln* (New York: D. Appleton, 1905); *The Table Talk of Abraham Lincoln* (New York: F. A. Stokes, 1894); and *Lincoln at Work: Sketches from Life* (Boston: United Society of Christian Endeavor, 1900). Part 1 of this book was published as *Inside the White House in War Times* (New York: Charles L. Webster & Co., 1890).

Also unlike Nicolay and Hay, Stoddard left few personal papers of which the whereabouts are known. The firm of Walter R. Benjamin, Autographs, offered some Stoddard papers for sale in 1967, but company records do not indicate who bought them or what they consisted of. *The Collector: A Magazine for Autograph and Historical Collectors* 80 (1967): 1. The Detroit Public Library owns the manuscript version of Stoddard's autobiography, referred to here as "Memoirs," and a handful of documents, including a letter by his son that states that Stoddard's papers "were lost or stolen during his sickness when Marshal of Arkansas." William O. Stoddard Jr. to David C. Mearns, 16 April 1954, copy.

2. In his introduction to *Dear Mr. Lincoln: Letters to the President* (Reading MA: Addison-Wesley, 1993), the editor, Harold Holzer, discusses at length the way in which the White House staff, including Stoddard, handled Lincoln's correspondence. Holzer fails to mention Stoddard's "White House Sketches," however, which contain much information on the subject. David Rankin Barbee, a journalist with a voracious appetite for original research, was one of the few writers on Lincoln to have used Stoddard's "Sketches."

3. Nicolay to Paul Selby, Washington, 11 March 1895, draft, Nicolay Papers, Manuscript Division, Library of Congress.

4. Don E. Fehrenbacher and Virginia Fehrenbacher, eds., *Recollected Words of Abraham Lincoln* (Stanford: Stanford University Press, 1996), 425, 427.

5. Mark E. Neely Jr., *The Abraham Lincoln Encyclopedia* (New York: McGraw-Hill, 1982), 291.

6. Reminiscences of William O. Stoddard Jr., quoted in Edgar DeWitt Jones, "Lincoln's Other Secretary and His Son," typescript, p. 3, Edgar DeWitt Jones Papers, Detroit Public Library. Stoddard was born in the town of Homer. Among the works of juvenile fiction he wrote dealing with Indians are *The Red Patriot: A Story of the American Revolution* (1897), *The Talking Leaves: An Indian Story* (1905), *On the Old Frontier, or, The Last Raid of the Iroquois* (1894), and *Two Arrows: A Story of Red and White* (1897).

7. Information on Stoddard's early years can be found in his manuscript memoirs, Detroit Public Library, and in *The National Cyclopaedia of American Biography*, 8:212. Though he did not spend his senior year on campus, Stoddard was allowed to graduate with his class in 1857.

8. William O. Stoddard Jr., ed., *Lincoln's Third Secretary: The Memoirs of William O. Stoddard* (New York: Exposition Press, 1955), 45; William O. Stoddard Jr., ed., "A Journalist Sees Lincoln," *Atlantic Monthly* 135 (Feb. 1925): 171. In the late 1860s, Scroggs (1817–74) served in the Illinois state legislature and as a trustee of the University of Illinois. Douglas L. Wilson and Rodney O. Davis, eds., *Herndon's Informants: Letters, Interviews, and Statements about Abraham Lincoln* (Urbana: University of Illinois Press, 1998), 770.

9. Stoddard, *Lincoln's Third Secretary*, 46, 193; Stoddard to Martin B. Anderson, Washington, 21 September 1861, Martin B. Anderson Papers, Rush Rhees Library, University of Rochester, Rochester NY.

10. Stoddard, *Lincoln's Third Secretary*, 47. Stoddard's name appears as coeditor for the first time on 18 August 1858.

11. Stoddard to Martin B. Anderson, West Urbana, 26 December 1858, Anderson Papers.

12. John W. Scroggs to William H. Herndon, Champaign IL., 3 October 1866, *Herndon's Informants*, 365.

13. *Central Illinois Gazette*, 4 May 1859.

14. Stoddard, "A Journalist Sees Lincoln," 172.

15. Stoddard to Mrs. J. B. Van Cleave, Madison NJ, 10 March 1909, enclosed in Oliver R. Barrett to Albert J. Beveridge, Chicago, 7 July 1926, Beveridge Papers, Manuscript Division, Library of Congress.

16. *Central Illinois Gazette*, 7 December 1859.

17. See "I Nominate Lincoln," in Stoddard, *Lincoln's Third Secretary*, 55–63; William Baringer, *Lincoln's Rise to Power* (Boston: Little, Brown, 1937), 48–89.

18. John W. Scroggs to William H. Herndon, Champaign IL., 3 October 1866, *Herndon's Informants*, 365.

19. Stoddard, *Lincoln's Third Secretary*, 62–63.

20. Stoddard, *Lincoln's Third Secretary*, 64–65.

21. Stoddard to Herndon, Champaign IL, 27 December 1860, Lincoln Papers, Manuscript Division, Library of Congress. Stoddard erred in his memoirs when he contended that Lincoln wrote him in early December, saying: "Close up your affairs and go to Washington and wait for me." Stoddard, *Lincoln's Third Secretary*, 65–66.

22. Stoddard to Trumbull, Champaign IL, 27 December 1860, Trumbull Papers, Manuscript Division, Library of Congress.

23. Stoddard, "Memoirs" (typescript), 2:332, Stoddard Papers, Detroit Public Library.

24. Donald W. Riddle, *Lincoln Runs for Congress* (New Brunswick NJ: Rutgers University Press, 1948), 81–90; James to Lincoln, Chicago, 27 September 1860, Lincoln Papers.

25. Henry C. Whitney to William H. Herndon, 23 June 1887, *Herndon's Informants*, 619.

26. Stoddard, "Memoirs," 2:429.

27. Stoddard, *Lincoln's Third Secretary*, 66–71. A photographic reproduction of his commission, dated 17 July 1861, can be found in *Lincoln's Third Secretary*, facing p. 74. His appointment was announced in the *Central Illinois Gazette* on 10 April.

28. Washington correspondence, 25 February 1861, *Central Illinois Gazette*, 6 March 1861. In this dispatch, Stoddard was especially critical of Norman B. Judd. See also Stoddard to Martin B. Anderson, Washington, 28 February 1861, *Catherine Barnes: Autographs & Signed Books, Catalogue 14* (1994), 15–16.

29. William O. Stoddard Jr., ed., "Face to Face with Lincoln," *Atlantic Monthly* 135 (Mar. 1925): 332.

30. Stoddard, *Lincoln's Third Secretary*, 76–77.

31. Nicolay to Paul Selby, Washington, 11 March 1895, draft, Nicolay Papers.

32. William O. Stoddard Jr. to William E. Barton, Detroit, 15 February 1930, Barton Papers, Regenstein Library, University of Chicago.

33. Stoddard to George P. Hambrecht, Madison NJ, 5 August 1921, copy, Lincoln Collection, Chicago Historical Society. Cf. Stoddard, *Lincoln's Third Secretary*, 196–97, and Stoddard, *Inside the White House in War Times*, 124–25.

34. Stoddard, "Memoirs," 1:307. In August 1861, Nicolay reported to his fiancée: "John Hay met me in New York. He himself has also been sick and was compelled to leave. He is going to Illinois to stay three or four weeks." Nicolay to Therena Bates, Washington, 31 August 1861, Nicolay Papers.

35. Stoddard, "Memoirs," 1:313. Stoddard replaced Nicolay, as Nicolay had replaced Hay during Hay's illness.

36. Hay to Nicolay, Washington, 25 September 1863, Hay Papers, John Hay Library, Brown University.

37. Hay to Nicolay, Washington, 7 August 1863, Hay Papers, Brown University.

38. Hay to Nicolay, Warsaw IL, 26 August 1864, Hay Papers.

39. Hay to Nicolay, Washington, 11 September 1863, Hay Papers.

40. Stoddard, "Memoirs," 2:364.

41. Stoddard, "Memoirs," 1:307.

42. Nicolay to Paul Selby Washington, 11 March 1895, draft, Nicolay Papers.

43. Stoddard to Hay, New York, 12 February 1885, Hay Papers.

44. Ida M. Tarbell, *All in the Day's Work: An Autobiography* (New York: Macmillan, 1939), 161–63.

45. Stoddard to Hay, New York, 25 March 1885, Hay Papers.

46. In 1955, Stoddard's son published *Lincoln's Third Secretary: The Memoirs of William O. Stoddard*, which contains some of the material in his father's two-volume, typed autobiography, "Memoirs."

47. Stoddard, "Memoirs," 2:411.

48. Stoddard, *Lincoln's Third Secretary*, 216.

49. Stoddard to his son-in-law, Harold S. Butterheim, Madison NJ, 22 February 1907, quoted in Jones, "Lincoln's Other Secretary and His Son," 9, Jones Papers.

50. Stoddard, "Memoirs," 2:331.

51. Caleb Lyon (1822–75) represented a New York district in the U.S. House of Representatives between 1853 and 1855 and served as governor of Idaho Territory between 1864 and 1865. Daniel E. Sickles (1819–1914) was a New York politician who served as a general in the Civil War. George Wilkes (1817–85) edited a New York newspaper, *The Spirit of the Times*.

52. Stoddard, "Memoirs," 2:346–48, 366.

53. Stoddard to Nicolay, Madison NJ, 17 December 1898, Nicolay Papers.

54. Stoddard to the Reverend Dr. J. M. Spencer, [1911?], quoted in Arthur J. Brinton, "Nation Called upon To Honor Mrs. Abraham Lincoln," undated clipping [February 1911?], William H. Townsend Papers, University of Kentucky, Lexington.

55. Stoddard, *Inside the White House in War Times*, 33.

56. See Michael Burlingame, "Honest Abe, Dishonest Mary," (pamphlet) (Racine WI: Lincoln Fellowship of Wisconsin, 1994), and *The Inner World of Abraham Lincoln* (Urbana: University of Illinois Press, 1994), 268–355.

57. Stoddard to Martin B. Anderson, Washington, 11 March 1862, Anderson Papers.

58. *Washington Star*, 12 March 1878.

59. *Washington Star*, 12 March 1878. On 14 October 1863, Lee and Meade clashed indecisively at Bristoe Station, Virginia.

60. Stoddard to the editors of the *New York Evening Post*, Brooklyn, 12 March 1878, *New York Evening Post*, 13 March 1878.

61. Stoddard, "Memoirs," 1:314–15. See also "Memoirs," 2:365–67. Stoddard's banker was Edward Wolf of the firm of Wolf and Dike.

62. As quoted in William O. Stoddard Jr. to William E. Barton, Detroit, 15 February 1930, Barton Papers.

63. As quoted in William O. Stoddard Jr. to William E. Barton, Detroit, 15 February 1930, Barton Papers.

64. Michael Burlingame and John R. Turner Ettlinger, eds., *Inside Lincoln's White House: The Complete Civil War Diary of John Hay* (Carbondale: Southern Illinois University Press, 1997), 64 (entry for 18 July 1863).

65. Stoddard to the editor of the *New York Tribune*, Madison NJ, 16 December 1912, *New York Tribune*, 20 December 1912.

66. Stoddard, "Memoirs," 1:312.

67. A Washington correspondent told the managing editor of the *Tribune*, "Stoddard wants his papers if you do not publish: has no other copy." Adams S. Hill to Sydney Howard Gay, [Washington], n.d., Gay Papers, Columbia University.

68. Undated Washington dispatch by "Illinois," *New York Examiner*, 4 June 1863: "I was prevented from sending my usual contribution last week by an 'experimental proof' that, under all this fine weather of ours, there still lurk those treacherous fevers which have been, from the beginning of the war, more fatal than sword or shot to the strength of our armies."

69. Stoddard, "Memoirs," 2:440. In the published version of the memoirs, Stoddard said: "Once again Lincoln employed me as a reporter. He directed that I make an inspection of the armies of the West and South." Stoddard, *Lincoln's Third Secretary*, 200.

70. Stoddard to Marble, [New York], 8 July 1864, Manton Marble Papers, Manuscript Division, Library of Congress.

71. Washington correspondence by "Illinois," 11 July 1864, *New York Examiner*, 14 July 1864.

72. Stoddard to Hay, Little Rock, 13 August 1864, Lincoln Papers. Orville Jennings is listed in the 1865 *Official Register of the United States* as U.S. attorney for the eastern district of Arkansas.

73. Washington correspondence by "Illinois," n.d., *New York Examiner*, 6 October 1864; Stoddard, *Lincoln's Third Secretary*, 215.

74. On 26 January 1865, Stoddard's nomination was submitted to the Senate for confirmation. Roy P. Basler et al., eds., *Collected Works of Abraham Lincoln*, 8 vols. (New Brunswick NJ: Rutgers University Press, 1953–55), 8:242 n.1. On 14 February 1865 his position as marshal was officially confirmed. A photographic reproduction of Stoddard's commission appears in Stoddard, *Lincoln's Third Secretary*, facing p. 216.

75. Reminiscences of William O. Stoddard Jr., quoted in Jones, "Lincoln's Other

Secretary and His Son," 5, Jones Papers. When Stoddard went to Arkansas, he intended "to be returned in due course as United States Senator." Biographical sketch of Stoddard, Stoddard Papers.

76. Stoddard, *Lincoln's Third Secretary*, 217.

77. Stoddard to Lincoln, Little Rock, 13–14 December 1864 and 16 January 1865, Lincoln Papers.

78. Stoddard to Washburne, Little Rock, 11 January 1865, 11 February 1865, Washburne Papers, Library of Congress.

79. Stoddard to Hay, Little Rock, 22 April 1865, Hay Papers.

80. "Having lost my health in the discharge of my duty," he told the president, he was forced to resign. Stoddard to Andrew Johnson, New York, 28 May 1866, photocopy, Illinois State Historical Library, Springfield.

81. Reminiscences of William O. Stoddard Jr., quoted in Jones, "Lincoln's Other Secretary and His Son," 6, Jones Papers.

82. This volume was subtitled *Dedicated by the Author to the Sachems of Tammany, and to the Other Grand Magnorums of Manhattan* (New York, 1869).

83. William O. Stoddard Jr. to Benjamin P. Thomas, 28 September 1953, copy, Stoddard Papers.

84. William O. Stoddard Jr., quoted in Jones, "Lincoln's Other Secretary and His Son," 6, Jones Papers.

85. Stoddard to Nicolay, Madison NJ, 3 November 1898, Nicolay Papers.

86. Stoddard to Nicolay, Madison NJ, 17 December 1898, Nicolay Papers.

Sketch 1

New York Citizen, 18 August 1866, p. 1, col. 3–5. All of the letters in part 2 are addressed to Charles G. Halpine, editor of the *Citizen*.

1. John Hay (1838–1905) was Lincoln's assistant personal secretary. He later became secretary of state under Presidents William McKinley and Theodore Roosevelt.

2. Col. Elmer E. Ellsworth (1837–61), a close friend of Lincoln, was killed in Alexandria, Virginia, on 24 May 1861, when he tore down a Confederate flag that had flown from atop a hotel.

3. At the battle of Ball's Bluff, Virginia, on 21 October 1861, Lincoln's good friend Col. Edward D. Baker was killed. Baker's death is discussed in sketch 6.

4. Gen. Benjamin F. Butler of Massachusetts (1818–93) first called on Lincoln at the White House on 4 May 1861.

5. An anonymous lyricist wrote the words to the loyal version of "Maryland, My Maryland." They can be found in Irwin Silber, *Songs of the Civil War* (New York: Columbia University Press, 1960), 73.

6. New York senator Preston King committed suicide on 12 November 1865.

7. The Radical Republican Owen Lovejoy (1811–64) represented an Illinois district in the U.S. House of Representatives between 1857 and 1864. He and Lincoln were close both personally and politically.

8. Scott died in 1866.

9. Stoddard served in a militia unit, the National Rifles (also known as Company A, Third Battalion), for three months at the beginning of the war. Stoddard, *Lincoln's Third Secretary*, 76–89.

Sketch 2

New York Citizen, 25 August 1866, p. 1, col. 1–3.

1. In the photograph alluded to, taken by Matthew Brady on 9 February 1864, Lincoln and Tad are actually perusing a picture album, not the Bible.

2. On Lincoln's "moral obtuseness" in choosing friends and making political appointments, see Jesse W. Weik, *The Real Lincoln: A Portrait* (Boston: Houghton Mifflin, 1922), 215–28.

3. On Lincoln's anger, see Burlingame, *The Inner World of Abraham Lincoln*, 147–235.

4. Stoddard comments at greater length on Mary Lincoln's character in *Lincoln's Third Secretary*, 110–16.

5. John G. Nicolay (1832–1901) was Lincoln's principal private secretary. A journalist described him as the "grim Cerberus of Teutonic descent who guards the last door which opens into the awful presence" and noted that he "has a very unhappy time of it answering the impatient demands of the gathering, growing crowd of applicants which obstructs passage, hall and ante-room." Noah Brooks, Washington correspondence, 7 November 1863, for the *Sacramento Daily Union*, in *Lincoln Observed: Civil War Dispatches of Noah Brooks*, ed. Michael Burlingame (Baltimore: Johns Hopkins University Press, 1998), 83.

6. In early 1864 Hay vainly tried to help reconstruct Florida in accordance with the Ten Percent Plan that Lincoln had proposed in December 1863. In July of 1864 Lincoln sent Hay to Niagara Falls to help deal with Horace Greeley's attempt to promote a compromise peace.

7. Stoddard portrays Edward McManus (whom he called Edward Moran) vividly in *Lincoln's Third Secretary*, 73–74. He was also known as Edward Burke.

8. Millard Fillmore of New York (1800–74) become president when Zachary Taylor died in 1850; he served until 1853.

9. In January 1865, Mary Lincoln had Edward McManus fired "for obscure reasons." Justin G. Turner and Linda Levitt Turner, *Mary Todd Lincoln: Her Life and Letters* (New York: Knopf, 1972), 197, 200 n.2. According to one account, she let him go in order to hire a replacement named Cornelius O'Leary, who would share with her his illicit earnings as a pardon-broker. *Union & Advertiser (Rochester NY)*, 16

March 1865. See also Noah Brooks's account of the scandal in Burlingame, *Lincoln Observed*, 171–74.

Sketch 3
New York Citizen, 1 September 1866, p. 1, col. 3–4.

1. Ward Hill Lamon (1828–93) was marshal of the District of Columbia throughout Lincoln's administration.

2. Mary Lincoln's ball took place on 5 February 1862.

Sketch 4
New York Citizen, 8 September 1866, p. 1, col. 1–3.

1. In Lincoln's White House, such "secretaries" included Nathaniel S. Howe and Gustave E. Matile. Howe and Matile, both of whom actually worked in the White House as assistants to Nicolay and Hay, were two of ten clerks listed as serving in the office of the Secretary of the Interior. *Register of Officers and Agents, Civil, Military, and Naval, in the Service of the United States on the Thirtieth of September, 1863* (Washington: Government Printing Office, 1864), 97. The Swiss-born Matile (1841–1908) was an assistant to Hay and is listed in the 1864 Washington city directory as a White House clerk. He had studied law with Abram Wakeman, whom Lincoln named postmaster of New York. Matile received a second-class clerkship on 1 September 1863, which he resigned on 31 March 1865; he then moved to Green Bay, Wisconsin, where he apparently served as the Swiss consul at one point. He later won appointment as a commissioner of the U.S. Court. William A. Steiger to Marion E. Brown, Springfield IL, 10 May 1955, Hay Papers. In 1863 and 1864 Nathaniel S. Howe of Haverhill, Massachusetts, was technically a clerk in the Interior Department as well. In the *Register* for 1865 he is listed as a pension clerk. Howe had been a lawyer and a probate judge in Haverhill and had served in the Massachusetts state senate in 1853; he sought a U.S. government post because he could not make enough money at his profession. After the war Howe served as collector of internal revenue in the sixth district of Massachusetts and was a political operative for Nathaniel P. Banks. See Howe to Charles Sumner, Haverhill MA, 1 January 1863, and Washington, 3 November 1864, Sumner Papers, Houghton Library, Harvard University; *Boyd's Washington and Georgetown Directory* (Washington, Boyd, & Waite, 1864); D. W. Gooch to William Henry Seward, Boston, 14 November 1861, Letters of Application and Recommendation during the Administration of A. Lincoln and A. Johnson, Record Group 650, reel 23, National Archives, Washington DC; Howe to Banks, Haverhill MA, 17 and 21 September and 29 November 1867; 8 January, 21 February, 12 and 13 March, 18 June, 3 July, 28 September, 12 and 28 October, and 9 December 1868; and 14 and 29 January and 16 March 1869, Banks Papers, Manuscript Division, Library of Congress.

2. Francis Elias Spinner (1802–90), a banker from Mohawk, New York, served in the U.S. House of Representatives from 1855 to 1861 and was U.S. treasurer from 1861 to 1875. His signature appeared on paper currency.

Sketch 5
New York Citizen, 15 September 1866, p. 1, col. 1–3.

1. John A. Dix (1798–1879) assumed command of the Baltimore District on 24 August 1861. He served as governor of New York from 1873 to 1875.

2. William Henry Seward (1801–72) was a prominent New York Republican who served as secretary of state from 1861 to 1869.

3. Lincoln occasionally went further than this in promoting new weapons such as the breech-loading rifle, rifled cannon, and a crude forerunner of the machine gun. See Robert V. Bruce, *Lincoln and the Tools of War* (Indianapolis: Bobbs-Merrill, 1956).

4. In 1860 Christopher Miner Spencer (1833–1922) invented a self-loading (repeating) rifle which the U.S. Army adopted. By the end of the war, over two hundred thousand Spencer rifles had been manufactured.

5. Elias Warner Leavenworth (1803–87), a friend of Stoddard's from Syracuse, was a brigadier in the New York militia and served in Washington as a U.S. commissioner in 1861 and 1862 under the convention with New Granada. Stoddard is referring here to Colonel Ellsworth's death.

Sketch 6
New York Citizen, 22 September 1866, p. 1, col. 1–3.

1. Simon Cameron (1799–1889) was a prominent Pennsylvania Republican who served as secretary of war in 1861 and 1862.

2. For Hay's first-hand account of the meeting, see Michael Burlingame, ed., *Lincoln's Journalist: John Hay's Anonymous Writings for the Press, 1860–1864* (Carbondale: Southern Illinois University Press, 1998), 122–23, and Burlingame and Ettlinger, *Inside Lincoln's White House*, 27.

3. David C. Broderick (1820–59), a senator from California between 1857 and 1859, was killed in a duel.

4. The news of Baker's death "smote upon him like a whirlwind from a desert." Lincoln deemed it the "keenest blow" he suffered in "all the war." Noah Brooks, "Personal Recollections of Abraham Lincoln (1865)," in Burlingame, *Lincoln Observed*, 215. Upon learning of Baker's fate, Lincoln emerged from the telegraph office "with bowed head, and tears rolling down his furrowed cheeks, his face pale and wan, his heart heaving with emotion" and "almost fell as he stepped into the street. . . . With both hands pressed upon his heart he walked down the street, not returning the salute of the sentinel pacing his beat before the door." Charles Carlton

Coffin in *Reminiscences of Abraham Lincoln by Distinguished Men of His Time*, ed. Allen Thorndike Rice (New York: North American Review, 1886), 172. At Baker's funeral, the president "wept like a child." J. Wainwright Ray to Nicolay, Washington, 18 October 1886, Nicolay Papers.

5. McClellan described Lincoln as "an idiot," "the original gorilla," and "'an old stick'—& of pretty poor timber at that." He spoke of "the cowardice of the Presdt" and said, "I can never regard him with feelings other than those of thorough contempt—for his mind, heart, & morality." McClellan to his wife, Mary Ellen McClellan, Washington, 16 August 1861; Washington, 31 October 1861; Washington, 17 November 1861; Berkeley VA, 17 July 1862; and Berkeley VA, 27 July 1862, *The Civil War Papers of George B. McClellan: Selected Correspondence, 1860–1865*, ed. Stephen Sears (New York: Ticknor and Fields, 1989), 85, 114, 135, 362, 374. To Gen. Montgomery Meigs, McClellan complained that Lincoln was indiscreet: "If I tell him my plans they will be in the *New York Herald* tomorrow morning. He can't keep a secret, he will tell them to Tadd [*sic*]." Montgomery Meigs, "The Relations of President Lincoln and Secretary Stanton to the Military Commanders in the Civil War," *American Historical Review* 26 (1921): 293, 295. On 13 November 1861 the general snubbed the president, an event which Hay described in his diary:

> I wish here to record what I consider a dreadful portent of evil to come. The President, Governor Seward and I went over to McClellan's house tonight. The servant at the door said the General was at the wedding of Colonel Wheaton at General Buell's and would soon return. We went in, and after we had waited about an hour McClellan came in, and without paying any particular attention to the porter, who told him the President was waiting to see him, went up stairs, passing the door of the room where the President and Secretary of State were seated. They waited about half-an-hour, and sent once more a servant to tell the General they were there, and the answer coolly came that the General had gone to bed.

Burlingame and Ettlinger, *Inside Lincoln's White House*, 32. This snub was not unprecedented.

6. Eighteen years later Stoddard gave a fuller version of the story about Lincoln's indignation at McClellan:

> [The president] was alone in his room when an officer of General McClellan's staff was announced by the door-keeper and was admitted. The President turned in his chair to hear, and was informed, in respectful set terms, that the advance movement [against Winchester] could not be made.
>
> "Why?" he curtly demanded.
>
> "The pontoon trains are not ready—"
>
> "Why in hell and damnation *ain't* they ready?"
>
> The officer could think of no satisfactory reply, but turned very hastily and left

the room. Mr. Lincoln also turned to the table and resumed the work before him, but wrote at about double his ordinary speed. William O. Stoddard, *Abraham Lincoln: The True Story of a Great Life* (New York: Fords, Howard, & Hulbert, 1884), 285.

7. Noah Brooks described the Soldiers' Home: "a large, fine building built of stone, in castelated style, about two and a half miles from Washington due North. The grounds are extensive and beautiful, and belong to the Government—which erected the large central building for disabled, homeless soldiers of the regular service, of whom a large number here rest from the services in the field. Near the central building are several two-story cottages, built of stone in the Gothic style and occupied by the Surgeon in charge, the Adjutant General and other functionaries, and one is occupied during the Summer by the President and family." Burlingame, *Lincoln Observed*, 57.

8. Butler suffered from an eye disorder known as strabismus.

9. Stoddard relates the story of the antismoking guard in *Lincoln's Third Secretary*, 150–52.

10. At the beginning of the war, Simon P. Hanscom had been a correspondent for the *New York Herald;* in 1862 he took control of the *Washington National Republican.* A journalist reported in 1865 that "[e]very day the irrepressible Hanscom, of the *Republican*, comes after news, and brings the gossip of the day. The *Republican* is the President's favorite paper, and he gives it what news he has, but very rarely reads it or any other paper." *Philadelphia Sunday Dispatch*, 25 March 1865. Many years after the war another journalist, Ben: Perley Poore, recalled that Lincoln's "favorite among the Washington correspondents was Mr. Simon B. [*sic*] Hanscom, a shrewd Bostonian, who had been identified with the earlier anti-slavery movements, and who used to keep Mr. Lincoln informed as to what was going on in Washington, carrying him what he heard, and seldom asking a favor. 'I see you state,' said the President to Hanscom one day, 'that my administration will be the reign of *steel*. Why not add that Buchanan's was the reign of *stealing*?'" Poore, "Reminiscences of the Great Northern Uprising," *The Youth's Companion*, 26 July 1883, 301.

Sketch 7
New York Citizen, 29 September 1866, p. 1, col. 3–5.

1. Gen. George Stoneman recalled that late one night at the telegraph office at McClellan's headquarters, Lincoln "arose from his chair to leave, straightened himself up and remarked: 'Tomorrow night I shall have a terrible headache.' When asked the cause, he replied: 'Tomorrow is hangman's day and I shall have to act upon death sentences'; and I shall never forget the sad and sorrowful expression that came over his face." Osborn H. Oldroyd, ed., *The Lincoln Memorial: Album Immortelles* (New York: Carleton, 1882), 221.

2. On 16 December 1862, shortly after the debacle at Fredericksburg, Lincoln exclaimed, "If there is a worse place than hell[,] I am in it"; on the eighteenth he lamented that "if there was any worse Hell than he had been in for two days, he would like to know it." William Henry Wadsworth to S. L. M. Barlow, Washington, 16 December 1862, Barlow Papers, Huntington Library, San Marino CA; Samuel Wilkeson to Sidney Howard Gay, [Washington, 19 December 1862], Gay Papers, Butler Library, Columbia University, New York. When the Governor of Pennsylvania described to him the "terrible slaughter" at Fredericksburg, Lincoln "groaned, wrung his hands and showed great agony of spirit. He . . . moaned and groaned in anguish. He walked the floor, wringing his hands and uttering exclamations of grief, . . . saying over and over again: 'What has God put me in this place for.'" Reminiscences of Andrew Gregg Curtin in William A. Mowry, "Some Incidents in the Life of Abraham Lincoln," *Uxbridge and Whitinsville (MA) Transcript*, 1913, clipping in the Harry E. Pratt Papers, University of Illinois. A War Department telegraph operator later wrote: "When it was learned that over 13,000 men were killed, the calamity seemed to crush Lincoln. He looked pale, wan and haggard. He did not get over it for a long time and, all that winter of 1863, he was downcast and depressed. He felt that the loss was his fault." Reminiscences of Edward Rosewater, in Victor Rosewater, "Lincoln in Emancipation Days," *St. Nicholas* 64 (February 1937): 13.

3. Ambrose E. Burnside (1824–81) and the Army of the Potomac were defeated at Fredericksburg, Virginia, in December 1862.

4. Gen. John C. Frémont (1813–90) freed the slaves in Missouri by decree in August 1861, and Gen. David Hunter (1802–86) did the same in his command along the coast of South Carolina and Georgia in May 1862; Lincoln overruled both of them.

5. Hay composed letters for Lincoln, including his famous message of condolence to Lydia Bixby, a widow who had supposedly lost five sons in the war. See Michael Burlingame, "New Light on the Bixby Letter," *Journal of the Abraham Lincoln Association* 16 (1995): 59–71.

6. Stoddard may be describing here the reception on 1 January 1865 that a journalist using the pen name "Puritan" covered:

The last levee [at the White House] is said to have witnessed an unusual spectacle[.] [F]or the levee of New Year's Day, two or three colored men for the first time in our country's history mingled with the throng and paid their respects to the President. On this occasion a colored woman presented herself, Mr. Lincoln shook hands with her and Mrs. Lincoln gave the invariable bow; on the passage of the second one Mrs. Lincoln looked aghast; and when the third colored woman appeared, Mrs. Lincoln sent word to the door that no more colored persons could be admitted to mingle with the whites. But if they would come at the conclusion of the levee, they should receive the same admittance. And I was told that quite a number availed themselves of the privilege to constitute a colored levee at the close of the white one.

Washington correspondence, 18 February 1865, *Boston Recorder*, 24 February 1865, p. 2, col. 6.

7. Lincoln to James C. Conkling, Washington, 26 August 1863, *Collected Works of Abraham Lincoln*, 6:406–10.

Sketch 8

New York Citizen, 6 October 1866, p. 1, col. 4–5.

1. In response to William H. Herndon's letter to Francis E. Abbott, dated 18 February 1870, Stoddard said:

[A]s my own acquaintance with Mr. Lincoln did not begin until he had graduated from the singular schools through which he is carried in Mr. Herndon's letter, I prefer to take him as they left him, and, see if he was indeed the sceptical and gloomy Deist that he is painted. Mr. Herndon says of him, to account for the way in which he swallowed so much "theism," from so many and such varied sources, that "he had no fancy or imagination, and not much *emotion*." A keen humorist, an eloquent speaker, fond of and effective in the use of figure and metaphor, he may certainly be credited with something of fancy and imagination, and for my own part I have always deemed Mr. Lincoln one of the most emotional of men. Who so ready to melt with pity and sympathy at any tale of suffering or sorrow? to flash out with angry scorn at meanness or wrong? to bow with unaffected and overwhelming grief over the disasters of his country or his friends? I have seen him only too often under the control of his emotions, and I am surprised at the opinion expressed by Mr. Herndon, even if that point is "essential to his case"—as I am inclined to think it is. But the letter goes on:

"Mr. Lincoln had not much hope and no faith in things that lie outside of the domain of demonstration; he was so constituted—so organized—that he could believe nothing unless his sense or logic could reach it. I have often read to him a law point, a decision, or something I fancied; he could not understand it till he took the book out of my hand, and read the thing for himself. He was terribly, vexatiously skeptical."

I cannot imagine what was the trouble with Mr. Herndon's reading. I have had occasion to read a great many things to Mr. Lincoln, and he not only never failed to understand them, but always seemed willing to believe that I had read correctly just what was written or printed, without any sort of skepticism.

I cannot at this moment recall any distinct assertions made by Mr. Lincoln, relating to matters of his religious belief, but we do not gather our conceptions of the religion of other men altogether from their repetitions of any formal creed; and this I can say, that after being with him daily for three years and a half, in all the wonderful variety of circumstances which marked his administration, I am convinced this day that, in the best and truest sense, Abraham Lincoln was a Christian.

That he had an abiding faith in the overruling providence of God, in His active interference in the affairs of men and nations, is beyond possible question. From the hour when in parting from his friends in Springfield, he asked them to "pray for him," to the day when he penned his last "Thanksgiving Proclamation,"—aye, to the very day of his death—he never failed, privately or publicly, to acknowledge our dependence on, and accountability to, our Heavenly Father; and his steadfast endurance under defeat and calamity, his unflinching firmness in the darkest hour of the nation's agony, were due, more than anything else, to his faith and hope—that "faith and hope" which Mr. Herndon denies him—that the God of Battles was on our side and that he would give us the victory. As to Mr. Lincoln's earlier views concerning the Bible I have nothing to say; most men are troubled at some time in their lives with the disease of skepticism, though it is only with weak or deformed mental constitutions that it becomes chronic, and Mr. Lincoln was neither of these. He read the Bible a great deal, and it was probably in that much abused book that he discovered the Divine command which he strove to obey in his famous "Sunday order," from which I quote as follows:

"The discipline and character of the national forces should not suffer, nor the cause they defend be imperiled, by the profanation of the day or name of the Most High."

Strange words for a gloomy Deist, who "sometimes denied the existence of a God!"

Quotations might be multiplied, but it is perhaps unnecessary, as the popular instincts, keener and wiser than any "theistic" lawyer, have long since decided that, contrary to Mr. Herndon's conclusions, Mr. Lincoln, first, believed in the God he prayed to, and on whose help he confidently relied; second, believed in the authority of the book which he quoted as Divine law, and whose mandate he not only strove to honor in his own person, but in the respect required for them of those under his authority; third, that whatever may have been Mr. Lincoln's vagaries of opinion in former days, the rubbish of New Salem atheism was burned out of him in the fiery furnace of long trial, great sorrow, and compelled acknowledgment of Divine power.

Let us hear no more of Abraham Lincoln's infidelity, under what name soever it be characterized; his life, his labors, his faith, his hope, his trust, alike forbid it. If he was not what some would admit to be a "Christian," he has at least left no record of illogical inconsistency between his public utterances, his private life, and his heart's belief.

Stoddard to the editor of the *New York Standard* (174 Chambers Street, New York), 18 May 1870, clipping, scrapbook of photostats of newspaper articles, Illinois State Historical Library, Springfield.

2. Phineas D. Gurley (1816–68) was the pastor of the New York Avenue Presbyterian Church, where the Lincolns often attended services. He preached the funeral service for Willie Lincoln in February 1862.

Sketch 9

New York Citizen, 13 October 1866, p. 6, col. 4–5.

1. Stoddard edited *The Central Illinois Gazette* of West Urbana (later called Champaign) and *The Ford County Journal*.

2. See Stoddard, *Lincoln's Third Secretary*, 51–54.

3. Stoddard's partner, Dr. John Walker Scroggs, was a colorful eccentric described engagingly in Stoddard, *Lincoln's Third Secretary*, 44–48. Dr. Scroggs initially favored Seward for president. Interview with Stoddard published in the *Boston Globe*, Madison NJ correspondence, 7 February [no year indicated], clipping, Lincoln Museum, Fort Wayne, Indiana.

4. Stoddard spoke with William Herndon and Leonard Swett to gather information for his editorial endorsing Lincoln. Stoddard, *Lincoln's Third Secretary*, 57–63; *New York Times*, 18 June 1931, p. 2, col. 3. The text of Stoddard's news article and his editorial about Lincoln can be found in Stoddard, *Lincoln's Third Secretary*, 59–62.

5. Francis Bicknell Carpenter (1830–1900) was a New York artist. His *First Reading of the Emancipation Proclamation* hangs in the U.S. Capitol.

6. In 1873 Stoddard took a more favorable view of Carpenter's work in testimony before the Congressional Committee on the Library. Stoddard, *Lincoln's Third Secretary*, 222–27.

7. Mary Boykin Chesnut objected vehemently to Mary Lincoln's intention to save money from her husband's salary. She confided to her diary:

Mrs. Browne & Mrs. Scott said Mr. Ledyard called on Mrs. Lincoln to request they would keep the present door keeper who has had the place since Jackson's time, the man having asked Mr. L to intercede for him. Mrs. Lincoln said no. She had brought her *help* with her & required no more except perhaps a *girl*. She intended to save at least twelve thousand a year out of Mr. Lincoln's salary. & whenever Dr. Blake [commissioner of public buildings] asks any thing about the Establishment, Mrs. Lincoln answers, *"Remember*, I shall not spend half the salary. We are poor; we must save! So make your calculations." The money was given by the people of the United States that their president should appear with becoming dignity to his high position as their *chief*—& to steal the money for her private purse is an *infamy*.

The Private Mary Chesnut: The Unpublished Civil War Diaries, ed. C. Vann Woodward and Elizabeth Muhlenfeld (New York: Oxford University Press, 1984), 31–32 (entry for 11 March 1861).

8. Lincoln, who lent money to several people, did file a foreclosure suit against a Springfield blacksmith named Samuel Sidener. Harry E. Pratt, *The Personal Finances of Abraham Lincoln* (Springfield: Abraham Lincoln Association, 1943), 76.

9. David Davis (1815–86) was a close friend and political ally of Lincoln's and the virtual manager of his 1860 campaign. Lincoln appointed Davis a justice of the Supreme Court in 1862.

10. *Citizen* editor Charles G. Halpine, to whom these sketches are addressed, was a good friend of both Hay and Nicolay.

Sketch 10

New York Citizen, 20 October 1866, p. 1, col. 3–5.

1. Stoddard's assessment of Lincoln differs from that of Hay, who wrote in 1866: "It is absurd to call him a modest man. No great man was ever modest. It was his intellectual arrogance and unconscious assumption of superiority that men like Chase and Sumner never could forgive." Hay to William H. Herndon, Paris, 5 September 1866, *Herndon's Informants*, 332.

2. On Lincoln's attitude toward women, see Burlingame, *The Inner World of Abraham Lincoln*, 123–46.

3. On 18 July 1863, Hay noted in his diary: "Today we spent 6 hours deciding on Courtmartials, the President[,] Judge [Joseph] Holt & I. I was amused at the eagerness with which the President caught at any fact which would justify him in saving the life of a condemned soldier. He was only merciless in cases where meanness or cruelty were shown." Burlingame and Ettlinger, *Inside Lincoln's White House*, 64. According to the judge advocate general of the Union army, the president, when reviewing court martial decisions, "shrank with evident pain from even the idea of shedding human blood. . . . In every case he always leaned to the side of mercy. His constant desire was to save life. There was only one class of crimes I always found him prompt to punish—a crime which occurs more or less frequently about all armies—namely, outrages upon women. He never hesitated to approve the sentence in these cases." Joseph Holt, interview by Nicolay, 29 October 1879, in *An Oral History of Abraham Lincoln: John G. Nicolay's Interviews and Essays*, ed. Michael Burlingame (Carbondale: Southern Illinois University Press, 1996), 69–70. Of the 276 Union soldiers executed during the Civil War, twenty-two were found guilty of rape. Robert I. Alotta, *Civil War Justice: Union Army Executions under Lincoln* (Shippensburg PA: White Mane, 1989), 30. Alotta notes that Lincoln "provided clemency for all types of military offenders, except rapists" (p. 31).

4. Stoddard describes Lincoln's fondness for children in *Lincoln's Third Secretary*, 126–27.

Sketch 11

New York Citizen, 27 October 1866, p. 1, col. 1–3.

1. Charlotte Saunders Cushman (1816–76) was a tragedienne especially renowned for her Lady Macbeth.

2. Edward Loomis Davenport (1815–77) was a celebrated Shakespearean actor. James William Wallack Jr. (1818–73), well known for his Othello and Iago, often toured with E. L. Davenport.

3. James H. Hackett (1800–71) was noted for his impersonation of Falstaff.

4. Basler, *Collected Works of Abraham Lincoln*, 6:392–93, 558–59.

Sketch 12

New York Citizen, 3 November 1866, p. 1, col. 1–3.

1. Frederick Steele (1819–68) commanded the Department of Arkansas. Cf. Stoddard, *Lincoln's Third Secretary*, 205–6. John B. Steele (1814–66) represented a New York district in the U.S. House of Representatives between 1861 and 1865.

2. Gen. Jubal A. Early (1816–94) commanded Confederate forces in the Shenandoah Valley. At the third battle of Winchester on 19 September 1864, Sheridan defeated Early.

3. Nathaniel Prentiss Banks (1816–94) served as governor of Massachusetts from 1858 to 1861. During the Civil War, he commanded a division and later a corps in the Army of the Potomac.

4. Stoddard himself was caught up in the speculative fever of the time. See pages xvi–xviii of the introduction to this volume.

Sketch 13

New York Citizen, 24 November 1866, p. 2, col. 5–6.

1. As a reform candidate, Halpine had just won election as the register of New York County, New York, handily defeating the regular candidate of Tammany Hall.

Index

Throughout this index, Abraham Lincoln is abbreviated as AL, Mary Todd Lincoln is abbreviated as MTL, and William O. Stoddard is abbreviated as WOS.